Comparative industrial relations in Europe

Comparative industrial relations in Europe

Edited by DEREK TORRINGTON

GREENWOOD PRESS
WESTPORT, CONNECTICUT

Library of Congress Cataloging in Publication Data

Main entry under title:

Comparative industrial relations in Europe.

  (Contributions in economics and economic history ;
no. 21)
  Includes bibliographical references.
  1. Industrial relations—Europe—Addresses, essays,
lectures. I. Torrington, Derek, 1931-
HD8376.5.C65   1978   331'.094   78-1359
ISBN 0-313-20366-0

Library of Congress Catalog Card Number: 78-1359

ISBN: 0-313-20366-0

English language edition, except USA and Canada
published by
Associated Business Programmes Ltd.
17 Buckingham Gate, London SW1

Published in the USA and Canada by
Greenwood Press, Inc.
51 Riverside Avenue,
Westport, Connecticut 06880

First published in 1978

Printed and bound in Great Britain.

Contents

Preface

The ambitious aim of this book is to paint a broad picture of industrial relations in Europe. It is also intended to provide for the needs of the student, in any part of the world, wishing to understand European industrial relations.

This task could not be done by one person, due to the need for a diverse and extensive background of scholarship to produce material of sufficient authority, so it has been undertaken by a team of twelve. I think the reader will agree that the range of the authority with which the contributors write is remarkable, not only in the substance of what they say but in the positions they hold.

Each chapter is original and published here for the first time. I am most grateful to the various writers for agreeing to participate in the venture in the first place and for writing so willingly to a frequently awkward editorial brief.

I would like particularly to acknowledge the parts played by Nicholas Chapman of Associated Business Programmes, who thought of the original idea; my UMIST colleagues Cary Cooper and John Goodman, who were so helpful in the formative stages; and Eddie Robertson of CBI, who commented generously on the outline proposal.

I think all of us would like to pay tribute to the skills of those who have turned a set of manuscripts into an immaculate, bound book. Every writer feels a sense of relief when his tortured notes are transformed into pristine typescript, followed by a feeling of profound satisfaction after the further transformation into print.

Derek Torrington

The Contributors : biographical notes

Professor Solomon Barkin

After graduating from the College of the City of New York Professor Barkin took his MA at Columbia University and later became a Fellow of that University. He held a number of posts, including twenty-six years as Director of Research for the Textile Workers Union of America, before moving in 1963 to the Manpower and Social Affairs Directorate of OECD in Paris, where he was Deputy to Director and Head of the Social Affairs Division. Since 1968 he has been Professor of Economics at the University of Massachusetts. He has published a large number of books, including *Manpower Policies and Problems in the Netherlands*, *Manpower Policy in Norway* and *Worker Militancy and its Consequences*.

Professor Cary L. Cooper

Cary Cooper is Professor of Management Educational Methods (a Chair funded by the UK Foundation of Management Education) in the Department of Management Sciences, University of Manchester Institute of Science and Technology. He is currently Research Co-ordinator for the Management Education and Development Division of the Academy of Management and is General Editor of a series of books entitled *Individuals, Groups and Organisations*, the European editor of the international quarterly *Interpersonal Development* and a member of numerous other editorial boards for scholarly journals. In addition to over fifty articles, Professor Cooper is author or co-author of six books *T-Groups: A Survey of*

Research, Group Training for Individual and Organisational Development, Theories of Group Processes, Developing Social Skills in Managers, OD in the US and UK (in press) and *Understanding Executive Stress* (in press).

W.W. Daniel

W.W. Daniel is the Leverhulme Research Fellow at PEP (Political and Economic Planning). He has now been engaged for some ten years in full-time research on labour relations and labour market issues both in Britain and in continental Europe. His publications include *The Right to Manage?*; *Beyond the Wage-work Bargain*; *Wage Determination in Industry*; *Scope for Labour/Management Co-operation in the Enterprise*; and *Racial Discrimination in England.*

Jenny Dorling

Jenny Dorling spent five years in industry as a Personnel and Training Officer, during which time she gained diplomas in personnel management and management studies. She has since been mainly concerned with manpower policies, training needs and training programmes and has held appointments with the CBI, IPM and, for the last three and a half years, the TSA. Throughout her career, Jenny has always taken an interest in the employment and training of women and has worked with the ILO and the Commission of the European Communities. Her activities in this area have ranged from advising girls and ITB's to the preparation of reports on the problems and possible solutions, including the drafting of the TSA's report on training opportunities for women. Jenny is currently involved in an action research project to promote the employment of women at managerial level and the development of a course for women returners.

John Gennard

John Gennard studied economics at the Universities of

Sheffield and Manchester between 1963 and 1968. He was appointed Research Officer, Industrial Relations Department, London School of Economics in 1968 and Lecturer in Industrial Relations at LSE in October 1970.

Professor J.F.B. Goodman

Professor John Goodman is Frank Thomas Professor of Industrial Relations and presently Chairman of the Department of Management Sciences at the University of Manchester Institute of Science and Technology. Prior to taking up this appointment in January 1975, he was Senior Lecturer in Industrial Relations in the University of Manchester. His previous appointments include a period as Industrial Relations Adviser at the National Board for Prices and Incomes, Lecturer in Industrial Economics at the University of Nottingham and as Personnel Officer in the motor industry.

Professor Goodman is joint author of two books on shop-stewards (*Shop-stewards in British Industry*, and *Shop-stewards*), and of *Rule-Making and Industrial Peace: Industrial Relations in the Footwear Industry*. He has contributed chapters to a number of books, and many articles to academic and management journals, covering a wide range of topics in the industrial relations field. Much of this research has centred on workplace industrial relations, but also includes other subjects such as wage indexation, local labour markets, strikes and industrial conciliation.

John Greenwood

After graduating from St John's College Oxford in Philosophy, Politics and Economics in 1965, John Greenwood spent two more years in Oxford reading for a BPhil in Economics. In 1967 he took up a post as Lecturer in Economics at the University of Sussex and moved to the Department of Management Sciences at UMIST as Senior Lecturer in Economics in 1976.

He has been an adviser to the Department of

Employment, NEDO and the National Board for Prices and Incomes and has worked on a variety of projects with the Institute of Manpower Studies. His publications include various papers on payment systems, equal pay, hours of work and wages councils, a book (co-author) on *The Small Firm in the Hotel and Catering Industry* and a book on *Worker Sit-ins and Job Protection.*

Terence P. Kenny

After education at Durham and Oxford Universities Terence Kenny took a first post as tutor at Bristol University Extra-mural Department and then spent six years with Albright and Wilson Ltd, being particularly concerned with training and management development. He joined Manchester University to help set up the School of Management and Administration, which was the predecessor of Manchester Business School. He stayed with the School for the first two years of its life as Senior Tutor, before joining the British Printing Corporation as Personnel Controller in 1967. He joined the main board in the summer of 1974.

While with the British Printing Corporation Terence Kenny was Deputy Chairman of the TSA's Research Advisory Committee, a member of the Industrial Relations Committee of the British Printing Industries Federation and of the Management Development Committee of the Printing Industries Training Board. He joined Brighton Polytechnic as Head of Department of Business Studies in June 1977, though staying on with The British Printing Corporation in an advisory capacity.

Peter Long

Peter Long is Director of Personnel for Don International Ltd. After gaining a Social Science Diploma at Swansea University College, he worked for a number of years in what was then the Youth Employment Service, first in Derbyshire and then in Luton. He joined his present

Company as Training Officer in 1958, and has had responsibility for training throughout the years since then. He is at present a member of the Training and Grants Committee of the Cotton and Allied Textile Industry Training Board. He is a Companion of the Institute of Personnel Management, and has been Chairman of the Manchester Branch and more recently of the Northern Region, as well as a member of the Institute's National Executive and Council.

Jack Peel

In 1973 Jack Peel was appointed Director of Industrial Relations in the Directorate-General for Social Affairs in the Commission of the European Communities. After an elementary education he spent his early working life as a locomotive foreman and engine driver and was a part-time Branch Secretary of ASLEF when he was twenty. He later became a weaver and read Social Science at Ruskin College Oxford on a TUC Education Trust scholarship. After becoming a full-time trade unionist of the National Union of Dyers, Bleachers and Textile Workers he was appointed General Secretary in 1966 and was a member of the TUC General Council from 1966 to 1973. He was also a part-time Director of the National Coal Board and the British Wool Marketing Board. As a member of the TUC General Council Mr Peel served on four government inquiries and studied industrial relations problems in many countries, including Israel, Japan, USA and USSR. He was awarded the CBE in 1972 and made Deputy Lieutenant of West Yorkshire in 1974.

Michael Rubenstein

Michael Rubenstein was born in New York and studied industrial relations at Cornell University and the London School of Economics. He is Managing Director of Industrial Relations Services and Editor of its five publications – *European Industrial Relations Review, Industrial Relations Review and Report*, *Industrial Relations Law Reports*, *Industrial Relations Legal Information Bulletin* and the *Health and Safety Information Bulletin*. He has delivered over 150 talks in the past two years on aspects of employment law to management and trade union groups and is the author of *A Practical Guide to the Employment Protection Act*. He makes frequent appearances on radio and television and is currently writing a book about sex discrimination in employment.

Derek Torrington

After education at Manchester Grammar School and Manchester University Derek Torrington began his working life as a management trainee in the engineering industry and subsequently spent five years as Manager, Personnel and Training Division with Oldham International Ltd before opting for a second career in education. A further five years as Principal Lecturer in Industrial Relations at Manchester Polytechnic was followed by his present appointment as Lecturer in Personnel Management at UMIST. Apart from journal and magazine articles he has written or edited six books: *Successful Personnel Management*, *Face-to-Face*, *Handbook of Industrial Relations*, *Handbook of Management Development* (with D.F. Sutton), *Administration of Personnel Policies* (with R. Naylor) and *Encyclopaedia of Personnel Management*. He has served the Institute of Personnel Management in a number of local, regional and national capacities.

Michael Wright

Michael Wright is a Research Assistant in the Department of Industrial Relations at the London School of Economics. He graduated in Economics from the Australian National University in 1972 and spent the next four years undertaking research and teaching part-time. His research centred on macro economic planning, especially manpower and employment studies in Papua New Guinea, and economic analysis within Australia. Earlier publications on employment and incomes in developing economies have been published by the New Guinea Research Unit of the Australian National University and the Institute of Applied Social and Economic Research in Papua New Guinea.

1   An introduction

DEREK TORRINGTON

In 1946 Churchill called for 'a kind of United States of Europe' because he saw the need for that kind of *political* unity. Since the Treaty of Rome was signed to create the European Economic Community the concern of member states has been almost exclusively with the potential *economic* advantages of unity, perhaps giving point to that penetrating comment by Mary McCarthy: 'The only really materialistic people I have ever met have been Europeans'. This book is concerned with one aspect of the *social* effects of Britain's entry into Europe.

Ever since it became possible that Great Britain would become a member country of the EEC there has been interest among politicians, managers, trade unionists and academics about the effect this would have on the structure and conduct of industrial relations in this country. The interest has usually been in the form of apprehension that being a part of Europe would make life even more tiresome. It is difficult to find any enthusiastic comments in the industrial relations debate of the last decade about the opportunities presented by Europe.

The focus of interest in Europe among industrial relations specialists has been prospective legislation, as we have contemplated the existing or proposed statutes and calculated the amount of trouble they will cause: again a rather negative attitude.

In this text we have attempted to take a wider and more positive view of Britain's European prospects in the area of industrial relations by examining a number of different aspects of the current situation and trying to discern future possibilities. In some ways this may present even more problems to the reader, as the contributors of the different chapters do not necessarily describe a trouble-free future, but we hope that the reader will get a full picture of the evolving European context of British industrial relations.

The structure of the book is of ten chapters, each dealing with a specific issue, followed by two chapters taking a synoptic view, one from Brussels and one from the United States. The book opens with *John Greenwood's* analysis of the development of manpower policies in Europe. Traditional concerns such as providing help for the unemployed were greatly altered with the growing need to focus on providing the manpower needed for economic expansion and on attendant problems caused by large scale labour migration. He explores all these issues and the types of manpower policy that have been contrived to deal with them before considering some of the developments underway to contend with a new employment crisis – employment protection, employment subsidies, early retirement and job release for education and training. He sees little evidence yet of a decline in the level of unemployment and considers the possibility of some of the experimental solutions now being attempted in work-sharing and work-rationing, whereby productivity 'pays off' in increasing leisure rather than increasing consumption.

John Goodman examines trade unions and the collective bargaining systems of Europe, finding a very wide variation, not only between countries but also within individual countries. To enable a useful degree of generalisation he concentrates mainly on arrangements for manual workers in manufacturing. After introducing the setting of collective bargaining in Europe he discusses trade unions and multi-employer bargaining structures before examining workplace bargaining and taking a look to the future. Despite the general dissimilarity in practice four signs of convergence are identified: the EEC with its objectives of harmonisation, the internationalisation of major companies, incomes policies and some elements of collective bargaining like the expanding role of legal regulation. The prospect of cross-frontier bargaining with multi-national companies is regarded as remote, and we are reminded that deep-rooted cultural influences will continue to make industrial relations practice differ markedly between countries.

The subject of *Bill Daniel's* chapter is probably the most familiar to readers as the alarm about the Fifth Directive was raised some years ago and the topic of industrial democracy has been of central interest in Britain in recent years as many people have made up their minds that some version of greater employee participation in the management of the enterprise was essential for the regeneration of British industry.

Participation may develop at the boardroom level, as is envisaged by industrial democracy proposals of the Bullock type, or it may develop in the workplace itself. *Cary Cooper* – one of the three Americans contributing to this book – provides a detailed and comprehensive assessment of current European developments in increasing employee participation in the decision-making processes of their work group by allowing them greater freedom in deciding how to organise and conduct their own jobs. After making comparisons with Sweden, the United States and Japan he concludes on an optimistic note with the assessment that this type of initiative produces results which benefit the organisation as well as the individual employee and that Britain is building up more varied experience in this field than her EEC neighbours.

The chapter on employee benefits looks at social security contributions and benefits, pensions and the age of retirement, holidays and hours of work, employee migration and company mergers, picking up and adding a little more information to some of the points mentioned by Mr Greenwood and Professor Goodman. Among the predictions of the future are a tendency for Europe to follow Britain in narrowing the distinction between manual and non-manual employees for social security benefit and contribution, while Britain may need to extend the period over which earnings-related benefit is paid during sickness.

A discrepancy is suggested between Britain and Europe on holiday pay but not the number of days holiday, and British non-manual employees are shown as being in a very favoured position on the basis of their weekly working hours.

Terence Kenny provides one of the most original and important chapters in the book as he deals with employer organisation for industrial relations, particularly the European personnel manager. After a dramatic beginning to symbolise the difference between personnel management in Britain and Italy, the chapter has substantial accounts of the situation in France and Germany providing an additional and different treatment to some of the themes in Daniel's chapter. In the closing section there is a general review of some European developments and comparisons that bears out the general divergence argument advanced by Goodman. We see, for instance, that social science qualifications are prevalent for personnel managers in Holland and Sweden and noticeably absent in France and Italy. Attitudes to trade unions are also different. The substantial majority of British and Dutch personnel managers see the unions as an aid to participation, while nearly half of the French and Italians see the unions as impeding the development of participation.

Our second American contributor is *Michael Rubenstein* who takes the theme of labour law. He begins with the uncompromising assertion that British personnel managers will have much more legislation to contend with on individual employment rights, despite the legal avalanche of the seventies, as the United Kingdom is still well behind the norm of Western Europe. Concentrating on the individual job property-right Rubenstein traces the various reasons for the development of this element in labour law in recent years, including the crucial effect of Europe, before describing why labour law will change further in the 1980s. He concludes by providing an ouline of the Employment Protection (Amendment) of (say) 1984.

John Gennard and *Michael Wright* survey the various

approaches in Europe to incomes policy. They first explore why incomes policies have been adopted as one of a number of anti-inflationary measures available to governments and then describe the four main forms of policy that have been attempted: exhortation, reports from neutral boards of experts, money incomes control and collective bargaining framework agreements. Turning to the problems that such policies produce, the authors consider how five countries – Denmark, France, the Netherlands, Sweden and the United Kingdom have tackled the three main difficulties, which they identify as pay differentials, the protection of real wages and the enforcement of the policy. After their concluding analysis they provide an invaluable chronicle of incomes policy developments in the five countries.

Jenny Dorling takes us into a different area by examining the employment of women across Europe. Whereas earlier chapters have been dominated by dissimilarity in practice between countries, Jenny finds the most striking feature about women and work in Europe to be the degree of similarity in their position and in the character of their employment: relatively poorly paid and trained as well as being concentrated in a narrow range of industrial and occupational sectors. She goes on to discuss the reasons for the inequality of women at work and some of the steps being taken to redress the balance.

The last of our chapters on specific topics is by *Peter Long*, looking at industrial training, following the introduction of this subject by Greenwood in the opening chapter. After a review of the growth of governmental interest in training as part of manpower policy in Britain, there is a comparison with the arrangements in Germany and in France. Because the EEC is seeking full labour mobility between member states there will be harmonisation of training and qualifications, even though this will be a slow process, and one of the means to be used is the Social Fund. In his final summary Long envisages increasing involvement by government and EEC.

Although the substance of our book is a comparison

between Britain and other member states of the EEC, with what do we compare Europe? The obvious comparator is the United States and *Solomon Barkin* provides us with an analysis of the contemporary scene in his country, where trade union membership levels are low yet the rate of industrial action is high. Public support for unionism and collective bargaining is declining and there is little centralisation of either trade union or employer organisation. Unions are primarily concerned with wages, hours and working conditions in the units for which they are bargaining agents. They do, however, support federal and state minimum wage and working conditions legislation – the latter with less determination – and advocate and support economic and social legislation and policies favourable to the working population.

Our book closes with an assessment of the whole picture by *Jack Peel*, looking from his unique position as Director of Industrial Relations for the European Commission. He begins by asking the rhetorical question about whether the formidable technology of the world can co-exist with its ramshackle social machinery. Then he reviews the ideological groupings of trade unions, multi-national companies and the evolution of European collective bargaining against the background of what the Commission is seeking to do in harmonisation. After turning to a consideration of future industrial relations trends Peel re-asserts a long-held conviction:

'... political power is linked to economic strength and economic success depends on good industrial relations. It is no accident that the richer countries like Germany, Sweden, Denmark, Austria and Switzerland have progressive, harmonious industrial relations systems. This correlation rests on the predominance of industrial trade union structures and more professionalism and economic realism in management and trade unions.'

We hope that the reader will find something in the following pages to inform and stimulate.

2 Manpower policy and the European economies

JOHN GREENWOOD

The pattern of economic development

The pattern of economic development in Western Europe since the Second World War may be described as one of three phases. The first phase of post-war reconstruction, of Marshall aid and the Korean war, was followed by a second period of economic growth and relative stability. This, in turn, came to an end with the economic recession of 1966–8 which introduced the third and current phase of greater instability, higher inflation and unemployment and a check to the previous record of economic growth. The second phase, of course, was the one in which Keynesian policies of macro-economic management were in the ascendancy, although the whole period has been characterised by cycles of boom and recession. These have been markedly less severe than in the period before the Second World War, but each successive recession has left the industrial Western world with a higher rate of inflation.

The recession of 1966–8 marks a watershed. By previous standards the check to output growth was relatively small and only in Western Germany did Gross National Product (GNP) in real terms actually fall. Elsewhere it proceeded to increase but at a slower pace. But the effect of the recession in output on employment was in most countries greater than previous experience had led them to expect. In addition this recession lasted longer, recovery was less pronounced and inflation in the succeeding boom was markedly higher than in previous post-war cycles. This was all the more disturbing in that the recession itself had very largely been deliberately induced by government economic policies as an anti-inflationary device in circumstances of increasing interdependence both of the national economies of Western Europe and of Europe as a whole with the rest of the Western industrial world.[1]

The 1966–8 recession also marks a watershed because it was succeeded by only a short boom before the still more serious recession of 1974 onwards. The intervening boom of the early 1970s was short but vigorous and highly synchronised between the major economies. It was accompanied by a worldwide explosion of prices, rapid expansion in the world's supply of money, and substantial increases in the prices of primary commodities including the fourfold increase in oil prices. Inflation had averaged between two and four per cent per year in the 1950s and then accelerated to three to five per cent in the first half of the 1960s but began to take off around 1967 and reached a West European average of thirteen per cent in 1973. Unemployment in the current recession, moreover, reached record levels by post-war standards (see Table 2.1). This has meant a distinct worsening, if not complete disappearance,

Table 2.1   Unemployment rates (%) selected European countries – 1962–73, 1975–76

Country	Average 1962 to 1972	1973	1975	1976 1	1976 2
Belgium	1.9	2.3	4.8 [a]	5.8 [a]	5.3 [a]
			11.0 [b]	14.2 [b]	14.3 [b]
Denmark	3.2	2.4	6.0	7.0	5.3
Finland	2.2	2.3	2.2	4.0	3.5
France	1.7	2.1	–	–	–
Italy	3.4	3.5	3.3	3.5	3.5
Netherlands	1.1	2.3	–	–	–
Sweden	2.0	2.5	1.6	1.8	1.5
United Kingdom	2.3	2.6	4.0	5.3	5.4
West Germany	1.0	1.3	4.7	5.7	4.3

Source: OECD   (a) Males only   (b) Females only

of the trade-off between inflation and unemployment presumed until now to exist.

Economic growth and the development of active manpower policy

Manpower policies have been developed and adapted in Europe to match these overall movements in their economies, although in many countries it was not until the mid 1960s that active consideration was given to the issues involved. Historically manpower policies have been very largely associated with the problems of 'relief' for the unemployed and other casualties of the labour market. Yet during the 1950s and early 1960s this preoccupation was mainly subordinated to that of providing the necessary manpower inputs for economic expansion. Concern in many countries was less with ensuring protection for those without work than with ensuring that there were sufficient people available to match the increasing demand for labour. Indeed by the end of the 1960s economists were reaching the conclusion that limited labour supplies themselves constituted an impediment to high or sustained economic growth.[2]

Economic growth during the second phase identified above tended to take the form of productivity growth in the secondary industrial sector, which in turn generated the capital for further investment in industry. The net effect of rising labour productivity and investment was to create additional employment. However the sources of additional labour supplies for industry proved problematical. Population growth was slow and increased participation by women in the labour force was to a large extent offset by increased education and lower activity rates among older workers. Instead, the new jobs created were filled by a substantial transfer of manpower from agriculture. An International Labour Office (ILO) study reported that in fifteen European countries between 1950 and 1960 this agricultural exodus provided 8,000,000 extra workers to industry and services and this was 1,000,000 higher than the total increase in their combined labour force. Only in Greece and Turkey did agricultural employment increase in absolute terms.[3] Moreover, on the European scale this transfer of manpower from agriculture took the character of a migration of workers from countries with large agricultural sectors – Greece, Ireland, Italy, Portugal, Spain, Turkey and Yugoslavia; the main recipients of such migration were West Germany, France, the United Kingdom, Switzerland and Belguim.

Labour mobility, however, proved only a partial solution in adapting manpower resources to a growing level and changing structure of economic demand. As the 1960s progressed policy makers switched their attention from the problems of sustaining a sufficient level of aggregate demand to ensure full employment, a problem which at least in the richer European countries appeared to be solved, to the more complex tasks of attempting to ensure a balance between supply and demand in each and every sector.

Increasingly a main concern became the possibility of an insufficient supply of particular skills or types of labour, since such shortages seemed likely both to establish 'bottlenecks' impeding the pace of economic growth and to add to inflationary pressures. Further concerns became those of winning continued consent to the adaptability required of workers if mobility were to continue to assist growth and with countering some of the less desirable economic and social by-products of such mobility notably the plight both of immigrant workers and of the depopulated regions from which some of them originated. Not surprisingly, interest in economic planning grew apace with the development of active manpower policies framed in terms of such selective, planning problems.

In France a Manpower Commission had already been well established as part of the planning machinery. This developed considerable expertise in forecasting manpower requirements by sector, occupation and region and hence in identifying likely surpluses and shortages during the currency of each plan.[4] Yet this was only a forecasting exercise and as each successive plan itself became more flexible and placed more reliance on market mechanisms so the need to add to the roles of France's employment and training agencies was appreciated. In both France and Belgium a planning and forecasting exercise has been supplemented by national level agreements between employers and labour organisations on such issues as job creation, protection and training. In the United Kingdom the National Economic Development Council turned its attention at an early date to manpower aspects of economic growth and suggested that to achieve faster growth there would need to be policies to assist in the movement of workers from declining to expanding sectors.[5]

To these powerful economic arguments for the development of active manpower policies the Organisation for Economic Co-operation and Development (OECD) added its voice and provided an additional institutional impetus by a recommendation on the subject to member countries in 1964. This was followed with a series of reports on the development of such policies in each country.[6] Member countries of the European Economic Community have also experienced the catalyst of manpower provisions in the Coal and Steel Community and Rome Treaties as well as, more recently, a Directive of the Council of Ministers on employment protection.

The OECD reports provide a comprehensive guide to the specific approaches of the different countries to the development of manpower policy. The battery of policy instruments is now large, but provision of a public employment service and some form of provision for industrial or vocational training remain the basic and common elements. In most countries both of these have been improved or reorganised sometimes by the establishment of wholly new administrative structures as in France with the National Employment Agency of 1967 or in Ireland with the An Co training authority. In other countries there has been more continuity as with the Labour Market Board in Sweden and the Federal Institute of

Labour in West Germany. Yet almost everywhere, with the notable exception of Sweden, it has proved difficult to establish manpower authorities with funds, skills, administrators and status comparable with those responsible for other economic policies.

Employment services

Attempts at renewing the public employment services have proved largely uncontroversial, although the attempt has been based not simply on improving their efficiency in helping employers to find workers or the unemployed to find jobs but also on introducing a new concept of their function. This was described by the ILO as 'to assist persons in the employment market to achieve their maximum potential and find their most productive employment'.[7] It is this concept which makes active manpower policy not only economic but also social in its aims and effects. It also reinforces the arguments for an extensive and comprehensive employment service. Yet, despite the fact that private employment agencies, where they exist at all extensively, have tended to cater to specialist occupations such as catering and entertainment, it has proved difficult for the public employment service to achieve a high degree of penetration in European labour markets. Part of this problem has been associated with the 'dole queue' image of many countries' public employment service. Hence in many countries, including the United Kingdom, Denmark and Ireland the authorities have taken steps to separate, at least physically, placement facilities from provision of benefit.

Improvements in employment services, therefore, have consisted very often in efforts to widen their appeal and increase their use as a precondition for extending the use of other public labour market policies such as training and re-training, incentives to mobility, etc. In addition the use of vocational counselling for adults has spread in a number of countries.

Industrial training

Developments in the field of industrial training have also largely taken the form of increasing provision and use. There are, however, important differences between countries in the type and mix of institutions providing the training and in adult entitlement to further training or retraining. Differences, in particular, arise in the extent of provision of training by or at the expense of the public manpower authorities. Thus in Sweden nearly all adult training, apart from that associated with the improvemens of skills within firms, takes place in the National Labour Market Board's own schools. In France adult training may take place either in one of the centres directly run by the Association for Adult Vocational Training (AFPA) or in other privately run centres and schools where the training is financed by the AFPA. In Italy a large proportion of training centres are run by the national trade union confederations, but finance is provided by subsidies from the *Istituto per la Formazione dei Lavorati*. In both Belguim and West Germany, apart from the initial training of young workers, industrial training remains largely the province of private firms and institutions.

Table 2.2 Government expenditure on manpower policies in selected countries as a proportion of gross national product.

Country	Years	Expenditure on manpower policy % of GNP
Belgium	1968	0.7
Denmark	1969—70	0.2
Norway	1968	0.7
Sweden	1969—70	1.4
United Kingdom (excl. Northern Ireland	1969—70	0.9
West Germany	1969	0.5

Source: OECD, *Reviews of Manpower and Social Policies: 14 Manpower Policy in Denmark,* OECD (Paris 1974) p.53

In part, these differences reflect the institutional characteristics and history of each country, in part they reflect differences in financial provision for manpower policy (see Table 2.2) and the distribution of this expenditure between 'active' measures such as training and 'passive' measures such as payment of unemployment benefit. In part, too, one suspects they reflect differences in ideology and political views on the appropriate role of the state in economic and social affairs.

State intervention in the labour market

The case for state intervention in the labour market is, of course, widely accepted and has become more widely accepted as labour economists have continued to reveal the inperfections of this market. Argument, however, continues to centre round the form of such intervention, whether it should consist largely of state provision free of charge, or whether it should operate less directly by means of taxes and subsidies. But it can be argued that both the tax and subsidy solution and direct provision run the risks of excessive bureaucracy, of the tutelage of individuals which restricts their choice and of widespread possibilities for abuse. All these criticisms, for example, were made of the levy-grant system of financing training in the United Kingdom, even though, in many ways, this was an ingenious method of attempting to provide a market solution by adjusting the distribution of private costs and benefits. It is also worth noting that a similar levy-grant scheme was introduced in Ireland.[8]

An alternative to these approaches suggested is that of 'drawing rights' under which individuals are provided with a credit on which to draw for labour market purposes such as job search, retraining, educational or other leave. The aim is to retain individual discretion and responsibility while reducing the risks and uncertainties of the labour market. Particular bottleneck problems could be tackled perhaps by reducing or waiving the charge on an individual's credit account for undertaking the necessery training and readjustment. Many recent innovations in the provision of paid educational and training leave have indeed incorporated some elements of the 'drawing rights' idea as have some well established schemes for early retirement with reduced pensions.[9]

Migrant workers

Economic growth in post-war Europe has been accompanied by structural change for which labour market adaptability was a prerequisite. As explained above it was a fear that this adaptability could no longer be guaranteed without effort that led to a serious consideration of active manpower policies. A further reason for this step was a growing awareness of the possible problems posed by the persistence of large-scale immigration which in the earlier years itself provided a crucial element of flexibility in the labour market.

Already by 1965 there were estimated to be over 5,000,000 migrant workers in Europe, over half of whom were from southern Europe and most of whom went to France, West Germany, Switzerland and the United Kingdom. They accounted for three and a half per cent of the West European labour force as a whole but for as much as thirty per cent of the labour force of Switzerland.[10] Moreover, the migrant workers tended to concentrate into specific industries and regions. In France, where the number of immigrant workers had risen to 1,800,000 by 1973, more than one-third work in construction where half the unskilled labour force consists of immigrants; but the main concentration is in manufacturing industry especially motor vehicles. Renault, in particular, employs thirty per cent immigrant labour.[11]

Immigration provided a source of mobility and flexibility in many European economies. The existence of administrative controls on the numbers of immigrants, on their subsequent jobs and lengths of stay in host countries itself should have ensured that immigrants only took jobs when and where there was a demand. But on closer inspection the bottlenecks which immigrant workers came to fill were largely in less skilled and less desirable industrial occupations which were increasingly being vacated by the more affluent indigenous populations. Thus between 1961 and 1968 the absolute number of blue-collar workers in the male labour force of West Germany fell and the proportion dropped from over sixty-three to sixty per cent. At the same time the proportion of foreign workers in Germany employed in blue-collar jobs rose from eighty-seven to ninety per cent. As Table 2.3 indicates, the general trend of employment in the richer European countries has been away from the secondary, industrial sector. In many cases there has been an absolute decline, but again this has been compatible with rising numbers of immigrant workers in rapidly declining industries such as textiles and clothing.[13]

The concentration of immigrant workers in particular industries and regions necessarily has far-reaching social consequences. Equally, it would seem that above some

Table 2.3   Index numbers of total employment by sector, selected European countries 1974 (1961 = 100)

| Country | Index of employment IN | | | |
	Agriculture	Industry	Others	Total
France	60.3	114.0	140.3	112.7
Greece	59.7	142.9	129.4	92.6
Ireland	67.0	125.9	175.0	100.3
Italy	50.1	108.0	119.2	93.5
Netherlands	67.7	97.5	132.8	111.4
Portugal	62.0	107.5	125.1	93.2
Sweden	49.3	99.1	137.9	109.1
Switzerland	65.0	103.1	132.4	109.2
United Kingdom	62.8	91.5	118.4	103.0
West Germany	54.6	96.2	115.0	97.9
All EEC	55.6	100.3	123.7	102.4
All Europe OECD	64.5	115.7	138.0	114.5

Source: OECD, *Labour Force Statistics 1963-74*

threshold immigration becomes irreversible and that once it assumes a 'structural' characteristic its use as a source of mobility and adaptability becomes questionable. This has been most notably true in Switzerland where initially immigration was thought of as temporary.

Later, as average lengths of stay increased, restrictions on the geographical and occupational mobility of foreign workers were relaxed and steps were taken deliberately to limit the inflow. Until recently in Switzerland, West Germany and other labour importing countries the net inflow had been regulated more or less automatically by the economic cycle. Thus in 1967 more than half of the decline of 790,000 in the West German labour force could be ascribed to an out-migration of foreign workers.[14] But contrary to this experience in 1974 the number of foreign workers in West Germany did not decrease.[15] In the EEC as a whole the number of migrant workers had dropped to 6,090,000 in 1976 from a peak of 6,600,000 in 1973, but of these the 4,500,000 migrants from outside of the EEC have proved less willing to return home during the current recession. Strict controls by a number of governments have meant a reduction in non-EEC migrants obtaining work permits but this is being increasingly offset by the natural birth rate of migrants already established.[16]

In addition to the substantial social problems generated in Europe's labour shortage countries, therefore, migration has been losing its value as a flexible and counter-cyclical component of aggregate labour supplies. Nevertheless, it clearly still retains some value as in Austria where the foreign labour force has been cut from 250,000 in 1973 to 180,000 by the end of 1975. On the other hand, the net effect will have been smaller because of repatriation of Austrian emigrants to neighbouring Switzerland and Germany.[17] Moreover, the opposite side of this coin is of course that migration tends to worsen unemployment levels during a recession in labour exporting countries, such as Spain.[18]

Indeed it is doubtful whether the overall effects of labour migration have proved beneficial to Europe's under-developed regions of labour surplus.

Emigration tends to be selective and most emigrants are prime age males. In some departments of Greece, for example, over eighty per cent of males in the fifteen to forty-four age group have emigrated. In two regions in Italy and Spain emigrants were exclusively active workers. True such emigration may provide additional job opportunities for those who remain. On the other hand it may also retard the displacement of underemployed rural manpower in such regions. Moreover, there is little evidence that returning migrants bring industrial skills relevant to the development of their home areas. Understandably those who acquire industrial skills tend to be least anxious to return.[19] Both on a European and a national level the lesson has been learned that migration and geographical mobility far from alleviating regional imbalances may, in the end, exacerbate them.

Manpower policy as a counter-cyclical device

The idea that indiscriminate deflation may produce a favourable 'shake-out' of labour from declining, low productivity towards expanding, high productivity sectors had only a short vogue and in only a few countries, notably Britain. Reliance on such minimal manpower devices as severance payments in the event of redundancy and more generous unemployment benefits to facilitate the transition of workers during such periods of supposedly accelerated structural change has proved insufficient. Experience and research suggests that workers already in employment can more effectively move to alternative jobs making better use of their skills than can most of those made unemployed 'through no fault of their own', that those shaken out tend to be older, less skilled and marginal workers least adaptable or able to undertake such a transition and likely, in many cases, either to retire from the labour force altogether or even to return to their previous employers once economic circumstances permit.[20] How to reallocate workers from declining industries to new jobs, especially where these involve a change of occupation and/or place of residence, has proved in the ILO's words 'the most refractory problem' for manpower policy.[21] In many ways the problem may be attenuated by the use of internal manpower planning, internal transfers and use of natural attrition. In this respect the public sector in many countries has scored some notable successes.[22] It was also, of course, one of the main concerns of the European Coal and Steel Community. But general deflation is as likely to hinder as to accelerate such a process of structural change.

For this and other reasons many commentators have suggested that manpower policy, particularly training policy should be used counter-cyclically. Once again it was the Swedish experience which indicated the efficacy of such an approach, supplementing the more traditional public works programmes in times of high seasonal unemployment or general recession with a substantial training programme which expanded and contracted counter-cyclically. This use of manpower policy as a counter-cyclical device can be justified on a number of grounds. First, an expansion of training during the recession can assist in providing sufficient trained manpower to overcome shortages and bottlenecks once circumstances allow a higher level of aggregate demand. Secondly, since taking part in a training course tends to be more acceptable than enforced idleness, the total decline in aggregate demand can be made greater; were those in training to be unemployed political pressures would prevent so tight a squeeze. Thirdly, training is not only more acceptable than unemployment it is also socially preferable.[23]

Such counter-cyclical devices, however, are not entirely unproblematical. In the first place, in order to have any counter-cyclical impact a public training programme has to be of a substantial size. In Sweden this has been the case and Austria has built up its training programmes rapidly for this purpose. Elsewhere the lack of public training facilities explains why they have been little used in this way until recently. On the other hand, a large volume of training need not necessarily imply a lavish provision of purpose-built, public training centres. Since training in private industry tends to be less during a recession, use can be made of employers' training centres. Use of shifts within training centres and use of temporary premises are other alternatives for ensuring the availability of adequate facilities.[24]

Public works programmes, too, may have their problems particularly in construction. Since planning, preparation and purchase of land takes time and substantially delay implementation, such a device may in the end be destabilising. The same argument applies to use of public sector investment projects to counteract the cycle. Another increasing difficulty is that at least half the labour now required on construction projects consists of skilled workers least susceptible to unemployment.[25] On the other hand, Germany's Federal Institute of Labour has had an obligation since 1969 to apply counter-cyclical principles in managing its expenditure and appears to have achieved some success in this direction with public works programmes.[26]

More recently a number of countries have been adopting various forms of employment subsidies in order to reduce the numbers of redundancies and lay-offs during the current recession. A pioneer country in this respect was Austria. The difficulty with such subsidies is that, should they become more than temporary, they may impede economic efficiency. Yet perhaps the major problem today is no longer that of discovering temporary counter-cyclical manpower policy instruments. On the contrary, the central issue may become how to convert these devices and to discover others which may safeguard employment in the face of a new longer-term and structural employment crisis.

The new employment crisis

The controversy in the United States of America between the exponents of a deficiency of demand explanation of unemployment, on the one hand, and those who explained it in terms of structural change, on the other, took place during and after the recession of 1958. An early consensus, at least among academic economists, favoured the aggregative, demand deficiency explanation, although there were those who concluded that rapid structural change caused by automation and other technical progress was the true culprit.[28] In Europe, too, there was concern during the 1960s over the possible effects of technological change on job opportunities, but again the conclusion was reached that the likely effect would be slight and that automation would tend to increase rather than reduce skills.[29] But more recent experience suggests that much of this optimism may have been misplaced and that there is now in Europe a significant structural element in unemployment which is unlikely to disappear with economic recovery. During the 1966–8 recession observers noted how shortages of specific skilled occupations in countries such as the Netherlands persisted despite high unemployment.[30] In Britain, as elsewhere, there were noticeable changes at this time in the relationships which had previously held between output and unemployment, employment and unemployment, unemployment and vacancies.[31] The present recession and the oil crisis, above all, have served to strengthen these doubts and the 'nagging suspicion' that the post-war employment levels enjoyed in Europe's richer countries have been only a temporary exception to the rule for modern industrial economies.[32]

However long it may continue, the new employment crisis seems set to strengthen the role of manpower policy both as a selective instrument for tackling the unemployment–inflation conundrum and as an alternative means of promoting employment to the well tried but now suspect measures of economic, fiscal and monetary 'management'. In particular, developments are already well established in four directions – employment protection, employment subsidies, early retirement and job release for education and training.

That redundancies were best minimised in extent or

carefully planned in advance when they occurred was recognised early in both West Germany and France.[33] The procedures established in these countries for consultation and examination with worker representatives and for advance notification to the public manpower authorities in the event of redundancies, to a large extent formed the basis for the EEC Directive on Employment Protection. This in turn has extended such provision to other EEC members. One effect of such measures is necessarily to increase the costs and difficulties of reducing employment within firms during a recession and this of course is nowadays reinforced by trade union pressure. They may also have the effect of restricting the overall growth in employment in organisations affected: by raising the fixed element in labour costs and reinforcing the tendency for labour to become a fixed rather than variable factor of production, such policies are likely to make employers increasingly cautious in making new 'investments' in additional manpower. But these considerations apply mainly to larger organisations and their full-time and longer service employees and to this extent will reinforce the duality of labour markets segrated into a primary sector of full-time, secure employments with fringe benefits, promotion and career prospects and a secondary sector characterised by insecurity, volatility, high turnover and poor prospects.[34] Employment protection therefore, remains only a partial and, at times, problematical response to the problems of employment promotion. A more comprehensive approach in recent years has been broached by the Italian trade unions in using the channels of company collective bargaining to negotiate both guarantees of employment levels and specific commitments to job-creating investment projects particularly in the underdeveloped South.

Increased employment protection has been accompanied in many countries by substantially more generous financial benefits for those who do lose their jobs through no fault of their own. Such provision tends to avoid the 'compensation principle' embodied in severance and redundancy payments as in Belgium and Britain, which may well encourage the selection for redundancy of those least able to find alternative work. The pioneer agreement was reached in France in 1974 providing unemployment benefits of ninety per cent of their former gross wages for workers dismissed for 'economic reasons' for up to one year.[35] But other countries, such as the Netherlands and Ireland, have followed the same path. Such more generous provision does not, of course, entirely remove the uncertainties and insecurity of labour markets. But in so far as they encourage voluntary redundancies there is evidence that they help. Both Chrysler in Britain and Volkswagen in Germany have recently made substantial use of voluntary redundancy in meeting the slump in the motor vehicle industry.

Employment protection, then, has applied a stick to employers and generous severance and unemployment payments a carrot to employees to reduce the scale of compulsory dismissal for economic reasons. A further device to avoid this resort has been increasing provision for early retirement. This, like most manpower policy devices, has been selective in providing for early retirement as an alternative to redundancy or to long-term unemployment. In Italy special allowances have been payable since 1975 to facilitate early retirements of workers in sectors temporarily affected by the economic recession.[36] In Belguim, as in Britain, there is now a temporary scheme allowing for early retirement where such a worker is replaced by a young, unemployed worker.[37] More general proposals for a reduction in retirement ages are, of course, being actively discussed almost everywhere.

Employment subsidies of various kinds, but especially for the employment of school leavers and unemployed youth, have also been adopted. In the Netherlands, the subsidies are directly tied to training in company schools, a narrower concept than in the British work experience programme or recruitment subsidy for school-leavers. Temporary employment subsidies to help firms ride out short-term difficulties without resorting to redundancy, however, are likely to be of more enduring interest in the framework of manpower policy. These have an obvious attraction to government in so far as their net cost to the budget is small and there are economic, as well as social, arguments in their favour. On the other hand, they raise knotty problems of state involvement in determining the likely long-term viability of particular firms, where mistakes will tend to lead to subsidies with more than a temporary character.

Education or training leave from work is the fourth area in manpower policy which has been stimulated by the new employment crisis. Such leave has been extended from provision for attendance at purely vocational courses designed to improve or add to existing skills, to providing retraining into wholly new skills and now increasingly for purely educational courses. In Belgium and Italy this includes attendance at Universities. This newer concept of adult study leave has only recently been introduced in Sweden.[38] Two important elements of such a policy are provision for reinstatement on comparable terms where leave is not on a day-release basis and compensation for any drop in income while studying. Usually this will involve some additional costs to employers, although with effective manpower planning they can be minimised. Study leave would also seem the prime candidate for the 'drawing-rights' principle and very often embodies it in so far as workers are given fixed entitlements of so many days per number of years. In France this is specified as a maximum proportion (two per cent) of an enterprise's workforce which may be on leave at any one time together with a maximum annual entitlement for each individual. Similar schemes have been introduced in Italy through collective bargaining. There the policy has been particularly important in allowing many workers to complete or to further their initial school education.[39]

Outlook

By the 1960s manpower policies in Europe's richer countries were being developed in response to actual or projected manpower shortages. Just as immigrant workers had become well established the desirability of permitting uncontrolled immigration as a source of additional labour supplies was questioned. Neither the rural exodus within some of the richer countries nor increased female participation seemed likely to fill the 'gap' between expected demand and supply of labour. Today the concern is with actual and expected manpower surpluses. Symptomatic of this is the British Manpower Commission's recent projection of labour supplies between 1976 and 1981 indicating the need to create an additional 900,000 jobs by 1979 if a target level of 700,000 unemployed is to be achieved.[40] Yet there are few indications that the present high levels of unemployment in post-war Europe are likely to decline significantly in the near future or medium-term.

Hence the central issues in manpower policy are no longer those of surmounting general shortages nor even of correcting inflationary imbalances, though this remains an important aim. Once again full employment is the central aim but in circumstances which seem to rule out demand reflation as a cure in many countries.

It is these pressures which have led to experimentation with the kind of solutions outlined above. Most of these now involve some form of work-sharing or work-rationing whereby it is hoped that a lower life-long commitment to work and increased spells out of the labour force for all will lead to fewer long-term unemployed. In effect this must mean that the fruits of any productivity increases will be taken in the form of increased leisure for the community rather than increased consumption of goods and services. The implications of such an alternative form of 'growth' are fundamental.[41] Moreover, the effectiveness of work-rationing depends crucially on how such schemes as paid educational leave and early retirement are financed. Invariably employers are required to bear at least part of the cost. But if such additional fixed employee costs do not restrain growth in employment or even reduce employment levels, they will be passed on as increased prices. In other words, there is little alternative to financing such schemes out of real wages and salaries either through additional taxes, reduced public expenditure in other areas or inflation. The same proviso operates with other work sharing schemes such as shorter hours of work, longer holidays, employment protection or increased availability of higher education where, as in Italy, it would seem quite genuinely to have become an alternative to unemployment.[42] Equally it applies to attempting to counteract unemployment with increased job opportunities in the public sector, when in many countries such policies are already encountering strong resistance to high rates of taxation.

In these respects, manpower policy cannot now, as it could not in the past, be isolated from the economic context and related monetary, fiscal and economic policies. But the change in this context has led to an important change in emphasis in manpower policies. What is not clear is whether the necessary consent of those who remain in employment will be forthcoming for helping to combat unemployment.

References

1. For a fuller account see Delors, J., 'Surveys and Analyses of Labour Market Developments During Recent Years (Selected Countries): A. Experience To Be Drawn From the Anti-Inflationary Recession in Europe 1966–8'. In OECD Social Affairs Division, *International Conference on Employment Fluctuations and Manpower Policy*, OECD (Paris 1969).
2. See Denison, E. F., *Why Growth Rates Differ*, Brookings Institution (Washington DC 1967).
3. International Labour Office, *Manpower Aspects of Recent Economic Developments in Europe*, ILO (Geneva 1969).
4. See International Labour Office, *Manpower Adjustment Programmes: 1 France, Federal Republic of Germany, United Kingdom*, Labour and Automation Bulletin No. 4, ILO (Geneva 1967), pp. 17–18.

5. See National Economic Development Council, *Conditions Favourable To Faster Growth*, HMSO (London 1963).

6. Organisation for Economic Co-operation and Development, *Reviews of Manpower and Social Policies*, OECD (Paris 1964 ff.).

7. International Labour Office, *Manpower Aspects of Recent Economic Developments in Europe, op. cit.*, p. 46.

8. Organisation for Economic Co-operation and Development, *Reviews of Manpower and Social Policies: 15 Manpower Policy in Ireland*, OECD (Paris 1974).

9. For a fuller explanation of the drawing rights approach see Organisation for Economic Co-operation and Development, *Reviews of Manpower and Social Policies: 13 Manpower Policy in Germany*, OECD (Paris 1974), pp. 33–6.

10. See United Nations Economic Commission for Europe, *Economic Survey of Europe in 1965*, United Nations (Geneva 1965)

11. Granier, R. and Marciano, J. P., 'The Earnings of Immigrant Workers in France', *International Labour Review*, vol. 111, January-June 1975, pp. 143–65.

12. Bohning, W. R. and Maillat, D. *The Effects of the Employment of Foreign Workers*, OECD (Paris 1974), p. 56.

13. *Ibid.* p. 101.

14. Delors, J., *op. cit.* p. 9.

15. Schiller, G., 'Channelling Migration: A Review of Policy with Special Reference to the Federal Republic of Germany', *International Labour Review, op. cit.*, pp. 335–55.

16. See Buchan D. 'Migrant Workers: First Victims of Recession', *The Financial Times*, 6 December 1976.

17. Organisation for Economic Co-operation and Development, *Economic Surveys: Austria 1976*, OECD (Paris 1976).

18. See Organisation for Economic Co-operation and Development, *Economic Surveys : Spain 1975*, OECD (Paris 1975).

19. Kayser, B., *Manpower Movements and Labour Markets*, OECD (Paris 1971), p. 127.

20. There is now a large literature on the effects of redundancy in Britain, but see in particular MacKay, D.

I., 'After The Shake-Out', *Oxford Economic Papers*, vol. 24, 1972, and MacKay, D. I, 'Redundancy and Re-engagement: A Study of Car Workers', *Manchester School of Economic and Social Studies*, Vol. XL, 1972.

21. International Labour Office, *op. cit.*, pp. 78–9.
22. See Bell, J. D. M., 'The Development of Industrial Relations in Nationalised Industries in Postwar Britain', *British Journal of Industrial Relations*, Vol. X111, 1975.
23. For a fuller account of the Swedish policy see, Mukherjee, S., *Making Labour Markets Work*, Policitcal and Economic Planning Broadsheet 532, January 1972, and for a more general discussion see Organisation for Economic Co-operation and Development, *Adult Training As An Instrument of Active Manpower Policy*, revised edition, OECD (Paris 1972).
24. See Hakanson, H., 'Industrial Training Programmes As An Employment Regulator', in OECD Social Affairs Division, *op. cit.*
25. Lachs, T., 'Timely Application of Compensatory Employment Programmes in Labour Surplus Areas', in OECD Social Affairs Division, *op. cit.*
26. Organisation for Economic Co-operation and Development, *Manpower Policy in Germany*, *op. cit.*, pp. 46–2.
27. See for example Ross, A., ed., *Unemployment and The American Economy*, Wiley (New York 1964).
28. See Rees, A., 'Surveys and Analyses of Labour Market Developments During Recent Years (Selected Countries): B. Recent American Experience' in OECD Social Affairs Division, *op. cit.*
29. See International Labour Office, *Labour and Automation Bulletins*, ILO (Geneva 1967); Organisation for Economic Co-operation and Development, *Manpower Aspects of Automation and Technical Change*, OECD (Paris 1966); Anderman, S. D., ed., *Trade Unions and Technological Change*, Allen and Unwin (London 1967); Reid, G. L., Hunter, L. C., and Boddy, D. *Labour Problems of Technological Change*, Allen and Unwin (London 1970).
30. Delors, J., *op. cit.*

31. See Bowers, J. K. *et al.*, 'Some Aspects of Unemployment and the Labour Market 1966–71', *National Institute Economic Review*, 62, November 1972.
32. Schiller, G., *op. cit.*
33. Mukherjee, S., *Through No Fault of Their Own : Systems for Handling Redundancy in Britain, France and Germany*, Political and Economic Planning, Macdonald (London 1973).
34. For a fuller explanation see Bosanquet, N. and Doeringer, P., 'Is There A Dual Labour Market in Britain?', *Economic Journal*, vol. 83, June 1973.
35. See *European Industrial Relations Review*, No. 11, November 1974, pp. 19–20.
36. *European Industrial Relations Review*, No. 32, November 1975, pp. 17–18.
37. *European Industrial Relations Review*, No. 32, August 1976, pp. 12–14.
38. *European Industrial Relations Review*, No. 14, February 1975, p. 11.
39. *European Industrial Relations Review*, No. 28, April 1976, pp. 17–18.
40. Manpower Services Commission, *Towards a Comprehensive Manpower Policy*, MSC (London 1976).
41. See J. Mouly and R. Broadfield, 'Employment Objectives and Policies in the Industrialised Market Economy Countries,' *International Labour Review*, Vol. 113, January-June 1976, pp. 85–95.
42. G. Birtig, 'Employment Problems and the Educational System in Italy,' *International Labour Review*, Vol. 114, July-December 1976, pp. 11–25.

3 Trade unions and collective bargaining systems

J. F. B. GOODMAN

The countries of Western Europe have many broad similarities such as parliamentary democracy, advanced industrialisation, high living standards and a predominant reliance on the market economy. In most of the countries similar political and economic forces are exerting strong influences, and elements of convergence can be discerned in certain contemporary industrial relations trends.

Despite the similarities, the countries remain a patchwork of individual histories and differing national institutional structures. Such differences are most marked in trade union organisation and in collective bargaining. The depth, form of organisation, scope and status of collective bargaining varies considerably between the different countries, although it is prominent in almost all of them as a means of determining pay and conditions of employment. Not only is there a difference in the exact forms of interaction between trade unions from country to country, there is a similarly wide variation *within* each national context between different sectors, industries, occupations and so forth.

European collective bargaining arrangements thus form a multi-coloured patchwork of different styles, tones and texture, which makes all-inclusive comment difficult. The search for appropriate generalisation and meaningful comparisons is hazardous and will necessarily be confined largely to manual workers in the manufacturing sector, with only few references to internal differences within countries.

The chapter begins by looking at the broad setting of collective bargaining in Europe. Then there are sections on trade union organisation and multi-employer bargaining structures. Comment on workplace bargaining is followed by a view of future trends.

Collective bargaining occupies a critical interchange position in Western European societies, influencing and being influenced by a myriad of characteristics of each society – economic, political, cultural, social, historical. It is related most fundamentally and directly to the pluralist political structures of Western democracies. Within these political systems collective bargaining represents the preferred method of organisation for handling the multitude of contentious issues ranging from income distribution to employee status, and constituting the primary means of institutionalising and containing social conflicts arising over employment and other issues in the industrial system. In most European countries the legal framework surrounding the conduct of industrial relations is both substantively more important and more detailed, whilst the extent of legal underpinning of both collective relationships between unions and employers and of individual employee rights is also deeper than in Britain. The extent of legal regulation tends, therefore, both to secure and to restrain collective bargaining activity and the associated exercise of sanctions. Further, some Continental trade unions, especially those on the Left, are far less wedded to collective bargaining than are British trade unions. For example, the CGT in France refuses to accept any limitation on its wider freedom of action as a consequence of reaching agreements on industrial questions with the employers, and refuses to feel constrained by 'peace clauses' or grievance procedures. In France, as in Italy, it is sometimes misleading to treat statutory enactments as describing the *de facto* reality of industrial relations whilst in other European countries the 'limits of the law' as a restraint on industrial strife have been observed with much greater frequency during the last decade than was the case in the two preceding decades. Holland, Belgium, Sweden and Denmark have all experienced outbursts of discontent and dissatisfaction at factory level, whilst the events in France in 1968 and during the 'hot autumn' of 1969 in Italy led many commentators to speculate about a new wave of militancy undermining the regulatory power of the established institutions. Industrial peace has once again been demonstrated to be contingent, and not permanently achieved by any temporary legal-social-institutional apparatus.

Collective bargaining is complex, and may be described or analysed from a variety of viewpoints, particularly within an international context. For example one of the major dimensions is the relative importance of the different *levels* of bargaining, descending from central national bargaining between confederations of trade unions and employers' associations to shop-steward activity within particular plants. Other important facets are the *scope* of collective bargaining, in terms of the range of subjects treated and the detail of their regulation, and in the sense of its *coverage* or extensiveness across different sectors of employment. Variations can also be found, for example, in the role and influence of third party agencies, tribunals, conciliation and arbitration bodies, in the legal status of agreements and their possible extension to non-signatories, in their duration, in the degree of co-ordination between bargaining units at different levels and in many other aspects. First, however, it is necessary to look at the organisation of the trade unions, for their varying power, both internal and external, exerts a profound influence on most of the dimensions of collective bargaining.

Trade unions

Although Britain has the oldest and probably the most complicated trade union structure, the trade union movements on the Continent also have their own intricacies. The absolute size of the British trade union movement is greater than that in any other European country, but it is by no means the strongest in proportionate terms. Further, although the British TUC has

achieved very considerable influence over the policies of the
Labour Government since 1974, the length of this influence
pales when compared with the longevity of the Social
Democratic governments in Sweden with which the
equivalent LO has close links. Finally, the British TUC
represents a major union centre with no rival centres of
power or of trade union representation. France, Italy,
Belgium and the Netherlands have competing
confederations of manual worker unions, and like
Denmark, Germany and Sweden they also have separate
minority confederations for white collar workers or civil
servants or both.

In Britain the main lines of union structure are
conventionally drawn on the basis of the groups of workers
each union seeks to organise, and these differing bases have
led to a complicated pattern of craft, ex-craft, general,
industrial and white collar unions, with the diversity often
being extended rather than reduced by merger and change.
Although the politics of British unions and particularly their
leaders are followed with interest it is seldom suggested that
a British union's political perspective outweighs industrial
or occupational attachment as a decision-rule for potential
union-members in Britain. On the Continent however, in
France, Italy, Belgium and the Netherlands, union structure
is drawn primarily along political and religious lines.
Within these divisions, internal union organisation is most
commonly structured on the industrial principle, but
clearly this does not produce single-unionism at plant level
for each confederation may be represented (certainly in the
larger establishments) and the willingness of the opposing
union confederations to work together varies between
countries. Currently the socialist, catholic and protestant
confederations in Holland are perhaps the closest to
overcoming their historical differences.

The simplest European trade union structure, and
certainly the one most familiar to British readers, is that of
West Germany, where the trade unions were re-established
on industrial lines after the war, following the destruction
of the earlier political/religiously divided movement in

mid-1930s. The sixteen industrial unions in Germany thus largely avoid both the divisions found in neighbouring countries and multi-unionism at plant level. All sixteen are affiliated to the DGB, including Europe's largest trade union I G Metall which covers the engineering sector, although the unions of salaried employees (DAG) and of civil servants (DB) remain outside. Like British unions affiliated to the TUC, DGB unions have autonomous bargaining powers and the DGB has only a limited co-ordinating role in collective bargaining. The Danish trade unions are primarily organised on the craft principle, although there are also industrial unions and a large general union as well, whilst the pattern of unionisation in Eire also has many affinities with the British structure. In Denmark, however, the central confederation, the LO, has substantial authority over member unions and plays a very significant role in the negotiation of multi-industry general agreements with the tightly disciplined employers' confederation (DA). In these countries trade unions are identified most closely with Labour or Social Democrat parties and whatever the influence of Leftist minorities they remain committed to collective bargaining and the adjustment of industrial grievances.

The largest Communist union confederations are the CGT in France and the CGIL in Italy. In France post-war industrial relations have been characterised by an atmosphere of overt class conflict. The general trade union picture is one of shifting stances, discords and schisms at the national level, built on relatively low levels of union membership and considerable weakness at plant level. The Marxist CGT competes with the socialist-reformist CGT-FO (which is strong in the public sector) and two other confederations with their origins in Catholicism – the now 'free' and increasingly radical CFDT, and the smaller CFTC which maintains its links with the Church. There are a number of other autonomous confederations as well. In Italy the unification of the re-established trade union movement after the war was short lived, and the three major union confederations split in 1947. The CGIL, which claims about four million members, competes with the CISL (mainly Christian Democrat) and the Social Democrat UIL with about 800,000. In addition there are several smaller trade union groups. The Dutch trade union movement also has a triple division – between (in descending order of size) the Socialist, non-denominational NVV, the Catholic NKV which is strongest in the South, and the Protestant CNV – although again there are other unions primarily of white collar workers outside these three confederations. In Belgium the two main confederations are the Christian CSC and the socialist FGTB, both with about one million members, plus the smaller CGSLB which has close links with the Liberal Party. In Holland and Belgium the internal structure of the confederations follows industrial lines, corresponding to the main lines of the bargaining structure below the central level.

The different union movements in different countries vary on a number of dimensions, not least in their membership levels. The highest level of union membership is found in Sweden with roughly ninety per cent. Belgium has the highest density of union membership of the original member countries of the EEC with about sixty-five per cent, whilst of the new entrants the level in Denmark (sixty per cent) is higher than that in Britain and Eire (fifty per cent). West Germany has about thirty-seven per cent, the Netherlands thirty-five per cent and both France and Italy with perhaps twenty-five per cent – though in these countries the levels are approximations at best for the union centres are inclined to exaggerate their size and union membership is often a more transient and spasmodic activity than it is in Northern Europe.

It is apparent from this brief outline that there is considerable variation in character, orientation and strength of European trade unions. Most European unions are heavily involved in national politics. The reformist ambitions of most are criticised by those to the Left as being moderate and pragmatic, and by those to the Right as departing from the examples of narrow sectional economic interest portrayed by the business unionism of the United

States. The CGT and the CISL perceive their role more as class organisations than as 'bargainers with capitalism' or as the protectors of sectional economic interests. Political differences between union groups have often limited the development of effective collective bargaining systems, and constrained the industrial achievements of the unions in France and Italy, particularly at plant level. Division and fragmentation amongst the unions have left the employers in a generally strong position in France, whilst in Italy the unions' concern with political differences and with external factors meant they were by-passed by rank-and-file revolts in the late 1960s. Both the CGIL and the CGT have faced dilemmas in reconciling ideological rectitude (which emphasises central policy direction) and grass-roots involvement. The latter has been in the ascendancy in recent years as the CGIL in particular has sought to re-establish its influence over the newly-emergent factory councils. Indeed recent developments in both Italy and in Holland have tended to mute inter-union differences. In Belgium the union confederations work closely together in the face of the employers, and (as in Holland) are firmly integrated in public economic and social planning bodies, but there is little immediate prospect of a formalised merger. The Christian – or 'confessional' unions as they are often called – are less concerned with radical social change, are more conventionally bargaining-oriented and less likely to be opposed to co-determination and co-decision-making than the socialist and communist union confederations.

Multi-employer bargaining structures

Collective bargaining takes place at a variety of levels, ranging from agreements reached between the central union confederations and central employers organisation, e.g. the LO and DA in Denmark, or the LO and SAF in Sweden, through various industrial, regional and company tiers to the works councils, shop-stewards or union delegations in individual factories. Again there is considerable diversity, not least at company and factory levels where the activities and scope of works councils (widely established by statute in European countries) interact in various ways with those of workplace trade union representatives. In many European countries formal collective bargaining by the trade unions stops short of the plant. Internal plant level issues are regulated by works councils which are not an integral part of trade union organisation and whose members are generally charged with promoting the most effective operation of the factories. The power to lead strikes or apply collective sanctions is typically witheld by the law from works councillors.

Just as no exact counterpart of the British (engineering) shop-steward can be found in Europe – although there are some approximations – another point of contrast is the importance of bargaining at the equivalent of TUC-CBI level. This is perhaps of greatest importance in the Scandinavian countries with their strong centralised trade union and employer organisations. The LO and DA in Denmark conduct their biennial negotiations within a Main Agreement – the first of which was reached in 1899, and which sets out the basic principles and procedures for the conduct of national level collective bargaining. The two central organisations negotiate over 'general questions', such as general wage increases, the nature of index-linking, hours, holidays etc., leaving 'special questions' to be negotiated simultaneously at industry level. Broadly similar arrangements apply in Sweden, where the high degree of centralisation and the synchronisation of the major negotiations has facilitated pursuit of an essentially bi-lateral incomes policy. In both countries, however, incentive payment schemes regulated at plant level are important. Nevertheless, these national negotiations constitute major strategic events in the calendar of industrial relations in the Scandinavian countries. National level, inter-industry agreements are also important in other countries, for example in Belgium where the three 'most representative trade union organisations' and the central employers organisation (FEB) have reached a number of agreements on subjects such as guaranteed incomes, pensions, manpower policy, holidays, time-off for trade union delegates and other subjects under a joint programme of social advance in industry, known as 'Social Programming'. Similar national level, inter-industry, *accords* have been a feature of negotiations in France in recent years, and for much of the post-war period national level negotiations over rates of wage increases have been important in Holland, which has a long history of nationally-regulated incomes policy.

Perhaps the major or most general feature of European collective bargaining is the extensiveness of multi-employer bargaining units – a sharp contrast with the predominant pattern of single company or plant agreements in the United States. In Italy the union confederations reached central agreements with the two main employer's organisations, *Confindustria* for the private sector and *Intersind* for the public sector, which were particularly important in the period until the early 1960s when a more 'articulated' system, including bargaining at lower levels began to emerge. This has subsequently been overtaken, although not replaced, by the rapid developments of workplace bargaining conducted by 'delegates' directly elected by work groups and often with only tenuous links with the trade unions. The present picture in Italy has been described by one writer as 'an unco-ordinated, multi-tiered system ranging from what are virtually political negotiations with the Government at the top to informal bargaining by workers' delegates at the bottom'. The pattern in West Germany is, predictably, somewhat more stable, with a relatively clear distinction drawn between external collective bargaining between employer associations and trade unions at industry and regional levels, and the internal role of works councils within companies. At the national industrial level, framework agreements covering such subjects as hours of work, shift premia, overtime rates, occupational classifications and other general issues are negotiated and often run for three or four year periods. Wage levels are negotiated, usually on an annual basis, at the regional (or *Land*) industrial level. A similarly clear pattern is found in Belgium, although it differs from the German pattern with the regional level being much less important. The high level of unionisation in Belgium has already been indicated, and the Belgian unions and employers have established a strong system of industry-wide bargaining, conducted in joint *Commissions Paritaires*. These industry-wide agreements are relatively comprehensive in their scope, and generally fix detailed wage levels, leaving relatively limited scope for plant bargaining. Recent agreements in textiles and the metal industry, for example, excluded company level claims, although the chemical industry is an exception. The bi-partite National Labour Council exercises an important supervisory role, and can conclude agreements for sectors where there are no *Commissions Paritaires*, as well as acting as an arbitral body on industry-level disputes. Union organisation, as opposed to the statutory works councils, is also influential in Belgian factories. Union delegates – although their formal powers of negotiation are limited and they have little of the autonomy of British shop-stewards – play an important monitoring role. The pattern of collective bargaining in Holland following the breakdown of the highly centralised bargaining structure in the mid 1960s, is much more diverse. There are important industry-wide agreements in building and engineering, but many of the large multi-national companies such as Philips, Shell and Unilever have company agreements. Historically the Dutch unions have not encouraged plant level bargaining, but the NVV in particular has recently pressed for workplace trade union representatives to be provided for in the collective agreements. As in Belgium, however, these representatives act primarily as points of contact for the external full-time union officers rather than as workplace bargainers.

The structure of collective bargaining in France is complicated. The clearest feature is the weakness of trade union organisation at factory level where the employers have generally retained considerable unilateral authority. As indicated earlier a number of multi-industry *accords* have been reached at national level, primarily on non-wage subjects such as retirement, staff status for manual workers, vocational training and employment and earnings security. These *accords* between the national employers' body, the CNPF, and the union confederations have usually been reached in close collaboration with the public authorities, and are left for detailed agreement and extension by the parties in specific industries. Industry level bargaining is the backbone of the French system, although the regional level has been most significant historically in the engineering industry. However, as in Germany, the regional industry agreements specify the wage levels (or rather the wage minima), but the determination of actual wages takes place within factories where – with a few notable exceptions – union organisation is weak.

Typically, collective agreements in European countries are legally binding on the parties, although the detailed provisions vary. It is also usual for the law to make a distinction between disputes about 'interests' and interpretative disputes about rights under existing agreements, and for binding arbitration to be used in the latter although industrial rather than court arbitration is more common in some countries. The three tier system of Labour Courts in West Germany is particularly prominent, and also plays a major role in interpreting and applying the extensive statute law on individual employment rights. Similar systems are also found in France, Denmark, Norway and since 1967 in Belgium. In Britain, which avoided special labour 'courts' for many years, the network of Industrial Tribunals now has an extensive role in individual disputes and can be compared increasingly with continental practice. Most European collective agreements contain 'peace clauses' prohibiting the exercise of sanctions during the currency of agreements, although as we have seen, the French CGT in particular rejects the notion of the trade union as a guardian of agreements or as an agent for worker discipline. Disputes about rights are conventionally referred for arbitration if they cannot be settled by informal means. Failure to agree over the periodic re-negotiation of new industry or inter-industry agreements typically involves national conciliation efforts, and not usually the participation of Government Ministers. In Denmark the Conciliation Board acts as mediator, and can order two consecutive postponements or 'cooling-off' periods when serious strikes are threatened. In the event of failure to agree over a new 'main agreement' a settlement drafted by the Conciliation Board may be put to a ballot. West German trade union rules normally require a ballot of members before strike action is taken, and often stipulate a seventy-five per cent majority before official strikes can be called. Further, there are other legal restraints and limitations on the constitutionality of strikes in West Germany. The recent changes towards legal enforceability in Belgium are underpinned by provisions in some agreements giving differential benefits to trade union members if the 'no strike' clauses are observed, and a recent agreement in the Belgian metal-working industry for example effectively gave the unions a direct financial incentive to get striking members back to work within a three day period. In a number of countries, notably Germany, Belgium and the Netherlands relatively prominent use is made of the legal provision for the extension of the substantive conditions specified in collective agreements to non-signatory employers.

Workplace bargaining

A major contrast between industrial relations at workplace level in Britain and in the countries of continental Europe is the almost universal presence in the latter of statutory works councils. In Britain the development of joint consultative bodies continued in many factories which had established joint production committees during the war, and in other cases they were created in the early post-war period to improve communications and facilitate discussion of topics not covered by collective agreements. Like many other aspects of the British system however, they were voluntary, and many fell short of managerial expectations and lost their impetus. The major development in workplace industrial relations in Britain in the post-war period is without doubt the increased numbers and enlarged bargaining role of shop-stewards. Whereas the traditional pattern of industry-wide agreements had inhibited shop-floor trade union activity, albeit with some exceptions, post-war conditions proved favourable for work-group pressure, and the shop-stewards acquired enhanced, if largely informal, bargaining rights over a number of important issues, not least overtime, labour utilisation, incentive payment schemes, discipline and other issues. British shop-stewards occupy an imperfectly defined role, being both representatives of trade unions and of trade union members, often in multi-union situations in which the unions have not developed adequate inter-union institutions at factory level. Their emergence and growth has been largely pragmatic and unplanned, but their presence adds greatly to the depth of trade union influence in Britain.

The works councils in Europe owe much more to deliberate legislative provision, and their powers rest unequivocally on statute rather than on trade union power or on collective agreements. In some countries trade unions have viewed the presence of works councils as a competitive threat to union organisation, and as a bastion against trade union influence in the workplace. The works councils in Germany are particularly strong, and have legally prescribed rights of co-determination over plant rules and discipline, the principles of remuneration methods and a broad range of issues ranging from productivity bonuses to welfare matters. The works councils are responsible for supervising the application of laws and collective agreements and have a major conflict-handling role, with access to arbitration where necessary. By comparison the union representatives at plant level, the so-called union 'trustmen' have no legal status and a very much more limited presence and role. The German works councils are exclusively employee bodies, elected by all employees though the great majority of works councillors are union members. The Councils are responsible to the 'works community' rather than to external organisations, and although their legal powers ensure them a central role in workplace bargaining, that bargaining is not underpinned by the availability of sanctions. They offer a highly formalised mechanism for the conduct of bargaining within factories – a system which offers obvious scope for consistency and clarity, and which German management generally considers conducive to efficient management. Like the German system, that in Holland has recently been strengthened, and is also similarly charged with promoting the 'best possible running' of the undertaking. Dutch works councils are joint worker-management bodies, with co-determination rights on certain issues (e.g. work rules, pension or profit sharing schemes, hours and holiday arrangements, and safety, health and hygiene matters) and prior consultation rights on other issues subject to their coverage in collective agreements. In both countries there is now legal provision for company councils in multi-plant companies. The works councils in Belgium are also joint bodies of workers and management, but only the trade unions can nominate candidates. Recent legislation has greatly extended the obligation on management to disclose economic and financial information, and they have co-determination rights on subjects like work rules, hours, holidays and welfare matters. There are also statutory Safety and Health Committees. In Belgium, however, the union delegations rather than the works councils tend to be more influential at factory level than is the case in Germany, and there is generally close liaison between the union delegates and the external full-time union officers who retain a strong position in the negotiation of agreements. French works councils have traditionally been regarded with some hostility by the employers and in the absence of strong unions within the factories have not been very effective. The CGT in France, like the FGTB in Belgium, has not favoured worker representation in collaborative structures. French law did not provide for workplace union representatives until 1969 – after the traumatic events in Paris a year earlier. The Italian works committees were largely consultative, and were similarly regarded with some ambivalence by both sides. In many factories they have in practice been superceded by the spontaneous emergence of a new form of work-place organisation – dependent neither on the unions nor on statute. The new 'factory councils' have challenged the external orientation of the Italian unions, and have sought to combine workers at shop-floor level independent of union membership or affiliation. The *delegatos* who formed the new factory councils secured agreements over many subjects via antagonistic bargaining. Denmark, like the Netherlands, has recently begun to experiment with employee representation at company board level, and at factory level the joint production committees have been superceded in the larger factories by 'co-operation committees' with more emphasis on participation in decision-making by the shop-stewards.

Future trends

This account has primarily described the main structural features of collective bargaining, and amply illustrates the diversity of forms, levels and orientations in European collective bargaining. It necessarily leaves many gaps, and the wider the canvas the greater the variations observed. One obvious difference is the substantive provisions established in collective agreements – the widely differing levels of pay, of holiday entitlements, and other benefits. If the diversity is apparent, what signs of convergence can be identified? Essentially perhaps four can be highlighted. The first of these is the existence of the European Economic Community and its long-term goals of harmonisation in the fields of company law and social policies more generally. The most immediately relevant of these, of course, are the draft directives on company law and the inclusion of employee representation at board level, but in the longer term legal regulation of employment issues more generally is likely to be enhanced. The Commission has also recently established a Collective Agreements Documentation Centre, which will facilitate international comparisons. Recent legislation in Britain, most notably the Employment Protection Act has established a higher and wider platform of legal rights for employees in many areas (e.g. redundancies, guaranteed wages, information disclosure etc.) which are already extensively covered by legislation in many European countries. Details may vary between countries, but legal regulation is increasing, generally in directions favourable to employees and unions rather than the reverse. The use of the law offers a more direct – if controversial – move towards harmonisation than piecemeal voluntarism. Certainly in the British context it is not an exaggeration to suggest that trade unions and their members have secured more through political lobbying and legislation than they have through direct industrial bargaining in the past few years. Significantly, if obviously, ground once occupied by the state tends not to be given up easily.

Secondly, of course, there is the growing internationalisation of major companies and of the West European economy as a whole. The managements of multi-nationals have generally resisted overtures from trade unions concerning 'cross-frontier' bargaining, and it is doubtful whether international trade union organisation will quickly develop the necessary strength and cohesion to achieve and sustain multi-national collective agreements. The international trade union secretariats' primary role at present is that of information collection and dissemination, although some attempts have been made to synchronise contract re-negotiation dates with multi-nationals in different countries. One feature of multi-national companies, however, is that they may introduce personnel policies and industrial relations practices which are innovative in a given national context, and to the extent that these large campanies act as pace-setters they may thus promote convergence indirectly. However, many multi-nationals have tended to de-emphasise corporate uniformity on industrial relations, and although there are some prominent exceptions, most have sought for fairly obvious reasons to integrate within local national industrial relations arrangements.

On the broader social front it is more difficult to anticipate the direction of future trends. At the macro-level many governments in Western Europe have sought to introduce direct wage policies aimed at slowing inflation rates, and as an almost inevitable consequence trade union and employers' leaders have been drawn more closely into tripartite bodies at government level. Trade union compliance has been secured only through increasingly greater influence on a wider range of economic and social policies. The dilemmas faced by the unions are similar to those anticipated by the prospect of greater involvement in corporate decision-making, namely the balance between participation and association and the retention of an independent adversary stance. Collaboration risks incorporation, and many unions remain uncertain of the optimal path. Indeed, displays of rank and file discontent have occurred in a number of West European countries, including several with traditionally stable industrial relations systems. Thus there are both centripetal pressures (associated with centralised incomes policies) and centrifugal forces (illustrated by increased bargaining activity at workplace levels), mediated in the different countries by differing social and institutional structures. Reforms, in collective bargaining structures, in union internal organisation and in the range and content of statutory provision on substantive matters, are likely to continue to seek to accommodate worker aspirations at lower levels of the system. In the past, rapid rates of economic growth and high levels of employment have obscured many of the underlying tensions and ambiguities, but these are increasingly being exposed. Overall the predominant trend is towards greater decentralisation, but this is generally of an additive rather than of an alternative kind.

Collective bargaining is an adaptive process and a flexible institution. Generally, once established, bargaining structures have proved relatively durable and stable, and shifts have been gradual and piecemeal. Given the diversity of the present bargaining arrangements in the different countries it is difficult to envisage any early development of what might be called a truly integrated European system of collective bargaining, even amongst member countries of the EEC. Certain points of convergence have been noted, for example the enhanced role of legal regulation (especially in Great Britain where it has traditionally been lowest), the medium term influence of the 'harmonising' policies of the Commission, and the developing strength of workplace union representatives in countries other than Britain. These and other trends are likely to diminish the differences, but deep-rooted attitudinal and cultural influences will no doubt persist. The prospect of cross-frontier bargaining with multi-national companies still appears to be remote in view of employer resistance, the localised focus of employee interests in these companies and the far from effective collaboration between union organisations in the different countries. If trans-national bargaining, which might initially develop on conditions and fringe benefits rather than on wages, seems improbable in the short-term the deeper, more detailed and more onerous regulation of employment issues through a combination of bargaining and legal prescription does not. From a British perspective this is likely to develop further, particularly in the areas of statutory minimum conditions and enterprise-based schemes of employee involvement in decision-making. Both issues, and a more explicitly predictive view, are covered more fully in subsequent chapters.

Bibliography

S. Barkin (ed), *Worker Militancy and its Consequences: New Directions in Western Industrial Relations*, Praeger (New York 1975).

International Labour Office, *Collective Bargaining in Industrialised Market Economics*, (Geneva 1974).

Commission on Industrial Relations, *Worker Participation and Collective Bargaining in Europe*, HMSO (London 1974).

C. Balfour, *Industrial Relations in the Common Market*, Routledge and Kegan Paul (London 1972).

4 Industrial democracy

W. W. DANIEL

Since 1970 legislation requiring some form of worker representation on company boards has been introduced or amended in seven European countries.[1] Many have simultaneously strengthened the powers of statutory works councils. In 1975 the Commission of the European Communities produced revised proposals for the harmonisation of company law in member countries and a draft statute for European companies.[2] Both sets of proposals were formulated on the principle that statutory provisions for worker representation on boards and for works councils are the normal requirements of company law in any modern industrial society. Even Britain, whose industrial relations traditions are alien to those which developed worker directors and works councillors, has not remained immune from the trend. In January of last year the majority Bullock report recommended parity representation of workers, appointed through trade union channels, on the boards of large companies.[3] The tide appears irresistible. Worker directors and statutory works councils represent industrial democracy. They will soon be required by similar laws in all countries within the European Community, and by many outside it. But, in practice the glittering prospect, or spectre, of most of Western Europe entering a new era of industrial democracy along the lines proposed by various EEC pronouncements will not be realised quickly or easily. Among those who favour greater industrial democracy there remains widespread disagreement about the best means of enhancing worker influence over decisions in the organisations that employ them. Many managers and employers remain jealous of their powers and fearful of the commerical consequences of increased worker influence. The differing industrial relations systems and traditions in different western European countries mean that an institutional innovation that may be wholly appropriate for a particular purpose in one country may have quite different consequences in another. It will not be possible in this short chapter to describe and evaluate all the competing notions of industrial democracy that have been postulated. We shall focus on what we shall term the *European model* of worker representation on boards and works councils because its influence and growth mean that the model warrants attention and not because it represents the only or the most effective way of ensuring that workers have a say over events. It will continue to compete with views that stress greater shop-floor participation; or self-management; or changes in ownership through nationalisation, producer cooperatives or wider share ownership. In Britain the European model will conflict particularly with alternative views that stress the importance of extending collective bargaining in order to ensure that the interests of workers are adequately represented relative to those of owners and managers. Such views have characterised the positions of organised labour in Britain during the post-war period. They arise from the distinctive features of the British industrial relations system compared to much of the rest of Western Europe. A brief account of these features will provide a framework indicating how proposed changes based on the European model are customarily evaluated by British trade unionists and their supporters. The account will also highlight the obstacles that exist to any rapid harmonisation.

The British industrial relations system

Three distinctive characteristics of British industrial relations are first the tradition of voluntarism, secondly the representation of workers through lay trade union officers at workplaces in the form of shop-stewards, and thirdly the organisation of trade union membership along occupational rather than industrial lines. In Britain trade unions have tended to seek to advance the interests and influence of themselves and their members through negotiation and collective agreement with employers. In continental Europe unions have been more disposed to look to the law as a means of achieving their ends. The British shop-steward is a unique institution. He represents workers across the full range of issues at workplace level including matters relating to pay, hours, grievances, discipline, workloads and so on. And he is an officer of the trade union. In continental Europe unions tend formally to represent workers in negotiations with employers and government only at the national, industrial and regional levels. Within companies and workplaces their influence is less direct. The formal channel of representation tends to be the works council, elected by union members and non members alike. Works councillors may or may not be trade unionists. In practice trade unions often exercise a major influence over elections and trade unionists often occupy key positions. But that pattern is by no means automatic. The works council system also means that there is one body representing all workers within any establishment. This again represents a major difference from the position in Britain where different unions tend to represent different sections of the workforce within companies and plants.

The British industrial relations system has led to the development of a distinctively British view of industrial democracy, based on the notion of countervailing power. This view was made explicit by Hugh Clegg,[4] but it is implicit in the behaviour of British trade unionism generally and particularly in its reactions to proposed innovations in industrial democracy. The view holds that in large, complex hierarchical organisations the ability of those at the base of the hierarchy to influence events is ultimately based on two pillars. The first is membership of institutions which are independent of the organisations for which they work. The second is the scope they have collectively to resist decisions until their consent is won. Accordingly the twin pillars of industrial democracy are independent trade unions and through them the scope to challenge and resist management decision-making where workers' interests are threatened.

Industrial democracy is advanced first by having strong representative trade unionists at every level of management decision-making: the shop, the plant, the divisional, the regional, the company and the national levels. Secondly worker influence is promoted by extending the agenda of collective bargaining to include the full range of management decisions. Conversely anything that weakens trade unions, or the scope of workers to organise and act collectively through trade unions, undermines industrial democracy. Innovations like worker directors and works councils are suspect. They create the illusion of greater worker influence while reducing the substance. They provide channels of worker representation which are separate from trade unions and likely to be more malleable to managerial control. For instance worker directors with no experience of board practice and no professional training in any of the specialisms involved in company decision-making are unlikely to make much impression on existing directors, particularly if they have no alternative ideological or institutional framework from which to derive a coherent position and some muscle to back it up.

The special features of the British industrial relations system and the distinctive view of industrial democracy to which it has contributed often results in mutual incomprehension between continental European and British trade unionists. People in the rest of Europe are astonished that Britons should reject and criticise the reforms for which they have struggled and which they see to be of such benefit to their members. The British are amazed that anyone should expect them to embrace institutional innovations that threaten their existing power by weakening their position within companies and plants and by limiting their scope to exercise sanctions. For instance the elected works council has a quite different meaning for British trade unionists than it does for their Swedish counterparts. In Britain it is often seen as a strategem for undermining shop-steward influence through the establishment of a separate channel of worker representation more favourably disposed to management. In Sweden, in the absence of a shop-steward system, works councils have been seen as means whereby unions can extend their influence within establishments and management decision-making may be made more accountable to workers' interests. They have been actively promoted by trade unions and integrated into their organisation. The opposite ways in which nominally similar institutions may be evaluated within different national systems of industrial relations underlines the formidable obstacles that stand in the way of the harmonisation of institutions and the legal provisions relating to them. Formally the British trade unions have modified their traditional view of worker representation on boards. They now favour the practice as long as representatives are appointed through trade union channels. The change was largely brought about by a recognition of the growth in the number and complexity of decision-making levels in business organisations, particularly transnational companies. While in principle trade union officers could represent workers' interests at all levels of management decision-making within national boundaries, through the traditional processes of collective bargaining, trade unionists recognised that to have influence on the transnationals it was necessary to be represented inside them at the highest levels. However, a substantial body of opinion within the British trade union movement still does not accept the case for worker directors. It still maintains that for employee interests to be effectively promoted representatives must remain independent of management and free to challenge and oppose management decision-making. It holds that the involvement of trade union representatives on boards will reduce that freedom. Moreover there remains a substantial gap between the form of board representation formally favoured by the TUC, and largely accepted by Bullock, and that operated or advocated in other parts of Europe.

Different forms of worker representation on boards

The reform of company law to provide for worker representation on boards has at least important symbolic implications. This has been apparent in the emotive response to the publication of the Bullock report in Britain. The appointment of worker directors formally and publicly recognises the right of workers to have a say over decisions affecting them at the highest level. And it formally recognises that companies should serve the interests of employees as well as shareholders. Whether it achieves any more than these symbolic ends is open to question. The one point on which all commentators and interest groups appear to be agreed is that board representation achieves little or nothing on its own. They argue that it needs to be integrated into an effective sub-structure of representation at other levels of decision-making and backed by other measures to promote involvement. Accordingly the establishment of a new system of board representation needs to be made congruent with other institutions. The existing national systems of worker representation on boards tend to be only one part of a set of measures to promote industrial democracy. It is always said that they have to be evaluated as part of the system as a whole rather than in isolation. But this may be because it is not possible to identify any hard evidence of board representation having had any particular effects. It has been perhaps cynically observed that the establishment of a legal requirement for workers to be represented on the boards of companies has invariably involved first the recognition of a right for workers to have an influence over decisions at the highest level, and secondly the specification of conditions and requirements which ensure that this right is not exercised.[5] Such requirements relate to the nature of the body on which worker directors sit; the proportion of worker directors on that body; their powers; the process whereby they are appointed; the limitations on those qualified to be appointed; and their legal obligations with regard to confidentiality and their primary interests. These have been the subsidiary issues which schemes for board representation have had to deal as they have sought to cope with the central issue of how to give workers an effective voice on the governing bodies of enterprises, at the same time as ensuring that the unity of direction in companies was maintained and its commercial interests in a market economy were not threatened.

The German system of worker directors was first instituted in 1952 and has the longest history of any. It provides a neat solution to the central dilemma. That is the two-tier board system involving a management board and a supervisory board. Crudely the management board runs the enterprise while the supervisory board acts as its watchdog. Employee directors sit on the supervisory board and make up a third of its membership. They are elected by the workforce as a whole. The indications are that supervisory boards have fulfilled a similar function in the operation of German companies as has the shareholders' meeting in Britain. Indeed the supervisory board has many of the formal powers that under British company law are vested in the shareholders' meeting, like the power to appoint or dismiss the management board. In practice under both systems this power has rarely been exercised. Professional management has remained firmly in command. It has retained control over the identification of policy options, the generation of information relating to these options and the implementation of policy. The supervisory boards tend to meet only about four times a year. And generally their role has been to approve the plans and performance of the management board. It is clear that in principle and practice the scheme is a long way from representing effective worker control over corporate decision-making. However, both German industrialists and trade unionists tend to agree that there are real benefits in the system. They say that it has encouraged managements to be more long-sighted in relation to manpower issues and to pay more attention to the possible effects upon workers of policy and change. And it has led to an earlier identification of problems associated with change. On the trade union side, however, there has been increasing dissatisfaction with the minority position of workers on supervisory boards and a growing demand for equal or parity representation. This has proved effective in the iron and steel industries where it has been established for many years. But so far German industrialists have successfully resisted its extension to the rest of German industry.

Other systems of worker directors in Europe have been established for too short a period for it to be possible to do any more than relate to some of their main features. Generally worker directors are in a minority position, are legally required to promote and defend the interests of the company as a whole and have constraints imposed upon the extent to which they can disseminate information gained in board meetings. All schemes formally separate the functions of the worker director and the trade union representative.[6] In the Netherlands neither employees of the company nor their union representatives may sit as worker directors on the supervisory board. Works councils may nominate people who have no direct connection with the company. The most common system of appointment is selection by works councils (the Netherlands, Austria, Luxembourg and France) followed by direct election (Denmark, Norway and most of German industry). Only in Sweden is direct involvement of the trade unions the chief means of appointment.

The Commission of the EEC has made two major sets of proposals relevant to worker representation on boards. The first is concerned with the harmonisation of company law in member countries;[7] the second with a statute for a European company.[8] The proposals for harmonisation will only come into being when and if they are accepted by all member countries. There is likely to be a lengthy period of negotiation and provision for flexibility to accommodate diverse forms of statutory requirement for worker representation before harmonisation is agreed. The draft statute will apply only to those companies that choose to register as European companies. It remains to be seen how far companies that operate in more than one member country will see any advantage in their doing so. However the provisions of the draft statute give an indication of the direction of Commission thinking on industrial democracy. It proposes a two-tier board system on the German model. This places the executive leadership of the company firmly in the hands of the management board, and leaves the supervisory board as a review body with particular rights of veto relating chiefly to closures, amalgamations, transfers and associations with other companies, and major organisational changes. The supervisory board will also have rights of access to management information. The supervisory board will be composed of one third shareholder representatives; and one third employee representatives; and one third co-opted by the other two groups to represent general community interests. Employee representatives will be appointed by election with all employees having voting rights. In addition the draft statute proposes a European works council having powers and functions similar to the works councils discussed in the section below.

It will be apparent that the majority Bullock recommendations for Britain differ from the European proposals in three important ways. First in opting for a single rather than a two-tier board system; secondly in specifying that the board members co-opted by shareholders and employee representatives should be an uneven number less than a third; and thirdly in proposing that employee representatives should be nominated by trade unions having negotiating rights in a company rather than elected by all employees. The little evidence that exists on the effects of employee representation on company boards in continental Europe suggests that whatever limited benefits they have brought about they have failed to achieve the goal of furnishing employee representatives with an effective say over decisions at the top. The minority position of employee representatives on boards has meant that they have always been outnumbered on issues of greatest concern. The bodies on which they have sat have often had limited formal powers and their effective powers have been even more restricted. Employee directors have tended to become isolated from constituents and identified with management partly as a result of the separation of trade union and director functions and the limits imposed on the dissemination of information. The Bullock proposals represent an attempt to reduce those limitations on the effectiveness of worker directors.

Statutory works councils

The second aim of the European Commission's proposals on industrial democracy is concerned with the establishment of works councils. According to the draft statute European companies would be required to set up a European works council. The council would have the right to co-determination on specified social and personnel issues; prior consultation on those matters subject to veto by the supervisory board; and information on a very wide range of other matters. Again the model is the German works council system which provides for statutory co-determination, joint consultation and the disclosure of information. Works councils are elected by employees as a whole, although trade unions wield substantial influence within councils. The operation of the co-determination principle can be illustrated in relation to redundancy. Before a management may declare a collective redundancy it has first to satisfy the works council that the redundancies are unavoidable. Secondly it must satisfy the council that an adequate social plan has been devised to provide for those to be displaced. Social plans will cover the criteria according to which the redundant will be selected, the compensation that will be paid to them, the measures that will be taken to help them find new jobs, and so on. If the works council is not satisfied with regard to either the need for the redundancies or the adequacy of the social plan then it may take the case to independent arbitration. However, associated with the council's rights to co-determination are strict limits on its powers to call for strikes and other sanctions against management. Secondly the co-determination provisions distinguish strictly between social or personnel issues and economic or technical ones. While managements are required to reach agreement with councils over matters like redundancy they have the right to unilateral decision-making in economic and technical matters. It is these features which make British trade unionists sceptical about co-determination. They suspect that works councils enhance freedom of management action rather than effective worker influence over events by requiring that workers are represented through elected works councillors and not trade union officers; by imposing limitations on the right to strike; and by providing for unilateral management decision-making in relation to technical matters.

In conception and origin the works council schemes operating in much of the rest of western Europe, such as those in France and the Netherlands, were even more unacceptable in British trade union terms. They were established by law or collective agreement to promote co-operation and common interests through joint consultation and the exchange of information. They were composed of elected employee representatives. In many ways they were the antithesis of the British shop-steward system of representation. Formally they resembled more the elected works councils that British managements have intermittently sought to establish for purposes of joint consultation separately from and parallel to negotiating machinery with union representatives. In Britain such councils have tended quickly to wither and die as a result of disenchantment and boredom on the part of both management and works councillors. Shop-stewards remained the worker representatives with powers to take action on issues that mattered to workers such as job rates, the allocation of overtime, workloads, grievances, discipline and change. Works councils were reduced to discussing peripheral and trivial matters about which they had no powers to do anything and were quickly castigated as irrelevant talking shops. In continental Europe, however, where there was no competing system of shop-steward representation, works councils developed in a quite different way. They filled a vacuum in the industrial relations system.[9] While having been established to promote co-operation through joint consultation they soon found themselves in negotiations to resolve conflicts. For instance in the Netherlands problems such as the introduction of an incentive scheme, job regulation, the recruitment of foreign workers, holiday arrangements and the need for overtime usually lead to some sort of negotiation in works councils.[10] In France council proceedings began to take on most meaning for members when some change was planned which threatened jobs or earnings or when there was some other issue or difference to resolve. The rate of industrial innovation and restructuring in the 1960s, combined with a rising demand for worker influence, made such issues more and more frequent. Within industrial relations systems where formal negotiations with unions were conducted at the national level works councils became involved in the collective bargaining necessary to make national agreements acceptable in relation to local conditions. More recently the formal powers of councils have tended to be enhanced by legislation. For instance the rights of French works councils in relation to redundancy have since January 1975 become very similar to those of the German works councils. In view of the way that continental European works councils have developed it is not stretching the nature of events too far to suggest that there has been some convergence between that system and worker representation in Britain during the past fifteen years.[11] Over that period the shop-steward system of representation has been changing in response to similar forces that modified the original purposes of continental works councils. These were most apparent in the productivity bargaining era of the 1960s.[12] Employers found that in order to bring about change at plant level it was necessary to bring shop-stewards into a process of consultation. There was a movement towards the establishment of joint shop-stewards committees representing all sections of the workforce. These were involved in the regular exchange of information, and joint consultation as well as the negotiation of changes. Accordingly from quite different starting points it was possible to identify similar institutions emerging to represent workers at plant level in Britain and in continental Europe. These were based on the following principles: a single channel of representation rather than separate channels for promoting co-operation and resolving conflict; the single channel being used for joint consultation, joint decision-making and negotiation; and a widening of the agenda of negotiation so that any issue was potentially the subject of joint regulation. However, while in practice it is possible to identify some convergence in the nature of industrial relations institutions at plant level in western Europe, the differences in principle remain marked as will have been apparent from the earlier parts of this chapter.

Conclusions

The pressures on governments within the EEC to advance industrial democracy over the next few years will be enormous. The pressures will come from fellow governments, from the Commission, and from domestic trade unions, workers and electorates. Governments will need more than ever the co-operation of organised labour and workers to help resolve the problems of inflation, unemployment and lack of growth which represent the biggest economic crisis for western Europe since the war. Granting workers and organised labour a part in decision-making is seen as a means of gaining that co-operation. The European model of industrial democracy is likely to be the main influence on initiatives taken by governments. First it is the dominant model in terms of the membership of the community. But beyond that it has powerful attractions for governments operating mixed economies and accountable to parliamentary democracies. The requirement for workers to be appointed to boards of companies achieves the maximum symbolic impact at the same time as imposing the minimum constraints on the pursuit by companies of their commercial interests in a market economy. Inspired as it has been by the German example the model is designed to enable managements to bring about the changes required by technical and commercial considerations with the co-operation and agreement of workforces. The election of worker directors and works councils by universal employee suffrage is consistent with the most popular notion of democracy. It will have been clear that adapting the model to British industrial relations traditions and institutions will not be easy. But the history of the worker director issue in Britain and its likely outcome suggest that the obstacles can be overcome. Experience of the European model of industrial democracy shows that employers and managers have little to fear and much to gain from its application to Britain. As far as workers are concerned it would be likely to make little difference in practice to sectors of employment where union representation is strong and well organised. But it would substantially increase the formal powers of workers in other sectors.

References

1. Eric Batstone and P. L. Davies, *Industrial Democracy*, Two reports prepared for the Industrial Democracy Committee, HMSO (London 1976).
2. In 1972 the Commission published Proposals for a Fifth Directive to co-ordinate the laws of member states as regards the structure of *sociétiés anonymes, Bulletin of the European Communities*, Supplement 10/72. In 1975 it published a Green Paper inviting discussion and

comments which would form the basis of a revised Fifth Directive; *Employee participation and company structure*, Bulletin of the European Communities, Supplement 8/75.

At the same time the Commission was drawing up proposals for a European Company Statute which would permit the creation of European companies by organisations which operated in more than one member state. In 1975 the Commission published its amended proposals; *Statute for European Companies*, Amended proposal for a regulation, Bulletin of the Europe Communities, Supplement 4/75.

3. *Report of the Committee of Inquiry on Industrial Democracy*, Cmnd. 6706, HMSO (London 1977).

4. H. A. Clegg, *A New Approach to Industrial Democracy*, Blackwell (Oxford 1960).

5. Eric Batstone (1975), *op. cit.*

6. Eric Batstone (1975), *op. cit.*

7. EEC Commission (8/75), *op. cit.*

8. EEC Commission (4/75), *op. cit.*

9. Y. Delamotte, 'The Content and Context of Co-operation', in *Prospects for Labour/Management Co-operation in the Enterprise*, OECD, 1974.

10. W. Albeda, 'Recent Trends in Collective Bargaining in the Netherlands', *International Labour Review*, March 1971.

11. W. W. Daniel, *Prospects for Labour/Management Co-operation in the Enterprise*, OECD, (Paris 1974).

12. W. W. Daniel and Neil McIntosh, *The Right to Manage?*, PEP/MacDonald (London 1972).

5 Employee participation and improving the quality of working life

CARY L. COOPER

We have heard a great deal in the last couple of years about the need to democratise or humanise the workplace in British industry, to improve the quality of working life by providing the industrial worker with greater participation in the decisions involving his work. This can be achieved by including employees on boards of companies and involving them in the long-term policy making issues of the organisations or by increasing their participation in the decision-making processes of their work group by allowing them greater freedom in deciding how to organise and conduct their own jobs. These two approaches to industrial democracy, which it might be added are not mutually exclusive, have been termed by Strauss and Rosenstein[1] as *distant* and *immediate* participation respectively. In the previous chapter we have heard about recent developments among our European neighbours to establish the mechanisms of greater 'industrial democracy' or 'distant participation' in industrial life. In this chapter, the intention is to consider the work that has been done in the field of *immediate* participation, for it is the opinion of this author that, at least in the initial stages of the 'participative revolution' (Preston and Post[2]), these developments are likely to have the most impact on increasing people's job satisfaction, performance, and improving the industrial relations climate generally.

A substantial number of employee or immediate participation programmes have been introduced throughout Europe and other countries under differing labels over the last decade; autonomous work groups, job enrichment schemes, work restructuring, etc. Each of these approaches to employee participation are attempting to meet any one or a combination of the following objectives which have been put forward by Herrick and Maccoby[3] as the four principles of humanisation at work:

1. *Security* – employees need to be free from fear and anxiety concerning health and safety, income and future employment;

2. *Equity* – employees should be compensated commensurately with their contribution to the value of the service or product;

3. *Individuation* – employees should have maximum autonomy in determining the rhythm of their work and in planning how it should be done;

4. *Democracy* – employees should, wherever possible, manage themselves, be involved in the decision-making that affects their work, and accept greater responsibility in the work of the organisation.

The experiments in the humanisation of the immediate work environment vary enormously from those which emphasise 'participative decision-making' to those that attempt to nurture 'work autonomy', from those which have been thoroughly conceived and planned to those which have developed out of political crises and expediency, from those which have been systematically monitored to those which have been uncritically praised, etc. Since we in Britain and in the European Community at large are likely to move increasingly toward greater participation in industry, for a variety of political and socio-psychological reasons (Davis and Cherns)[4], it might be worthwhile exploring some of the examples and results of the recent work undertaken to humanise the workplace in different countries, so that we may be able to plan and organise more effective programmes in the future. We will be exploring firstly the developments in the EEC countries and then we will go further afield and examine those in Sweden, the US and Japan – where these approaches to participation and quality of working life have been extensively used and may be of particular value to us in Britain. In reviewing these examples, we will attempt to restrict ourselves to those cases which have been relatively systematically evaluated and reported in the literature and, in particular, to those where data are available on the organisational (e.g. productivity, absenteeism, etc.) and/or personal (e.g. perceived job satisfaction) consequences of such industrial interventions.

European Economic Community

Many companies within the EEC have begun to experiment with employee participation and 'quality of working life' programmes, indeed many of the Community countries have introduced legislation to set up governmental agencies to encourage this development. Although there are a growing number of participation programmes being initiated and in progress, the systematic documentation of them in most EEC countries has not kept up with this growth. What we will attempt to do here, therefore, is to provide a 'thumb nail' sketch of one or two of the better documented examples in each of the Community countries, to give us some flavour of their approach and assessment of their effect.

Denmark

Denmark is moving, as other Scandinavian countries have, on both 'immediate' and 'distant' participation fronts simultaneously – in the late 1960s on shopfloor humanisation and in 1973 on company law associated with boardroom participation. In 1969, representatives of various trade unions, employers' organisations, and the staff (managers and workers) of a select number of companies were encouraged by the Danish Productivity Fund to tour the United States and assess the work system re-design programmes there. As a result of this experience, a number of these companies formed the basis of pilot experiments in their own companies in new forms of work organisations along the lines of autonomous work groups.

The three most notable examples are Foss Electric Co., Sadoin and Hohmblad, and Colon Emballage (Taylor)[5]. Foss Electric is a small manufacturer of dairy product testing equipment. In 1969 they introduced semi-autonomous work groups for natural parts of the production process. These groups planned and manufactured their segment of the operation, were paid on a flat rate, had flexible working hours, recruited staff, and had a say in designing the immediate socio-technical system. It was found that labour turnover dropped in one year by ten per cent and quality errors were reduced by thirty-five per cent. Not as much information about results is available about the Sadoin and Hohmblad (paint manufacturers) experiment, but they introduced a major change in their structure by creating interlocking managerial groups throughout the organisation. Jenkins[6] reports that production improved as a result of solving more quickly and efficiently the production problems generated. The final example of Danish efforts at work humanisation took place in a small corrogated board plant, Colon Emballage, in southern Jutland in 1970. Autonomous work groups of between seven and eight workers were formed to decide on work roles, wage system (shifted from piece rates to uniform flat rates), etc. – they were restricted however on production scheduling. It was found that production rose eight per cent and the employees expressed greater satisfaction with their work.

On the basis of these and many other work humanisation examples, the Danish government introduced a Working Environment Bill in 1974 to promote further improvements in the quality of working life in industry. At roughly the same time, 'distant' participation legislation was also passed for limited liability corporations (of over 500 employees) in which the employees were eligible to appoint two members to the board of directors to represent their interests. Denmark seems to be one of the few countries to be pursuing a policy of introducing worker participation programmes at all levels of the organisation, dealing with political as well as human issues.

The Netherlands

Since the early 1960s the Netherlands have been involved in work humanisation programmes, stemming mainly from the activities of the Philips Company but also from work system design experiments in the Dutch steel industry, post office, and railways. As Butteriss[7] points out much of the stimulus to these attempts to improve the quality of working life in Dutch companies and government/quasi-government agencies, was due to the problems of the time such as 'graduate unemployment, failure of the government to adjust the quality of labour supply to the demand requirements, the discrepancy between the high quality labour force and the low quality jobs with resulting absenteeism, turnover, etc.'. By far the most extensive and interesting examples of work re-design and participation programmes come from Philips, the manufacturers of electrical appliances and other equipment – mainly in their assembly operations but there is also an example from among their clerical workers. Most of these· experiments took place during the 1960s in different assembly departments. For instance, autonomous work groups were set up in the bulb assembly and finishing departments where thirty individual jobs were combined into groups of four, with a certain amount of job rotation. It was found (den Hertog)[8] that production costs were reduced by twenty per cent, rejects were halved, and output increased; worker satisfaction was not any higher but workers indicated a strong preference for the current job design in contrast to the old. In the black and white television factory they had the same sort of results with the autonomous work groups introduced there between 1969 and 1972. They formed seven person work groups with twenty-minute work cycles and multiple job tasks (e.g. quality control, work distribution, material ordering, etc.). The 1972 evaluation programme in this department revealed that there was significantly lower absenteeism, lower waiting time for materials, better co-ordination and improved training, and component costs reduced by ten per cent; unlike the bulb department, greater job satisfaction was expressed as well (den Hertog). Also worthy of note was the white collar experiment in the order department of Philips. There, the department was reorganised by product, three operational lines became three product lines. Within each product line every employee learnt all the tasks and rotated them; and each unit decided on their work group leader who, in conjunction with his team, was responsible for delivery of a complete product. They found that productivity doubled and the majority of employees expressed a preference for the new system, although some indicated that the supervision was 'too close'.

The Netherlands have a commendable record in Europe for their work humanisation efforts, both in terms of the experimental work carried out by Philips and others, and in attempting to establish detailed documentation of their progress.

France

It was not until the early 1970s that the French government introduced legislation setting up the *Agence National pour L'Amelioration des Conditions du Travail*, whose main task was to provide information, carry out research, and assist companies to improve the quality of working life (e.g. re-organisation of work and working hours, improving the physical environment of companies, encouraging employee participation and methods of assessing and changing working conditions). This agency is trying to collate information on employee participation schemes and to encourage more systematic data collection on the consequences of the different approaches. Presently there are only a few well-documented cases in France (Jenkins). There are two, in particular, that we might briefly explore here which best illustrates the current work in France. Guilliet SA, a woodworking machinery manufacturer in Auxerre, introduced semi-autonomous work groups of between seven and ten persons covering the manufacturing process of their machinery. Each of these work groups assembled nearly an entire piece of equipment by themselves. The programme was carried out in 1969 and covered nearly 800 employees. The most positive outcomes for the company were increased sales and substantially enhanced job satisfaction. Another example (Taylor)[9] was that of a nylon spinning plant of 100 workers. The employees introduced a work re-design scheme (with the co-operation of management) in which each worker carried out a larger number of skills including maintenance (replaced five jobs with two), and in which the work group took on the decision-making responsibility in the areas of quality control, staffing, and work assignments. The experiment was carried out between 1969 and 1972 with the following encouraging positive results: absenteeism was reduced by two-thirds of traditional levels, no grievances or strikes were initiated, and labour turnover was significantly reduced, indeed workers refused transfers to other plants. Many more cases of worker participation programmes are in process in France and as the National Agency for the Improvement of Working Conditions gets some momentum we will be seeing more detailed accounts of their strategies and effects. Presently, however, not many detailed accounts of such schemes are available from France.

West Germany

Although West Germany has been the model of Western European countries for worker participation at boardroom level (i.e. distant participation) or what they term 'co-determination of employees in the economic enterprise' (*mitbestimmung*), they have progressed very slowly indeed on immediate or shopfloor participation. It was not until the Federal Government carried out a research programme into job satisfaction in the early 1970s, which indicated that the low paid were the least satisfied with their job (e.g. income, security of employment, participation, etc.) and their career prospects, that any immediate participation programmes were encouraged. It was in the middle of 1974 that the Federal Ministry of Labour and Social Affairs planned a programme for Research for the Humanisation of Work, which was similar in objectives to the French *Agence National pour L'Amelioration des Conditions du Travail*. Its 'brief' was to collate information on issues related to stress at work, worker participation, work and job design, etc., and to stimulate further research. There is very little work reported on German experiments of employee participation, mainly because this is ·not particularly strongly supported by the German Federation of Trade Unions (DGB), as Mire[10] has emphasised 'the DGB continues to pay lip service to the demands for direct representation of the workplace, but only as part of its broader demand for worker participation at the top .... Most efforts of the trade unions are directed at this aspect of their legislative programme rather than at bringing about worker participation at the plant level.' Indeed, there is only one well reported case of employee participation and that is the work at the Singer Company of Germany (Ruehl).[11] At Singer they introduced autonomous assembly work groups of electric and electronic equipment, precision parts and house appliances – these were described by the company as assembly islands. Unfortunately, no information is available on the objective consequences of these innovations, so we are left with very little evaluative data.

The Germans are very much aware of the need to develop their programme to improve the quality of working life and participation generally, even though to date their record in this area is far from progressive. This was particularly highlighted when Chancellor Brandt in the early 1970s set up a working party (sponsored by the Economic and Social Research Institute) of five employers' representatives, five trade unionists, and seven academics to consider new approaches to the organisation of worklife (Butteriss). Work from this group should help to provide the foundations and framework for work humanisation in the future.

Italy

The Italian government has only recently set up an agency to explore quality of working life issues, the *Instituto di Studi di Lavero*. It has some of the same objectives as other government institutes which have been established in other countries. Italy, like some of the EEC countries, has not been at the forefront of employee participation schemes, with the exception of a very few large companies, particularly Olivetti and Fiat. The most widely known example of work re-design in Italy took place at Olivetti's Ivres plant in the parts workshop and two assembly departments. There, Olivetti abolished the 'long assembly line' on two product lines and introduced what they called 'integrated assembly units' or 'assembly islands'. These are composed of a group of thirty people whose job is to assemble, inspect, and maintain the whole product. The entire output needed is produced by a number of identical integrated units. A detailed account of Olivetti's work re-design programme can be found in Butera[12], including an assessment of its success. Briefly, the following changes were evident from the work system change programme: (i) increase in the speed of the product through-put and decrease in-process time to less than one-third of the time of the line system (ii) quality of product improved significantly, lower wastage (iii) increased job satisfaction and worker motivation under the new schemes (iv) per capita costs had increased and also training costs and (v) there was a greater flexibility in the system for allocating human resources in the plant. These activities are still in progress in Olivetti and indeed other departments within the organisation are experimenting with new work systems.

As the work of the working parties set up by the *Instituto di Studi di Lavero* begins to come to fruition, it is anticipated that many more examples of work humanisation will emerge, but at the moment it is still early days for these innovations in Italy.

Belgium

From a central government point of view not much is happening in the way of quality of working life policies or practices in Belgium. The *Office Belge pour L'Accroissement de la Productivito* has responsibility for the dissemination of information in this area but little is known about the work of firms in Belgium to humanise the workplace. The only exception to this is the apparel manufacturer, Inbelco, at Poperinge. They are reported (Jenkins) to have re-structured their organisation in a series of nine inter-locking management groups, each of which was broken down into three or four sub-groups. Within these groups joint decisions are made about job tasks with opportunities for job rotation and enlargement encouraged. There is very little objective data available about this particular experience, however, except that measured job satisfaction seems to have increased since the introduction of the experiment.

Ireland

Ireland is another country in which work humanisation projects are not very well-developed. This is inevitably due, to some extent, to the absence of larger scale industrial organisations in the Republic. Butteriss suggests that this is also partly a function of the prevailing attitudes of management and trade unions, which have been less than enthusiastic about work re-design and quality of working life issues generally. This is ironic in view of the fact that the Council of Europe have agreed the creation of the European Foundation for the Improvement of Living and Working Conditions and have centred it in Dublin. The only documented evidence of Irish interest in the quality of work environments comes from a government working paper on Job Enrichment in June of 1974 and proposals (on the 'distant' participation side) in July of 1975 for a Bill on Worker Directors.

Luxembourg

Of the documented work available to us in the quality of working life field, we are unable to find any evidence of government activity or individual industrial projects being pursued in Luxembourg.

United Kingdom

In a recent report by the Work Research Unit[13] on work restructuring projects and experiments in the UK, they claim to have traced 111 industrial examples; schemes relating to job rotation, job enlargement, job enrichment, and autonomous work groups. The industries in which these programmes most frequently occur are the chemical, food and drink, manufacturing, engineering, electrical, paper and printing, and electronics. Of these 111 experiments in UK firms, only slightly over a dozen seem to be documented or to show sufficient objective economic and human results to draw any firm lessons. Like Sweden, the US and Japan, the UK has a longer history of work humanisation efforts than is realised. The work of the Tavistock Institute of Human Relations in the early 1950s (Trist and Bamforth;[14] Trist, Higgin, Murray and Pollack[15]), in terms of the application of socio-technical system concepts, is the most notable example of early quality of working life research and practice. But it is only recently that these and other UK approaches to employee participation and humanisation have been systematically encouraged to develop, mainly through the Department of Employment who set up the Work Research Unit for this purpose in 1974 at the recommendation of a Tripartite Steering Group of the TUC, CBI and Government. The stated overall objective of the WRU is 'the stimulation of changes in the ways in which work is organised in industry and commerce .... In practice this often means introducing such things as: allowing some degree of discretion and responsibility; giving scope for learning and development; introducing challenge and variety in the job; and by giving the individual an opportunity to make an identifiable contribution to the end product' (Butteriss). It might be worthwhile here to examine some of the UK examples of work restructuring to humanise the workplace and encourage employee involvement and participation. One of the best documented (Hill)[16] and well-designed programmes in a UK company was one carried out by Shell UK Ltd., at their Stanlow Refinery. This took place in their micro-wax department, where until the work system re-design, morale was very low, costs were high, and maintenance poor. A major restructuring of job tasks was then introduced whereby the employee worked as a team to complete *all* of the job tasks as opposed to only *part* of them. The workers were given more decision-making power about their jobs and in respect of running the plant generally. As a consequence the company got more commitment and increased morale. On objective criteria, sickness and absenteeism were down fifty per cent, off-plant wax testing was reduced by seventy-five per cent, output increased by between thirty and a hundred per cent in various units, and occasionally significant reprocessing costs were saved. Another recent example was that of Ferranti's avionics plant in Edinburgh between 1968 and 1972. They introduced group cell technology, with teams of four workers controlling six machines to deal with 300-400 different components. Each group cell was left to organise the job tasks and methods of production. It was found (Clutterbuck)[17] that the time taken to reset tools dropped by sixty per cent, production time for each component was cut by thirty per cent (and delay in getting parts), and quality improved steadily.

Although the bulk of the UK experiments in this field are production or assembly orientated, there are also some notable white collar ones as well. For example, ICI in 1967 introduced greater autonomy and responsibility for their sales representatives in order to increase the sales efforts. Sales representatives were given discretion on reports, complaint refunds, and some pricing policies, etc. A job reaction survey showed a significant increase in job satisfaction and also an 18.6 per cent increase in sales (a control group of salesmen showed a drop in sales of five per cent) (Paul and Robertson)[18]. Other white collar humanisation projects in the UK have been undertaken, for example, among design engineers and researchers (Paul and Robertson), managers (Taylor)[19] and stock control office staff (BOC)[20], etc.

The UK, therefore, has a reasonable history and breadth of work humanisation projects, which should stand them in good stead for future developments in this area.

Summary of EEC Countries

The Council of Europe has recently acknowledged the importance of work humanisation programmes in member countries by passing resolution 565 which states 'in view of changing worker attitudes and aspirations, that some working conditions have an adverse effect on health and attitudes therefore there is a belief that some work should be dramatically changed to take into account worker attitudes'.

The Resolution recommends the following objectives:
1. The removal of soul destroying jobs as social progress depends on the interest workers take in jobs.
2. That government authorities together with employees and work organisations promote the humanisation of working conditions.
3. More opportunities should be given to participate in the methods and conditions of work.
4. Assembly work should be eliminated and consideration given to job enlargement, job enrichment and autonomous work groups.
5. Pay structures should be re-examined in the light of these proposals (Butteriss).

To this purpose the EEC has established the European Foundation for Improvement of Living and Working Conditions, to provide the stimulus and funds to encourage these recommendations.

Developments in other countries

There are a number of other countries outside the EEC who have been extensively involved in quality of working life projects over the last decade, notably Sweden, the United States and Japan. A brief account of their developments might be instructive in putting the European cases in perspective.

Sweden

There are literally hundreds of examples of serious, systematic efforts at work re-design and participation in Sweden (Agervold)[21]. Although many of these have not been published in English or have not been fully evaluated by objective criteria, Sweden has certainly been at the forefront of recent ventures in this field. Much of the work done there was initially prompted by the country's need to 'overcome an inability to recruit Swedish workers to Swedish factory work (particularly in the 1960s) and to respond to union demands for better quality of working life' (Taylor)[5]. One of the best documented Swedish examples is, contrary to general expectations about Volvo, the Saab engine assembly line (at the Sodertalje truck and bus plant). The process of moving toward autonomous work groups began in 1969 with the expansion of the works council, the formation of development groups, and of small team production groups of between seven to eight workers – where job tasks were decided by foremen and workers in collaboration. By 1974, the plant had ninety development groups and 200 production groups, where decisions about work organisation were jointly reached. In the first year of the change programme, capital costs were higher and absenteeism/turnover were about the same as previously, but significantly more labour was attracted into the plant (and a more flexible work system was materialising). By the third year, labour turnover was reduced from seventy to twenty per cent, unplanned stoppages were down from six to two per cent, production had increased, costs were five per cent below budget, and absenteeism was markedly improved (Norstedt and Aguren)[22]. Another interesting Swedish example, which involved a comparative analysis of two different forms of work restructuring was carried out in Granges AB, a die casting foundry near Stockholm. They introduced in one unit of the plant a job enrichment scheme and in another, autonomous work groups (Jenkins). They found that labour turnover rose from sixty to sixty-nine per cent and productivity dropped by seven per cent in the former case, but productivity rose twenty per cent for the self-managed work group with turnover dropping from sixty to eighteen per cent (in addition absenteeism dropped five per cent and quality spoilage dropped two per cent in the latter case).

There are many other encouraging examples of successful quality of working life cases from Sweden, as they build up an impressive catalogue of work environment changes which are the model for other countries. Indeed, the Swedish government enacted legislation in 1971 to set up the Work Environment Fund to sponsor more research and work in this field. In addition to immediate participation programmes, Sweden is also moving rapidly toward boardroom or distant participation by acts legislated in 1973.

United States

There are a large number of industrial cases of work humanisation projects in the US, some dating back to the late 1940s (Coch and French)[23] and 1950s (Morse and Reimer)[24]. Most of these examples are found in small plants of up to 250 employees and involve predominately assembly or production operations. Many of these can be found in O'Toole's classic book *Work in America*[25]. An example of the kind of programme carried out in the US is best illustrated by the Corning Glass and Texas Instruments experiments. At the Corning Glass factory in Medfield, Massachusetts they introduced autonomous work groups in their electric hot plate assembly department. Groups of six workers

assembled an entire electric hot plate and had the freedom
to schedule work any way they chose. Absenteeism dropped
from eight to one per cent, rejects dropped from twenty-
three to one per cent and expressed job satisfaction
increased. A similar experiment was carried out among 120
maintenance workers in the Dallas plant of Texas
Instruments. The maintenance workers were organised into
nineteen member cleaning teams, with each member
having a say in planning problem solving, goal setting and
scheduling. It was found that turnover dropped from one
hundred to ten per cent and cost savings were $103,000 in
two years between 1967 and 1969.

There are also some examples of quality of working life
experiments outside an industrial context in the US, for
instance, in government departments. An example of this
was a programme carried out by the Operations Division of
the Ohio Department of Highways. They established three
experimental construction crews with differing degrees of
self determination of work schedules and division of labour,
and compared them to three crews who maintained the
traditional assignment of duties and work schedules. It was
found (Powell and Schacter)[26] that as participation increased,
so did morale and job satisfaction (but not productivity).

The most important contribution of many of the
American examples, lies in their concern rigorously to
evaluate the objective (e.g. productivity, labour turnover,
etc.) as well as subjective (e.g. perceived job satisfaction)
outcomes of such experiments. In this respect, the Survey
Research Center of the University of Michigan and the
Quality of Working Life Unit at the University of California,
Los Angeles are the focal points for much of the execution
and collation of research in this field in the US. In addition,
as a consequence of the Work in America report findings
(commissioned by the Department of Health, Education
and Welfare), the US government has established a National
Commission on Productivity and Work Quality to promote
increased productivity and to enhance the quality of
working life. To this end legislation has been introduced
recently in the US Congress to encourage the allocation of

federal funds for work humanisation projects in the private sector.

Japan

As a result of the economic and social devastation of the Second World War and the immediate post-war upheavals, Japanese industrial life over the last couple of decades has been in transition, in a process of change. During this period there has been a strong wave of opinion for the democratisation of work life in firms. The largest national labour union *Sohyo*, has been at the forefront of promoting and encouraging *hatarakigai* or the quality of working life. In the latter part of the 1960s the younger Japanese workers declared that work was only a means to their ends and that it was the responsibility of all working people to encourage the creation of humanising environments at work by reducing alienation, monotony, and increasing the greater involvement and participation of all employees. Since then a large number of quality of working life experiments have been initiated in Japanese industry. One of the better known examples (Kato)[27] was initiated within the large Mitsubishi Electric company in 1968. At their Fukuyama plant, a nine-position conveyor line system was reorganised into autonomous work groups of seven workers. Although the work teams received monthly production goals from top management, they were given the authority to set immediate work targets, to take on quality control and inspection, to organise and supply parts and materials, etc. The scope of the worker's job was immeasurably widened with only periperal services provided centrally. It was found that productivity increased by over fifty per cent, while errors dropped by nearly eighty per cent. In addition, perceived job satisfaction had increased and industrial relations problems minimised. Another well-documented example is Kanto Seiki, an auto parts manufacturer. The engineers at Seiki decided to carry out a comparative study of two work restructuring approaches. In one part of the plant they maintained their traditional conveyor belt system for assembling speedometers and in another they reorganised themselves into autonomous work groups of differing sizes (seven- four- and three-workers modules). In contrast to the conveyor system, productivity increased between seventy and ninety per cent for the autonomous work groups (with the three-man modules producing the largest increase), with absenteeism and labour turnover significantly decreasing as well.

There are an enormous number of quality of work life projects in process at the moment in Japan (Takezawa)[28], and they are likely to increase in the future. In a recent Japanese government survey of 700 influential national leaders from the unions, industry and the institutions of higher education, it was concluded that wages and salaries would be less important in the 1980s than job satisfaction and working conditions – this was particularly strongly supported by the trade union officials.

What have we learned from this work?

After surveying briefly some examples of work humanisation and employee participation schemes in various countries, it is important to attempt to answer a number of more general questions raised by them. First, why were these programmes undertaken in the first place, that is, what did they hope to achieve? Second, how successful were they in achieving their objectives? Third, and finally, what are some of the problems raised by the implementation of such innovations in industry and how might they be improved upon in the future?

Reasons for implementation of QWL experiments

If we examine in detail most of the published work in this field (Taylor; WRU; O'Toole; Davis and Cherns), we can begin to answer the first question we have set for ourselves about the objectives of quality of work in life experiments, that is, what organisations hope they will achieve. A survey of the best-documented and most quantifiable of the available studies reveals that there are a wide range of reasons firms give for doing this kind of work; recruitment difficulties, high costs, poor quality, low productivity, demarcation disputes, high labour turnover, automation, introduction of new technology, etc. By far the two most common reasons given are low productivity *and* high absenteeism and labour turnover. These two together represent something of the order of fifty per cent of the overt stated reasons why organisations are undertaking these change programmes. The next category of expressed overt problems is comprised of industrial relations difficulties (e.g. poor worker-management communication) and lack of worker job satisfaction, which together represent roughly twenty-five per cent of the problems needing resolution. Of the remaining twenty-five per cent, the following are given as reasons for introducing change (in order of frequency of expression): experimentation of new work designs, poor quality, to encourage participation, unnecessarily high costs, inability to recruit, introduction of new equipment, productivity deals, etc.

It can also be seen that most of these innovations apply to manufacturing or assembly type operations with few white collar, clerical, or middle management programmes. This supports Taylor's survey of the hundred best documented international cases of work restructuring, in which he found that most of them were in assembly operations (thirty-three per cent), semi-skilled machine tending (twenty-three per cent), and process operating (twenty-one per cent); while only nine per cent of them were among white collar workers and maintenance tasks were a poor fifth at three per cent.

How successful are these quality of working life experiments?

There are several reasons why it is unwise of us to draw any firm generalisable conclusions about the efficacy of the quality of working life and participation projects which are available to-date. First, it may be the case that we are only

Figure 5.1

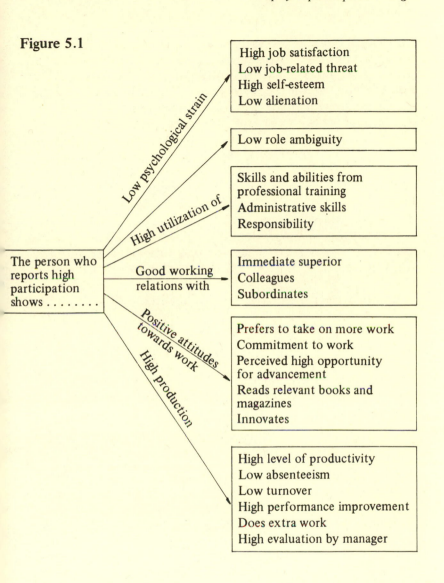

Source: French, J.R.P. & Caplan, R.D. 'Organizational Stress
and Individual Strain'. In Marrow, A.J. *The Failure of
Success,* AMACOM New York 1973, p.52.

hearing about the successful interventions, while the ones which are less successful or of marginal benefit are buried under piles of reports or forgotten altogether. Second, that not enough of the reported work has objective criteria measures by which we can confidently judge them. Third, not enough of the work in this area is comparative, that is, where one approach, for instance, to absenteeism reduction is compared to another or two other possible approaches.

Nevertheless, given these *caveats* there still is convincing evidence that many of the participative and work humanisation projects (which meet some of the criteria discussed above) have had positive individual and organisational consequences. The empirical work associated with these types of experiments was recently summarised by two University of Michigan researchers in Figure 5.1.

It can be seen from the above that many of the sources and manifestations of stress for the individual at work are minimised (e.g. job-related threat, alienation, etc.) and many of the organisational objectives are achieved (e.g. lower absenteeism, higher productivity, etc.) when the conditions for improving the quality of working life through involvement and participation at the work site are introduced.

Problems associated with work humanisation

In spite of the fact that we have reason to believe that QWL experiments have many beneficial outcomes there are a number of problems and difficulties associated with their implementation. The following are only the tip of the proverbial iceberg of potential problem areas:

1. Difficulties associated with the consequent changing roles of management and workers occasioned by these interventions.
2. Problems of designing and re-creating training programmes to meet the specific needs of the different varieties of work humanisation projects.
3. Coping with the fears of first line supervisors.

4. Dealing with the resistance of the unions who may feel threatened that some of these approaches may affect the number of jobs and manning levels.
5. Increasing costs during the initial phase of these interventions.
6. Organisations may have to pay more for workers taking increased responsibility.

Because of all these potential problem areas, there are a number of stages that should be gone through in introducing employee participation and QWL schemes (Ottaway)[30]. First, vital to any successful change project is that there is a *psychological contract* between those changing and those advocating or implementing the change. This will involve all employees concerned with the change, discussing the 'what', 'how' and 'when' of the change programme. One way to ensure success at this stage is to encourage the formation of a working party of all interested participants, to oversee the quality of working life intervention to fruition. Second, it is important to diagnose the *quality* of working life problem areas: job design, style of management, quality, industrial relations difficulties, etc., and then to introduce a small scale project as a pilot scheme. Third, to *design* the change effort with the full participation of those who are going to be involved in the change programme. Fourth, before implementing the new programme, it is essential to 'take back' any possible proposal for change to top management and the unions, who first contracted the change programme and established the working party, to endorse the suggested project. Fifth, once the programme has been accepted, training must be introduced to prepare those concerned with the skills necessary to carry through the experiment successfully. Shop-floor workers may need to learn, for example, how to make decisions in groups or first line supervisor how to facilitate greater worker involvement or how to relinquish decision-making power. And finally, in addition to helping to create the work structure in which change can take place and preparing people for the change by training, it is necessary to *reinforce* the appropriate new behaviours that emerge. These six steps should ensure that many of the potential difficulties associated with humanising the workplace are minimised or to some extent contained. In addition to these sequential implementation stages, and something that permeates the whole process of change in the worker participation and quality of working life field are four underlying principles which must be adhered to throughout (French and Caplan):

1. The participation or change programme *is not illusory*, that is, it is not used as a manipulation tool (for example when management asks employees for advice and then ignores it).
2. The decisions on which participation are based *are not trivial* to the people concerned (e.g. management asking workers to decide on the colour of the paper to be used for the company's newsletter).
3. Those aspects of the work environment on which participation are based are *relevant* to the needs of the workers.
4. The decisions which people participate in are perceived as being *legitimately* theirs to make.

These conditions seem critical guidelines in designing programmes which encourage involvement and work sharing.

The nature of future British developments

We can finally consider some of the implications of the foregoing for the managements of British organisations operating within an EEC framework. It remains to be seen how influential Resolution 565 will become and to what extent it becomes a requirement as opposed to simple exhortation. Some of the other implications of this study are, however, the following:

1. The overwhelming conclusion must be that work humanisation initiatives pay off in terms of greater organisational effectiveness and enhanced employee satisfaction with the work to be done. Notwithstanding

the reservations mentioned on page 86, it is difficult to discount the hard evidence that we have seen of the work humanisation pay-off. One implication for British managers is therefore that there should be continuing and wider attention to this feature of managerial initiative.

2. Britain is one of the few countries in the EEC demonstrating satisfactory experience of a variety of work humanisation experiments that have been successful. Other EEC countries have experimented mainly with autonomous work groups and similar methods, while Britain has a variety of experiments comparable in scale with those of Sweden and the United States.

3. Although the use of autonomous work groups appears to be the most widely used successful method of improving the quality of working life, it may not necessarily prove to be the most popular among managers because of the questions it raises about control. Autonomous work groups and what we have termed distant participation both reduce the degree of managerial control of the work place itself to a greater extent than such methods as job enrichment, re-design of the individual job and altering methods of payment. It may be significant that Western Germany has moved further than other EEC countries on distant participation and has neglected, until recently, autonomous work group methods. One can at least speculate that managers can adapt to one or the other but not to both at the same time, and if we are to see legislative moves via the Bullock report on board-level participation, these may inhibit moves towards work group autonomy.

4. No contemplation of the future can ignore the views of trade unions. In Britain the TUC can be regarded as late-in-the-day converts to both forms of participation and still showing relatively little enthusiasm for the work humanisation developments of the type we have considered.

5.   We must also consider what is likely to be the main stimulus to participation. Innovations in the Netherlands were attributable directly to problems of graduate unemployment, high-quality employees engaged on low-quality jobs and so forth. It may be a stimulus of this type that will emerge in Britain, or it may be the need for greater productivity, the need to innovate or a feeling after some sense of greater social responsibility. According to the social imperative that emerges there could be varying directions to the development of work quality programmes.

6.   We must always remember that the experiments we have studied have been carried out in certain types of work in certain types of industry, and we need very much more data before we can generalise about the type of work humanisation programme which is likely to be appropriate in specific environments.

References

1. Strauss, G., and Rosenstein, E., 'Worker Participation: A Critical View', *Industrial Relations*, 1970, 9, pp. 197–214.
2. Preston, L. E., and Post, J. E., 'The Third Managerial Revolution', *Academy of Management Journal*, 1974, 17, pp. 476–486.
3. Herrick, N. Q., and Maccoby, M., 'Humanising Work: A Priority Goal of the 1970s', in Davis & Cherns (Eds.) *The Quality of Working Life*, Free Press (New York 1975), Volume 1, pp. 63–77.
4. Davis, L. E., and Cherns, A. B., *The Quality of Working Life*, volumes 1 and 2, Free Press (New York 1975).
5. Taylor, J. C., 'Experiments in Work System Design: Economic and Human Results'. Unpublished paper, University of California (Los Angeles 1975).
6. Jenkins, D., *Industrial Democracy in Europe*, Business International SA (Geneva 1974).
7. Butteriss, M., *The Quality of Working Life: The Expanding International Scene*. Work Research Unit Paper Number 5 (London 1975).

8. den Hertog, F. J., 'Work Structuring Philips' Gloeilampenfabrieken', *Industrial Psychology*, 1974.
9. Taylor, J. C., 'Quality of Working Life: Annotated Bibliography'. Unpublished paper, University of California (Los Angeles 1972).
10. Mire, J., 'Trade Unions and Worker Participation in Management', in Davis & Cherns (Eds.), *The Quality of Working Life*, Free Press (New York 1975) Volume 1, pp. 416–438.
11. Ruehl, G., 'Work Structuring II', *Industrial Engineering*, 1974, February, pp. 52–56.
12. Butera, F., 'Environmental Factors in Job and Organization Design: The Case of Olivetti', in Davis & Cherns (Eds.), *The Quality of Working Life*, Free Press (New York 1975). Volume 1, pp. 166–200.
13. Work Research Unit, *Work Restructuring Projects and Experiments in the United Kingdom*, WRU (London 1975).
14. Trist, E. L., and Bamforth, K., 'Some Social and Psychological Consequences of the Long Wall Method of Coal Getting', *Human Relations*, 1951, 4, 3–38.
15. Trist, E. L., Higgin, G., Murray, H., and Pollack, H., *Organisational Choice*, Tavistock Publications (London 1963).
16. Hill, P., *Towards a New Philosophy of Management*, Barnes & Noble, (New York 1972).
17. Clutterbuck, D., 'Creating a Factory with a Factory', *International Management*, October, 1973.
18. Paul, W. J., and Robertson, K. B., *Job Enrichment and Employee Motivation*, Gower Press (London 1970).
19. Taylor, L. K., *Not for Bread Alone: An Appreciation of Job Enrichment*. Business Books (London 1973).
20. British Oxygen Company, Stock Control Office, Manpower Development Unit Paper, November 1971.
21. Agervold, M., 'Swedish Experiments in Industrial Democracy, in Davis & Cherns (Eds.), *The Quality of Working Life*, Free Press (New York 1975), Volume 2, pp. 46–65.
22. Norstedt, J., and Aguren, S., *The Saab-Scania Report*, Swedish Employers Confederation (Stockholm 1974).

23. Coch, L., and French, J. R. P., 'Overcoming Resistance to Change', *Human Relations*, 1948, 1, 512–532.
24. Morse, N. C., and Reimer, E., 'The Experimental Change of a Major Organisational Variable', *Journal of Abnormal and Social Psychology*, 1956, 52, 120–129.
25. O'Toole, J., *Work in America*, MIT Press (Boston 1973).
26. Powell, R. M., and Schacter, J. L., 'Self Determination at Work', *Academy of Management Journal*, 1971, 15, 165–173.
27. Kato, H., 'Job Enlargement as Viewed from Industrial Engineering', Paper delivered to the Japan Psychological Association, 38th National Conference, 1974.
28. Takezawa, S., 'The Quality of Working Life: Trends in Japan'. Unpublished paper, Rikkyo University, 1974.
29. French, J. R. P., and Caplan, R. D., 'Organisational Stress and Individual Strain', in Marrow (Ed.), *The Failure of Success*, AMACOM (New York 1973), p 52.
30. Ottaway, R., 'Working in the Right Direction', *The Guardian*, 15 September, 1975.

6 *Some comparative aspects of employee benefits in Europe*

DEREK TORRINGTON

This chapter is concerned with two aspects of employment in Europe. First financial benefits other than direct pay and secondly general provisions to safeguard the individual employee.

The treatment will be eclectic rather than comprehensive. Not only is this necessary to embrace the material within one chapter, it is also because some aspects are dealt with elsewhere in this book. The chapter will be in the following sections:

a. The social situation in the Community
b. Social security contributions
c. Social security benefits
d. Pensions and the age of retirement
e. Holidays and hours of work
f. Employee migration and company mergers
g. Some future implications

a. The social situation in the Community

Although various European countries have had some provision for poor relief for centuries, with state responsibility developing by the beginning of the twentieth century, the report of William Beveridge in 1942 can be seen as the basis for the type of social security provision we have in Western Europe today. Although it was a report on the British situation, the ideas were taken up in a number of other European countries. Beveridge brought about a shift in attitude so that social security payments became not a disbursement of charity to the poor, but a means to achieve social and economic stability by giving everyone a right to a minimum level of subsistence.

As the people of Europe began to re-order their affairs after the 1939–45 war, they welcomed a state initiative in providing the minimum subsistence level Beveridge had envisaged, together with the sense of security that came with it.

In 1957 the Treaty of Rome gave individuals in member countries the freedom to work anywhere within the European Economic Community. This required that the social security systems of the different countries should be both compatible and sufficiently co-ordinated to enable the transfer of individual rights from country to country. Gradually this transferability has developed and general moves towards consistency in levels of benefit can be discerned.

While harmonisation of social security provision was one of the very first examples of barrier-lowering in the Community, recent years have seen different features taking shape, mainly the Social Action Programme of 1974 and promulgating the approximation of company laws within member countries with the eventual aim of creating European company law.

b. Social security contributions

In all countries of the Community expenditure on social security falls within the range of eighteen to twenty-two per cent.[1] Clearly the amount of benefit distributed must be related to the level of contribution made. This requires not only appropriate actuarial preparation but a periodic review of the scheme's assets and liabilities to ensure against erosion through inflation. The International Labour Conference of 1952 adopted the Social Security (Minimum Standards) Convention which required governments to evaluate periodically the assets and liabilities of schemes to ensure their solvency and to fix both benefits and contributions on the basis of actuarial estimates. As social security has to provide for benefit during sickness and unemployment, such evaluation is difficult. Although it is possible to predict with reasonable accuracy the calls upon a fund to compensate for unemployment through sickness, the level of unemployment through the non-availability of work is susceptible to greater fluctuations requiring greater reserves.

Social security schemes are financed by transferring income from the economically-active and rich sectors of the population to those individuals affected by the particular situation of sickness, unemployment or injury for which the scheme provides benefit. This transfer is undertaken by taxation, by levying a contribution or by a combination. The standard method of obtaining the contribution is to make it a joint employer/employee contribution. This is a method invented by Bismarck in Germany in the latter part of the nineteenth century, which has now been adopted throughout Europe. Although the proportions contributed by the different parties may vary, there is no likelihood that the basis will alter. The employee contribution sustains his sense of responsibility as a contributor and his dignity as a recipient of benefit. The employer derives the benefit of the security felt by the employee and is helped by the medical benefits that the scheme provides for individuals in maintaining their productive potential. The third element in financing is the contribution the state makes from taxation. This not only expresses social solidarity, but also helps to cushion schemes against the fluctuations of industrial prosperity.

The Social Security (Minimum Standards) Convention provides specific guidance:

'The cost of the benefits provided in compliance with this convention and the cost of the administration of such benefits shall be borne collectively by way of insurance contributions or taxation or both in a manner which avoids hardship to persons of small means and takes into account the economic situation of the member and of the classes of persons protected.'[2]

The same Convention sets a maximum level for the employee contribution:

'The total of the insurance contributions borne by the employees protected shall not exceed fifty per cent of the total of the financial resources allocated to the protection of employees and their wives and children.'[3]

Any up-to-date comparison of the source and level of social security finance is made very difficult by the variety of national schemes, to say nothing of the rate of exchange, but one indication of the historical disparity in funding within some of the Community countries can be seen in Table 6.1[4] showing the origin of funds in social security schemes in 1963.

Table 6.1   Receipts of social security systems in selected countries in 1963. Percentage from each source

Country	Employee contribution	Employer contribution	State & public contribution	Income from capital etc.
BELGIUM	20.0	44.6	28.0	7.4
DENMARK	12.9	9.6	76.9	0.6
FRANCE	16.4	63.7	19.0	0.9
GERMANY (FDR)	26.8	44.4	25.0	3.2
ITALY	15.1	63.3	15.3	5.3
UNITED KINGDOM	21.9	20.3	54.4	3.4

Two recent examples of changes in social security arrangements in member countries of the community illustrate a general trend towards the rising cost of social security for the economically active, particularly for the employer.

In October 1976 social security contributions in France were increased to combat the heavy cost of the social security system to the central government. This was the second increase in nine months and raised the level of employer social security contribution to nearly thirty per cent of what the employer paid to the employee, himself paying as much as ten per cent of his earnings as contribution. In France, however, there are a number of other compulsory contributions – apart from income tax – that the employer has to meet in connection with each member of his payroll, ranging from wages tax to an employer's building levy, which means that for every 1,000 francs he pays in wages to an employee with a gross annual salary of 36,000 francs he pays an additional amount of some 450 francs in various contributions. For higher-paid management staff the figure is proportionately slightly less.[5]

In Belgium contribution rates for manual workers at the same time were set at twenty-eight per cent of gross earnings to be paid by the employer and 8.9 per cent by the employee. The contribution rates for white-collar workers (*travailleurs intellectuels*) are somewhat lower.[6]

By comparison the current contribution rates in the United Kingdom are 8.75 per cent of gross earnings from the employer and 5.75 per cent from the employee, although it would be naive to say that this is the extent of the employer contribution. The relatively high contribution from central taxation is partly made up of employer – or company – taxation. Also employer contributions have an additional two per cent surcharge in 1977–78.

c. Social security benefits

Social security benefits are those payments made to cover the following:

sickness	family allowances	death
maternity	unemployment	
disability	retirement	

As with social security contributions, standards of benefit vary considerably between one country and another. One reason for such variety is the nature of health care provision, another is the distinction already referred to that many countries make between manual and non-manual employees. Some comparative tables help to explain the range of provision. First there is the duration and amount of sickness benefit, country by country (Table 6.2)[7].

Table 6.2   Sickness benefit in EEC countries, July 1974

	Duration of benefits	Amount
Denmark	Unlimited	90% of average weekly earnings with a ceiling of 792 Dkr per week.
Ireland	Flat-rate benefit Unlimited if 156 contributions paid. Earnings-related benefit limited to 147 days	Flat-rate of £7.75 per week plus earnings-related benefit of 40% of earnings between £14 and £50. Family supplements.
United Kingdom	Flat-rate benefit limited to 312 days, if less than 156 contributions have been paid; otherwise replaced by invalidity benefit after 168 days entitlement. Earnings-related supplement limited to 156 days	Flat-rate of £8.60 per week, plus earnings-related benefit at $33\frac{1}{3}$% of average earnings between £10 and £30 and 15% of average earnings between £30 and £42 weekly. Family supplements.
Netherlands	12 months	80% of average weekly earnings up to a maximum of 778.50 guilders per week.
Germany	78 weeks over a three year period	Employer pays wage for 6 weeks. Thereafter 75% of earnings on which social security contribution is assessed. Family supplements.
Belgium	12 months	60% of earnings on which social security contribution is assessed.
France	12 months over a three year period	50% of earnings on which social security contribution is assessed. Family supplements.
Italy	6 months per year	50% of earnings. $66\frac{2}{3}$% after 21st day of sickness.
Luxembourg	52 weeks.	The *gross* salary the insured person would have earned if he had continued to work.

The information in this table is the most up-to-date available at the time of writing and indicates the disparity in benefit provision. Now we can compare it with unemployment benefit (Table 6.3)[8].

Table 6.3   Unemployment benefit in EEC countries, July 1974

	Duration of benefits	Amount
Denmark	Up to 2½ years	Varying up to 90% of average earnings.
Ireland	Flat-rate limited to 312 days. Pay-related benefit limited to 147 days.	Flat-rate of £7.75 per week plus pay-related benefit of 40% of earnings between £14 and £50. Family supplements.
United Kingdom	Flat-rate limited to 312 days. Earnings-related supplement limited to 156 days.	Flat-rate of £8.60 per week, plus earnings-related benefit at $33\frac{1}{3}$% of average earnings between £10 and £30, and 15% of average earnings between £30 and £42 weekly. Family supplements.
Netherlands	Up to a maximum of 118 days a year.	80% of average weekly earnings up to 155.70 guilders a day.
Germany	312 days, if employed for 24 of previous 36 months.	Varying up to 80% of average earnings, dependent on family situation. Family supplements.
Belgium	Unlimited	60% of average earnings, reduced to 40% after first year if not head of a household.
France	Unlimited, but with progressive annual reductions.	10 francs a day during first three months. 9.10 francs a day thereafter. Family supplements.
Italy	180 days a year.	800 lire a day.
Luxembourg	26 weeks in twelve months.	60% of average earnings.

d. Pensions and the age of retirement

The payment of retirement pensions and the age at which retirement takes place are topics necessarily considered together, as the first is so dependent on the second.

The ideas intrinsic to pension schemes are those of incapacity and merit. First there is the idea that every employee reaches an age at which he is not able to continue working, simply due to his age. Secondly there is the idea that long service in a particular field entitles one to a benefit beyond that of the pay bargain that has existed during active service: a retirement pension. Governments have entered the area of pension provision relatively late and pension schemes run by employers in conjunction with insurance companies have been developing over many years. In the United Kingdom, for instance, there are some 65,000 such schemes providing retirement pension provision for half the employed persons in the country. Government intervention has come to maintain minimum standards and to preserve the rights of the individual, as well as providing for those employees not covered by employer-run schemes.

The 1970s have seen some movement towards employees being entitled to draw retirement pension at an earlier age, and the criteria for determining what that age should be have developed beyond the simple definition of the ILO in 1944:

'The prescribed age should be that at which persons commonly become incapable of efficient work, the incidence of sickness and invalidity becomes heavy, and unemployment, if present, is likely to be permanent.'[9]

In the three decades since that definition was enunciated the conventional opinion of retirement has been changing. The long-standing view of retirement as a condition in which one was 'thrown on the scrapheap', 'pensioned *off*' or even the old workhouse category of 'ready to die' has been modified by greater life expectancy, generally increasing leisure and, most recently, rising unemployment.

Very recently there have been changes introduced in various community countries to enable earlier retirement for certain categories, and these are described later in this chapter. Two long-standing features of pensionable age, however, have been the frequent provision for women to retire earlier than men. Britain is one of only three EEC countries with this feature and the passing of the 1975 Sex Discrimination Act has caused many questions about this apparent anomaly. The traditional reason for such distinction has rested on both the difficulty that elderly women have in obtaining employment in many of the occupations usually followed by women and on the more generalised assumption that work is not as important to women as to men. The reason for it not being readily altered is the considerable cost of extending the benefits to an increased number of men, assuming that the men would then elect to receive them.

It has been pointed out by the International Labour Office that nearly all pension schemes fix pensionable age at a multiple of five. A survey they conducted in 1967 found that all but eight of eighty-four schemes were set up this way, despite the considerable financial implications. The same level of pension could cost the scheme forty to fifty per cent more if pensionable age is sixty than it would if pensionable age were sixty-five because of the difference in the number of people surviving beyond those ages.[10]

Another long-standing aspect of pensionable age has been to distinguish between different occupations. In Britain we are familiar with an earlier-than-usual retirement age for members of the armed services and the police, even though it is common for such retired persons to take up other employment. The principle that certain occupations require physical strength or other characteristics that make continued employment im-practical beyond a relatively early age has been applied more widely in other countries for some time. Several European countries have created special arrangements for the retirement of coal-miners at up to ten years before the normal retirement age.

In the Community countries pensionable age has a range of thirteen years (Table 6.4).

Table 6.4   Pensionable age in countries of the EEC (1974)

MALE		FEMALE	
Country	Age	Country	Age
Denmark	67	Ireland	68
Ireland	65	Denmark	67
Belgium	65	Luxembourg	65
Luxembourg	65	Netherlands	65
Netherlands	65	Germany	63 – 67
United Kingdom	65	Belgium	60
Germany	63 – 67	France	60
France	60	United Kingdom	60
Italy	60	Italy	55

The option for retirement at sixty three instead of sixty five has been available in Germany since 1972 and has resulted in a steep increase to the economically active in the cost of pensions. Against the background it is interesting to look at the position on retirement age in other Community countries where there is currently some action on the matter.

In France both men and women qualify for a social security pension at sixty, but this is only at the level of twenty-five per cent of previous earnings and is increased by five percentage points for each year of service beyond the age of sixty, reaching fifty per cent at age sixty five, when most private pension arrangements begin payments. In July 1976 the French began a programme of generally lowering the retirement age and the first step was to enable those employed in *taches penibles* to retire at sixty on the same terms as if they had continued to sixty-five. The criteria for eligibility are strict – although they include all manually-employed mothers of three or more children – and only 60,000 men and 15,000 women were affected by the scheme when it was introduced.

In the Netherlands an arrangement has been introduced whereby an employee aged fifty-eight or over who becomes unemployed will then receive benefit of at least seventy-five per cent of their former earnings until they reach pensionable age. This is not a right to a pension at an earlier age, but is another feature of making more tolerable an early withdrawal from economic activity.

The Belgian government has enabled older workers to retire early in order to free jobs for younger people because of the high level of unemployment. Introduced in 1976 the scheme allows for men to retire at sixty and women at fifty-five on condition that their job is filled by someone under thirty. Although the employee retires he does not receive his pension, he receives unemployment benefit until retirement age, plus half the difference between that level and their former earnings. Initially this scheme was introduced to permit retirement at sixty two instead of sixty-five, but within months it was extended to cover those of sixty or over. This extension was because the offer had proved relatively unattractive to older workers.

A similar scheme came into operation in the United Kingdom in January 1977, when the 'job swap' arrangement was introduced to make a payment of £23 a week, tax-free, to any employee who opts to retire a year early; his employer being required to replace him or her with someone from the unemployed register. It was estimated that 78,000 volunteers could be eligible.

At a time when there has been a much-publicised move towards earlier retirement for some British miners it is interesting to note some estimates made by the Deparment of Health and Social Security on the disparity between retirement age of men and women.[11] They estimate that the annual cost to public funds of reducing retirement age for men to sixty would be £2000 millions a year and that reduction to age sixty-four would be £350 millions a year. Also the employed population would shrink by one million men and many of their wives.

The general European position on pensionable age is thus confused. The age varies from sixty to sixty-seven for men and from fifty-five to sixty-eight for women. The general tendency is for retirement age to come down, particularly for those in heavy manual work, and for differences in entitlement between men and women to even out. This tendency has been fought for vigorously by trade unions and in very recent years governments have been inclined to co-operate not simply because of the moral justice of the case for earlier retirement but also to ease problems of unemployment. Whereas the moves to earlier retirement in Germany and Italy have proved relatively popular to employees and costly to implement, the more recent schemes that have been introduced mainly or partly because of anxiety about unemployment have been less popular.

The early weeks of the British job swap scheme showed that only 5500 applications had been approved and over 4000 of these had been from men who were already unemployed and who were using the scheme to take themselves off the unemployed register without producing an employment vacancy. Less than 1500 applications were men with a job to give up.

The Belgian government estimated that their 1976 scheme would be taken up by 30,000 older workers, yet the first four months of operation produced only 380 volunteers. The Belgians have since introduced legislation enabling retirement on full pension at sixty-four instead of sixty-five for those who have spent either twelve years in their whole career or five of the last fifteen years in particularly arduous or unhealthy work.

This raises important questions for the future. Does the Begian experience suggest that there is a lower practical limit to pensionable age and that in the 1970s the employee of sixty years or more is reluctant to retire? This would suggest that the DHSS calculations are misleading. There is perhaps an alternative explanation: that being eligible to retire on pension at sixty-three or sixty (Germany and Italy) is a different matter from being able to draw a reasonable level of unemployment benefit until retirement age. Also employers may feel that they prefer to retain the sixty-year old they know rather than engage the thirty-year old they do not know. Whatever the true reason the connected issues of pensionable age and pension level have begun to receive sufficient attention to be sure that there will be considerable change in the next few years.

e. Holidays and hours of work

In 1974 Anthony Barry was able to write:

'Britain is a poor relation compared with her partners in the EEC when it comes to holidays, both annual and public. Employees in most other countries not only seem to enjoy more public holidays and generally longer annual holidays, particularly in the case of manual workers, but usually also have far more to spend while on holiday.'[12]

Within two years the discrepancy had become less stark, as is shown by this comparison between the EEC countries in April 1976 (Table 6.5)[13]:

Table 6.5   Annual and public holidays in EEC countries (April 1976)

Country	Annual leave in days* by law or collective agreement	Annual leave in weeks	Days of public holiday
Belgium	24	4	10
Denmark	24	4	9½
France	24 – 30	4 – 5	7 – 10
Germany	18 – 26	3 – 4 +	10 – 13
Ireland	15 – 18	3	7
Italy	24	4	17
Luxembourg	20 – 22	4	10
Netherlands	20 – 22	4 +	7
United Kingdom	15 – 20	3 – 4	7

*Days of leave are calculated on the basis of a five day working week in the Netherlands and the United Kingdom, five *or* five and a half in Ireland, five and a half in Luxembourg and six days elsewhere.

Although there is still a clear gap, it has begun to narrow and eight-one per cent of British manual employees had achieved a holiday entitlement of more than three weeks by May 1976.

Barry's other comment was on the amount of pay employees receive while on holiday. In the United Kingdom holiday pay is calculated in a variety of ways. For salaried employees it is usually paid at the same rate as for a working week but for manual employees there are complications of overtime, shift and incentive earnings to be taken into account and most organisations pay on the basis of some formulation which produced a level of payment for holiday periods approximating to average earnings, although there are situations in which holiday pay is less than average. In other EEC countries the employee may well receive a higher rate of pay on holiday than at work. In Belgium and the Netherlands the level is *twice* earnings and in both Denmark and Germany the employee will receive appreciably more than average earnings whilst on holiday.

Another difference between the United Kingdom and Europe has been a wide differential on holiday provision between manual and non-manual employees. In 1974, for instance, fifty-four per cent of manual male employees had holidays of more than three weeks compared with seventy-five per cent of non-manual males. This practice is very rare in other Community countries and is becoming less common in the United Kingdom.

We can therefore visualise a situation in which British employees steadily move to a holiday entitlement with less variation between industries and categories of occupation, possibly supported by legislation as has happened in other countries. Although British collective agreements customarily include many of the features that are provided by statute in other countries, the lack of legislation in the United Kingdom means that there is no statutory minimum and little standardisation. In other countries there has been a tendency for legislation to follow collective bargaining as a means of extending to all employees additional benefits included in certain collective agreements.

It is also reasonable to assume that there will be further pressure on holiday pay. Although the practice of paying employees basic rate only for their holiday periods is disappearing rapidly, the incoming norm of average earnings is not as good a deal as in four of the Community countries. On public holidays the gap has narrowed significantly and from 1977 onwards there will be eight public holidays annually, for employees in Britain.

There used to be an argument which sought to justify shorter holidays in Britain because of a longer working week elsewhere in Europe. This is no longer valid as the following comparisons indicates (Table 6.6)[14]:

Table 6.6   Average weekly hours of work per manual worker

October 1972		October 1975	
Country	Hours	Country	Hours
France	45.0	France	42.4
Luxembourg	43.9	United Kingdom	41.8
Netherlands	43.9	Italy	41.5
Germany	43.2	Germany	40.9
United Kingdom	43.0	Luxembourg	40.9
Italy	41.9	Netherlands	40.8
Belgium	41.7	Belgium	37.1

The above figures are for hours worked: not the length of the standard working week, where the United Kingdom reached the forty-hour goal a little ahead of her European partners, notwithstanding the lack of legislation.

There is a further variation from practice in other Community countries that has to be noted. In most there is little or no difference between the standard working week for manual employees and that for non-manual and it is interesting to note that the standard for German public service non-manual employees was reduced from forty-two to forty hours a week in 1974, seven years later than the forty hour week was introduced in the engineering industry. In the United Kingdom a shorter working week for non-manual employees is the norm and standards of thirty-six to thirty-eight weekly are common.

f. Employee migration and company mergers

One of the earliest effects of the Treaty of Rome was to develop the transferability of social security rights between Community countries. Although such transferability already existed between some countries as a result of bilateral treaties, the effect of EEC Regulations of 1959 and 1972 has been to enable the free movement of workers throughout the Community. If an employee moves to another Community country for up to twelve months he will continue to be insured in the country from which he has moved. After that he will either transfer to the social security system of the country to which he has moved or there can be an extension of his cover by the system in the country from which he has transferred for up to a further twelve months.

Benefits can be paid in any Community country and rights acquired in one country are not lost on moving to another. One of the main aims of the Regulations is to ensure that the immigrant worker receives the same treatment as the national in the country to which he has moved. The acquired rights are especially important when there are qualifying periods for certain benefits, like unemployment pay or retirement pension. The regulations apply to the family of an insured person as well as to the insured person himself.

As recently as December 1976 the Council of the EEC approved a new directive intending to harmonise legislation in member countries about the protection of a different set of acquired rights: those of employees of companies merged with others. The aim is that employees should not suffer as a result of a change in the ownership of their company. In February 1977 the British House of Commons Select Committee on European Legislation considered this directive and recommended that it be considered further by the House.

g. Some future implications

This chapter has considered some of the more important features of employee benefit provision in the EEC. There has been no mention of retirement pensions other than those provided from public funds, and no mention of private medical insurance schemes. These omissions are part of the eclecticism mentioned at the opening of the chapter.

One way in which we may see continental practice following Britain is in the distinction made between manual and non-manual employees for social security contribution and benefit, where British practice does not make the same type of discrimination and it is other countries which will be under some pressure to match up.

The comparison of benefits is a hazardous task because of the varying type of social provision in different countries. However, a simple comparison on sickness benefit provisions suggests that there may be a need to extend the period of earnings-related benefit fairly soon, although unemployment benefit compares more favourably with our European partners.

It seems safe to predict that the age at which retirement becomes possible for men will come down in the United Kingdom, but it will presumably be a progressive reduction over a number of years rather than a dramatic drop. Also present indications are that it will be a move toward *retirement* rather than *guaranteed unemployment pay* until retirement, which does not seem an attractive proposition.

European developments provide little reason for predicting a big increase in holiday entitlement, either in annual holidays or statutory days, although annual holiday entitlement will probably continue to edge up in some areas. Holiday pay is an area where a discrepancy *can* be seen, with four of our European partners providing holiday pay that is greater than average earnings.

In considering hours of work we find near-harmonisation with the rest of EEC for manual workers, while British non-manual workers are in a favoured position. It is presumably unlikely that there will be an increase in the hours of the British non-manual working week, but there is certainly no justification for a further reduction yet on the basis of a comparison with the rest of Europe.

There remain a number of questions relating to the subject matter of this chapter, though not covered in it. Will we reach the situation of a statutory minimum wage? This operates in France by a link to the prices index and in the Netherlands by relating a statutory minimum to average earnings. How will statutory compensation of employees for short-time working and lay-off, introduced by the 1975 Employment Protection Act, compare with arrangements for similar situations in other EEC countries? The economic recession of the seventies has brought to light differences in national practice that were not previously significant. And then there are other questions relating to matters treated elsewhere in this volume. A point on which to end is to make one comparison. Many British employers were alarmed by the maternity provisions of the 1975 Act which provided for paid maternity leave at ninety per cent of previous earnings and rights to return to work within forty weeks. In Italy paid maternity leave is five months at eighty per cent of previous earnings and on return to work the mother can have up to two hours off work each day to look after the child until its first birthday. This time off is at the employer's expense and the mother has *absolute* protection against dismissal in that period.

References

1. Callund, D., *Employee Benefits in Europe*, Gower Press (Epping 1975).
2. *Social Security (Minimum Standards) Convention* (International Labour Office) 1952, Article 71, para. 1.
3. *Ibid.* Article 71, para. 2.
4. Adapted from *Introduction to Social Security*, International Labour Office, (Geneva).

5. *IDS International Report No.41* (Incomes Data Services Ltd) 1977. p. 7.

6. *IDS International Report No.37* (Incomes Data Services Ltd) 1976. p. 7.

7. *Comparative Tables of the Social Security Systems in the Member States of the European Communities*, 8th ed., Commission of the European Communities (Brussels 1974) p. 42–43.

8. *Ibid.* pp. 120–123.

9. *Income Security Regulations*, International Labour Office (Geneva 1944).

10. *Introduction to Social Security op cit.* p. 80.

11. *Pension Age*, Memorandum to the Equal Opportunities Commission from the Department of Health and Social Security, 1976.

12. Barry, Anthony, *Holidays and Hours of Work in the European Community*, Institute of Personnel Management (London 1974) p. 2.

13. *Comparative Tables Relating to Hours of Work in Community Industries*, Commission of the European Communities (Brussels 1976) pp. 3–7.

14. *Hourly Earnings, Hours of Work*, vol. 2. Statistical Office of the European Communities (1976) p. 93.

7 Management organisation for industrial relations

TERENCE KENNY

Di Marco knew from the moment he entered Lambrate that they meant to murder him. And now there he lay on a dusty street in this Milan suburb, shot down by his would-be assassins.

Such might be the beginning of a thriller about the Mafia and drug operations in Milan. But Valerio di Marco did not belong to that world. He was personnel director at British Leyland's Italian branch, Leyland Innocenti, and was engaged in lengthy discussions over the possible closure of the factory, when he was shot down by left wing fanatics.[1] British personnel directors naturally have difficulties over emotive issues such as closures, but it would need a considerable leap of the imagination to see them facing assassination squads over any industrial issues. While it is not contended that bullets have yet replaced the normal industrial relations procedures in Italy, there is something of great significance for the subject of this chapter in that assassination attempt. Clearly one principal way in which European managements of many medium sized, and most large firms, organise themselves for dealing with industrial relations is to set up a personnel department, often headed by a personnel director. As will be seen, there are very great immediate similarities in the way these departments work and the various responsibilities they discharge. Yet the di Marco shooting reminds us that what may appear to be the same in a list of comparative activities may mask very different realities.

It has long been argued that Italy is a more 'revolutionary' country than Great Britain[2] and that industrial relations in consequence take forms quite different from our own. The Italian personnel manager will thus be faced with a different job from that of his counterpart in Britain and may be a different kind of man. One way in which he certainly is different from his British counterpart is in his social origins. He is much less likely to have come from a working class background than a personnel manager in Britain or from many other European countries.[3] In this he is similar to his colleagues in the other management functions, and the question is inevitably raised as to whether his role in the firm is compromised in the eyes of some sections of the labour force, a question the ILO will now study further.[4] Certainly, granted a more revolutionary society in Italy than in Great Britain, and a greater social divide between the manager and the managed, then a somewhat more dramatic style of industrial relations becomes more explicable.

The differences alluded to so far, between personnel managers in Italy and in various other European countries are just examples from a numerous literature which has grown up in recent years on 'comparative management' and 'cross-cultural' studies in management. Before any more examples of the same kind are quoted it needs to be said that much of this literature needs to be treated with great caution. A great deal of the 'evidence' produced rises little above the level of personal opinion, and most of the surveys in the field – including, unfortunately, those quoted here – leave a very great deal to be desired as valid research instruments. Even where the surveys across cultures appear at first sight to be reasonably sound, there are still difficulties in the very definition of culture, and on many sides there is a readiness to assume too easily that attitudinal differences spring from this 'culture', that behavioural differences spring from such attitudes and that these behaviours are directly relevant to management effectiveness.[5] In this chapter we are more concerned with understanding some differences in European personnel management than trying to judge effectiveness, so that cautious use of comparative literature need not lead us too far astray.

It is not possible to advance far into a discussion of this kind before facing the issue of the supposed convergence of industrial societies. Granted that the cross cultural studies already mentioned show us a wide variety of differences, nevertheless these are said to be either vestigial or ultimately not important. Modern industry involves a certain scale, certain technologies, certain educational requirements, certain work relations, work discipline and the like, all of which ensure that industrial societies become ever more rapidly like each other. Management in general, and as far as we are concerned here, personnel management in particular, will thus tend to become much more similar throughout the world, including Europe, over the coming years. There is not the space to discuss this issue here. The weight of academic opinion in England seems to be against the convergence theory, although it must be said that there is an enormous amount of evidence in the development of personnel management to lend credence to some form of the theory.

A major problem facing anyone wishing to assert the convergence of personnel management organisation in Europe is the prior problem of explaining personnel management organisation in one's own country in the first place. Much of the traditional organisational literature used in Britain has tended to assume that there was some 'right' type of organisation founded on certain basic principles of management. Much British personnel literature has discussed personnel management from within this tradition, using a highly prescriptive approach. Thus, for example, even an otherwise first class introduction to personnel management, Terry Lyons's *Personnel Management in a Changing Environment*,[6] significantly fails to discuss the implications of this changing environment for the structure and functions of the organisation of personnel management. Clearly, personnel management as much as any other aspect of organisation must be considered from the point of view of contingency theory.

This is not to say that the idea of, if not the term, 'contingency' is new to personnel management. Like the

Molière character who was so delighted to find he had been speaking something so important sounding as prose all his life, so personnel managers delight in discovering that they have long been 'contingency theorists'. After all, what does contingency theory mean in the last resort but that 'it all depends ...'?[7] But personnel managers in Britain have undoubtedly been slow to re-think their behaviour and organisation in the light of their intuition of the contingency concept.

While echoes of the current debates on convergence and contingency will never be far away, only a rapid and relatively superficial survey of personnel management in Europe can be attempted here.[8] Some broad knowledge of the personnel function in Britain will be assumed. It will be helpful to examine the historical development of personnel management in two particular countries – France and Germany – before attempting a comparative sketch across a wider range of European countries. Many of the problems associated with personnel management throughout Europe can be seen in the developments within these countries.

Development of personnel management in France

Although the very word 'personnel' is itself French, it would be a mistake to infer from this that the modern concept of personnel management has come to us from France.[9] It has been said that 'the development of personnel administration, both as a specialised function and as an approach to manpower problems to be used by all members of management, roughly parallels the degree of industrialisation of individual countries'.[10] This broad truth holds at least for a comparison between France and Britain. France experienced its 'industrial revolution' some decades after England so that it is not surprising that the personnel function developed later. When it began to develop, the lines along which it did so were affected by the fact that since industrialisation was later there was some possibility of drawing lessons from early English experience of some of the social evils of rapid industrialisation.

The French tradition of industrial welfare was by no means the creation of their industrial revolution. Colbert, at the beginning of the eighteenth century had anticipated much of the welfare activities of the nineteenth century.[11] This tradition lasted through the industrial revolution in one form or another to present times, (although the modern French personnel manager is as uneasy and ambivalent about his heritage as is the British personnel manager about his own). Earlier in the nineteenth century Louis Philippe had only seen the need for repression of the workers, but other contenders for power had seen the workers as possible allies, and many 'legitimists' at that time founded charitable institutions and became involved in the development of a new Catholic social thinking. However, Louis Napoleon in his exile in England was, amongst other less reputable activities, taking a close look at British industry and its social problems.

With the return of Louis Napoleon to France, industrial welfare became a calculated part of his social and political policy. This was far more than a matter of personal style, as exemplified by his imperial tours of factories and handouts to old or injured workers, or of his wife's heavy involvement in charitable organisations. Government officials, for example, frequently organised local festivals to honour workers for their achievements or for loyalty to their employers. Thus, in 1854, we see the Prefect of the Department of the Somme assuring some *braves ouvriers, braves soldats de l'industrie* of the Emperor's keen concern for their welfare.[12] Government officials and factory owners had little scruple in linking their vaunted welfare with the need for the workers' votes, while being thankful for the contribution this welfare made to social peace. In the sixties and seventies the workers were clearly less and less content with welfare and philanthropy. A fascinating glimpse of this can be seen in a French newspaper report of 1869.[13] This contrasts the wild words at public meetings of the new class conscious workers movements with the peace and harmony at a meeting of the 1500 workers of Leclaire, who has often been held to be a forerunner of personnel management in

France. 'There', the report says, 'antagonism, hate, over
excited passions ... here ... harmony, contentment, moral
and material well being, and in the workers' mouths
eloquent and enthusiastic words to know social peace and
to express the most ardent gratitude and the most sincere
respect to their employer.'

By the time the First World War began it was clear that
welfare had not brought peace and harmony to the work
place or to society. It had been used cynically and
manipulatively, and those who boasted one day that their
companies looked after its workers from the cradle to the
grave, were quite capable of sacking workers the next day
for political activism for the 'wrong' party.[14] But welfare
always had another side. Its Colbertian origins have been
mentioned. The Alsace manufacturers of the first half of the
nineteenth century who had not only attempted to improve
welfare in their own factories but had banded together to
make a more forceful social intervention, were motivated
by quite different concerns than pure class interest or
politics. But the Christian origins of European welfare work
of this kind, associated as it is with considerable social
thinkers like Le Play and La Tour du Pin, is not to be simply
equated with apparently similar origins in Britain. The
influence of Catholic social thought in Europe on social
developments in industry has been little investigated here,
but remains one of the keys to understanding some
differences between British and European developments in
industrial relations. For example, in this country the names
of Lamennais, Lacordaire and Montalembert are known
principally as footnotes to the religious history of the
nineteenth century, while in a new standard French work
on trade unions, they appear as important figures in the
early growth of trade unionism.[15]

During the First World War in France there was great
interest in British experience of welfare work in munitions
factories. Our example was copied, a training school to
train such welfare workers was set up and an association,
L'Association des Surintendantes en France was founded.[16] In
many companies there had already been recently founded a

service de personnel, usually headed by a *chef du personnel* which was largely an administrative department concerned with records, payroll and often recruitment. The new welfare workers sometimes joined these departments, sometimes worked alongside them in a *service sociale*, and in some places formed the one and only functionally separate personnel type of department in the firm. After the war those social departments which had been separate from the *service du personnel* soon coalesced with them.

French writers on personnel management tend to think of the period between the two world wars as the first age of personnel management,[17] an age where personnel management is characterised by restricted, administrative work on the one hand and paternalistic welfare work on the other. They do not commonly stress what from here looks a very interesting development, the influence of the 'scientific management' school as evidenced by Le Chatelier, the Michelin brothers and Raoul Dautry. Dautry, for example, was not only a brilliant manager and convert to scientific management, but a social reformer with interests in a whole range of welfare and educational services. The new made an interesting marriage with the old. The second age is looked on as the age of techniques and the decline of welfare, with heavy borrowing of ideas from America, during which time recruitment, selection, training and certain human relations techniques were developed and refined. The third age is in effect the age of organisation development, with the personnel manager as a change agent within his company.

Before looking more closely at these second and third stages of personnel management in France, it is necessary to review some of the factors which shape it in its daily operation. The establishment of the works' committees (*comités d'entreprises*) in 1945 has provided a non-paternalistic handling of the welfare side of the company, although giving rise to a new concern that workers spending time and energy on social matters will be slow to seek a more meaningful participation. The structure of collective bargaining has meant that the French personnel manager spends much less time on plant bargaining than his English colleague. It is interesting that Clegg has explained the relative infrequency of plant bargaining by the successful determination of the employers to keep the unions out.[18] However, while collective agreements may be on a regional or national basis, or imposed by law, this does not exempt the personnel manager from a great deal of work related to their application within the plant and the complaints and problems which arise from them.

The horizon of British personnel managers has of late been dominated by trade unions and the law. Whatever the structure of bargaining, the French personnel manager is also very sensitive to trade union problems, not so much because of the complexity of a movement split along political and religious lines, but because of the rejection by some of these unions of capitalism in general and personnel management in particular. For them the personnel manager is part of an exploitive and manipulative team, and should only exercise his indubitably important functions within the firm as a jointly appointed, ideologically uncommitted technician in the service of the workers and the management – or perhaps only of the workers.[19] Again, while British personnel managers have been deluged by legal change, there are still profound differences between us and them in the role of law in industrial relations, and behind this, in the concept of the state and its relation to individual citizens and associations of various kinds. Alongside this, it would be interesting to explore certain particularly French attitudes which complicate the situation within which personnel managers in France have to operate, that is those concerned with the so-called 'bureaucratic phenomenon' about which Crozier has written so revealingly and with the concept of 'unity of command'.[20]

A good example of the stage which French personnel management had reached towards the end of its second stage can be found in the 1960 International Labour Office account of the organisation and practice of the personnel function in a large undertaking.[21] The author explains that a personnel function needed to be set up at the centre of this big company mainly because the setting up of a central works committee including representatives from the various works committees in the plants had provided the need for co-ordination to avoid discontent over differences in methods of wage determination, discipline, representation and the like. This central department only needed one senior person with two or three employees. Within the plants the first problem of organisation was that of authority. 'The need for unity of management is universally recognised in French undertakings. At each echelon in the undertaking there can be only one chief.' Thus the French personnel manager, as here, is essentially in a staff role as an adviser. He is held responsible for human relations, and must therefore have a good knowledge of men. He is responsible also for personnel policy in a firm bound by technological and economic constraints so that he should know something of technology and economics, and responsible also for the observance of labour laws and regulations so that he must have knowledge and ability in that area. The author explains that these requirements have led in his experience to the recruitment of engineers, ex-soldiers and lawyers to the personnel function.

The duties of the personnel function in this large organisation are seen as typical for other countries. There is a good deal of human relations training for supervisors and heavy involvement in recruitment with a psychological testing service in addition. A special responsibility of the personnel department arises from the law on collective dismissals, since it must prepare the lists for submission to the works committee. The personnel manager also gives assistance to the works committees on the discharge of their welfare functions, and works closely with the secretary of the committee in drawing up the agenda for its monthly meetings. In addition, it is to the personnel manager that the individual or collective complaints are forwarded from the employee delegates, and a monthly meeting is also held with these. In addition to all this the personnel manager must address himself to specifically trade union problems. Incidents likely to give rise to union claims are dealt with by him, and in the regional collective bargaining he is often the company man on the employers' federation side of the negotiations. Health and safety services operate under a safety engineer who is answerable to the head of personnel. Training, while heavily technical and vocational, is under the general direction of personnel.

This second period did not end abruptly in 1968 – since elements from all three ages of personnel management, not to mention its pre-historical period, can and always do co-exist – but from that time a new era of personnel management can increasingly be distinguished, much more open to the future of social change and the need to plan for it. If French management was an absolute monarchy before 1936 and a constitutional monarchy afterwards, since 1968 French personnel managers at least have increasingly seen it in participative terms.

A study of the organisation of the personnel department of another large French group, Rhone-Poulenc, in the early seventies displays some interesting differences from the 1960 study. Naturally, it is not an 'ideal type' but an actual operating organisation and so is bound to bear marks of earlier history.[22] The department's title is *La Direction Administrative et Sociale*, and as its name suggests it is not purely a personnel department but includes responsibility for various legal and property matters which in Britain would normally be dealt with by the company secretary. However, it defines its *mission general* as that 'of assuring the harmonious functioning of the different parts of the organisation in order to allow them to effectively reach the objectives corresponding to their *vocation* in the Rhone-Poulenc group'. While the clerical overtones of *mission* and *vocation* can no more be avoided in French than in English, they would presumably be far from the mind and intention of the Rhone-Poulenc management, yet even so it is interesting to note the definition of the purpose of the department in terms of 'harmonious functioning'.

The department is organised beneath the personnel

director into four main sections. The first of these is a general secretariat dealing with legal and property matters and head office administration, including sales to personnel. The second section covers *gestion du personnel et emploi* (personnel management and employment) and includes a nuclear section named *service administratif du personnel* dealing with pay and employment administration, as well as many welfare matters and relations with (non-union) committees and representatives. The third section is for 'social relations'. It is very much smaller in numbers than the *gestion* section, but this is the section which deals with documentation and studies on the labour side, and with what we in Britain would think of as typically 'industrial relations' work, including negotiation of collective agreements, handling labour problems concerning claims and industrial action, relations with the relevant employers' organisations and the like. The fourth section is concerned with training and information, which includes the responsibility for a permanent inventory for training needs, keeping in touch with training organisations outside the company and seeing that the training required by the employment function is provided. It provides a house journal, and co-ordinates internal information.

The Rhone-Poulenc group sees this personnel organisation as 'defining, promoting and controlling the human policy of the firm. To this end it collects all necessary documentation, ensures all useful relations between the plants and the group and outside bodies; it makes studies of the status of personnel as much as methods of management and human relations, notably in order to improve the conditions of the life and work of the work force, to encourage their growth and development and to maintain a good social climate ... ' (It is incidentally significant that between 1970 and 1973 the personnel director saw fit to eliminate from the written responsibilities of his department concern for the 'simplification of tasks' and to add to the duties of the personnel managers in the factories a concern for 'job enrichment'.)

Is the Rhone-Poulenc personnel department a third stage

organisation? A closer study of it shows many features which would qualify for this label – the high level of the head of the department within the total organisation, a concern for strategic as much as tactical policies, a concern for job enrichment, and the like.[23] On the other hand much of the department's concern, the language in which its aims are expressed, even the titles of the sections of the department are traditional enough. The simple truth is that, as in Britain, one needs to see an organisation in operation before any such judgements can be safely hazarded. But even from the written account of its structure and functions it is possible to appreciate much of the current concern among French personnel managers about their attempt to bring personnel management from the second stage of absorbtion in techniques and heavy involvement in administration to the third stage of a personnel management more open to the environment, more flexible and open to change, more concerned with policy making in the company at the highest level.[24]

In 1976 a whole number of *Personnel*, the journal of the French national personnel managers' association, was devoted to the present position of the personnel function in French management.[25] The worries expressed by Bosquet in 1971[26] about the difficulties of moving from *administration* to *gestion* still loom large to the authors. They seem ready to believe that Anglo-Saxon and German personnel managers have broken through sooner to an effective policy making level, but some of their hopes for achieving their concept of the right level for personnel management may seem to us rather optimistic. One writer, for example, sees an appropriate title for a third stage personnel manager to be no longer 'director', a title achieved frequently enough in the second stage, but now the title 'assistant managing director' (*directeur-général adjoint*) is looked for.

One of the most interesting recent surveys on personnel management in France was published in 1972 by the research organisation, *Entreprise et Personnel*.[27] This study found that there were still two quite distinct ways of looking at the personnel function in France, one which saw it as concerned with a clear vision of the future, with an integration of short and long-term objectives, the other which was a product of a very short-term view of the future, where the personnel function was created to meet an immediate constraint or because everyone else had one. The problem with the latter view is that once staff have been appointed for such a type of personnel function it is a matter of many years before it is practical to remove or re-educate the staff involved. The survey concludes that 'the personnel function as it has been known so far is now put in question. Its evolution has led to numerous contradictions, notably between intentions and results, between the profound needs and the many short-term constraints.'

We are left with a paradox. Some aspects of social change in French industry – for example, mensualisation, moves to raise the dignity and ease the burden of the manual labourer, the proposals of the Sudreau report for industrial reform – all seem to suggest a big and rapid change in industrial attitudes, but the personnel manager seems to have doubts about the capacity of his function to operate with full effectiveness in this new climate. An understanding of how this paradox might be explained and resolved would take us deep into the social problems of modern France. This is not the place to attempt such a study, but it nevertheless remains a fact that if, for example, the proposals of the Sudreau report are to be put into practice, then despite the fact that the report did not look at it in this way, it will be the personnel managers of France who will be most concerned in seeing that the industrial application of the proposals is practicable and effective.

Development of personnel management in Germany

Hans Friedrichs, the Director of the German national association for personnel management sees the development of personnel management in his own country as falling into three stages, very similar in practice to the French stages already discussed.[28] The first period he calls the *Verwaltungsperiode* (administration) which he dates to about 1950, and from then until 1970 he describes an *Anerkennusperiode* (recognition) with the third and current stage being as *Integrationperiode* (integration). The content of these necessarily somewhat arbitary divisions is again very similar to what we have seen in France. From an English perspective it would seem that Herr Friedrichs gives equally short shrift to his first period just as French personnel managers are apt to do with their own. For if the whole period starting at the turn of the last century, which saw the adaptation of American 'scientific management' ideas to European industry, is to be the first period, what then are we to call developments in the nineteenth century? Perhaps we can call this period the pre-history of personnel management, but it is to this period we have to go to see the roots of modern personnel management in Germany.

Hans Friedrichs includes welfare in his 'administration' period but although he does not dwell on it, it is quite clear that a special study of nineteenth century welfare would be rewarding. Clearly the German personnel manager will be ambivalent about this tradition. To read now, for example, about Alfred Krupp's speech to his employees in 1877,[29] in which he advises them to eschew politics except in so far as they elect candidates recommended by their superiors, and to remain in the circles of their families, is to be brought sharply up against one aspect of the reality of the paternalistic approach of the time. But the same historian of the German labour movement who quotes Krupp as above, does not seem much more pleased with the current position – 'the fact remains that the worker (and employee generally) leaves his freedom in his locker along with his overcoat',[30] no essential difference remains for her between that day and this in the role of welfare which she sees as part of 'a trend towards modern industrial feudalism along paternalistic lines'.

A study of the development of German industry, from the earlier mining organisations to the giant chemical and other concerns which were in position at the end of the nineteenth century, shows how essential it was that the range of welfare measures were taken if it were to be possible to recruit, train and retain the necessary work force. These measures were not frills, not devices to lure workers to forget the basic wretchedness of their lot, but the only means by which such rapid and effective industrialisation could have been built up.[31]

Much of this is clear from one of the best accounts in English of European welfare work.[32] The writer contrasts the paternalistic nature of German welfare work with that of the French, citing in evidence the 'democratic' work of Leclaire. He may be a little misguided here. There are some features of French industrial development which could be cited to prove how much more democratic it was than elsewhere, e.g. the use of working men, ·after special training courses, as factory inspectors in the late nineteenth century, but we have already seen how the work of Leclaire must have seemed at the time to French trade unionists being berated to follow his example. Yet in the same decade as the Leclaire meeting the death rate in Essen was fifty-five per thousand, and the Krupp housing and other welfare measures made a powerful contribution to the public good, as well as being clearly good for Krupp. It is by no means clear that recipients of the Krupp welfare were less ready for self-government than other German workers less favoured in this respect, and one English observer thought they were more so. (*op. cit.*, p.109).

We know from the work of Geck that welfare officers of one title or another had already been appointed soon after the middle of the century, and that from 1890 to the First World War there were developments in some way parallel to those in the United States and England. War time needs forced Germany towards the use of welfare ladies in war factories in much the same way as in England and France. But there were a variety of developments in German factories and it is interesting to see some of these in one particular German firm. A fascinating account of the development of personnel work has been written by von Beckerath in the Bayer centenary history.[33] From this we learn that the Bayer early welfare arrangements were needed in the comparative absence of state regulations – in the whole period from the regulations on young workers of 1839 to the October revolution of 1918 there were only 103 laws and orders of a social policy content in Germany, and only thirty-seven of these were in the period 1839–1900. It is not only the detail of the growth of the personnel function through the centralising of payment and recruitment arrangements and the setting up of a committee on workers' affairs which is important, but also the glimpses of employee involvement which are highly significant, especially from the first appearance in 1873 of two workers on the board which ran the sick scheme. The stability of the Bayer company during the period of unrest after the First World War is attributed by the author, not so much to the material welfare which the workers had enjoyed, but more specifically to the great number of committees which Bayer had set up with the set aim of letting workers co-operate in various areas.

The relevance of the inter-war period to the development of personnel management in Germany is greater than might at first sight appear, although it can only be glanced at here. The works councils of 1920, which were theoretically non-union, rapidly became union dominated, and were dominated by the more narrow interests of the workers.[34] This experience was to be significant for the future. There was also much about the Nazi period which was interesting, leaving aside the horrors of forced labour and other excesses. Although the welfare and cultural arrangements of the 'strength through joy' movement were once a target for scorn, many of the preoccupations of the movement now have a very modern look in an age of concern for the environment and the quality of life. Some of the practices were if anything a little too democratic for modern British industrial taste – it is hard to see a British managing director of a large concern drawing lots with his workers to decide who was to have the privilege of a cabin on the works' holiday cruise![35]

The beginning of the new German industrial system after the Second World War is relatively well known in England, the more so since our own part in its creation has been much, perhaps too much, lauded by ourselves. The concept of *mitbestimmung* has dominated the post war era, though it has not been without its critics. Max Weber was worried by the dominant 'welfare' approach of his own day, and Ralf Dahrendorf has been worried by the dominant industrial idea of post war Germany. He sees the *mitbestimmung* movement as the search for an impossible if not undesirable conflict-free consensus. But as Arndt Sorge[36] has pointed out, the supporters of *mitbestimmung* have been right in predicting less conflict through the institutionalisation of their aims, and Dahrendorf has been wrong.

How does German personnel management work in a co-determination age? Some critics from the labour side claim to find little evidence of systematic personnel policies in all but a few large companies.[37] However, there is no doubt that personnel management is now solidly founded. The German employers' confederation (BDA) suggested to their members in 1962 that a full time personnel manager became necessary when the number of employees reached 500[38] and went on to give sound and comprehensive advice on the matter, though clearly within the social work and personnel techniques tradition which Heinrichs has led us to expect of that time. A traditional type book on management organisation appearing in 1971, similar to many others which could be quoted, lists the so called vast problems with which a personnel department must deal[39] and it is probably a good inventory of the concerns of a personnel manager, but the character of some of these problems, e.g. establishing different pensionable ages for different groups, almost immediately juxtaposed to the problem of the introduction of a systematic approach to the evaluation of personnel, seems to put the concept of the personnel function into the administrative and recognition phases of Friedrichs, hardly the integration period. A very thoroughgoing approach to the organisation of the personnel function was published in 1973 by the German national association of personnel managers.[40] In this a great deal of information is given on different forms of organisation according to size (there is, as one would naturally expect, no recognition of the contingency of personnel organisation) and a trend is shown towards structuring personnel departments according to subject specialism – planning, training etc. – rather than having separate sections of the personnel department dealing with separate sections of the work force as had been usually the case. The result is that the organisation charts of personnel management in medium and large sized German companies do not look at first sight very different from those we see in Britain. This still leaves the question of how far they are in their actual operation akin to those we are familiar with in Britain.

There is no doubt that the operation of works councils and the whole co-determination movement has had a profound effect on personnel management in Germany. As Friedrichs puts it 'the *mitarbeiter* has become the subject and not the object of personnel work'.[41] The works council has had a vital role in personnel management from the start, and even more so since 1972. This can be interpreted as a form of joint decision making, or can be more pejoratively described as the functioning of the councils as 'agents for personnel management',[42] on the hypothesis that since the councils are not essentially trade union bodies, their apparent area of freedom is a sham. This is not the way it appears to German personnel managers in general. An example of how differently even the more routine aspects of personnel management work in Germany can seem is given us in the ILO study already quoted, in respect of French experience. With regard to the engagement of a new employee, for example, 'the personnel department first obtains particulars regarding the applicant ... and puts these on record. If the applicant appears to be suited to the vacant post he is immediately introduced to the works council (or more often, its chairman) as well as to the medical officer of the factory and the head of the training division. The works council or chairman is thus able to talk with the applicant and put questions to him. If the works council has an objection to the applicant it must, under the Works Constitution Act, state this in writing, giving reasons, within a week. The statement must be made to the employer, represented in this case by the chief of personnel. The reasons which justify the works council in refusing its consent to an appointment ... are listed in the Act.'[43]

The precise relationships between the personnel department and the works council will differ according to a variety of factors to do with the previous history of the firm, the type of worker and the values of the management, the product and technology, the market and other aspects of the firm's environment. It will differ internally between matters which are for co-decision, those for consultation and those simply for information. The aim is, however, to involve the works council in the whole field of personnel policy. A good example of this can be seen in an address of the Personnel Director of Krupp to his central works council.[44] In this the emphasis is very much on the need for better personnel planning and a more profound study of work in the organisation, but in meetings such as this the whole range of personnel policy becomes involved.

Personnel managers do not only work with works councils, and the existence of these have not solved German industrial problems. In the address of the Krupp director already quoted from, there is anxiety expressed about the 'alienation' of much of the work force, and our own newspapers here have carried reports of a rapid loss of interest in their jobs by many German workers.[45] This is not the place to examine the trade union structure within which the personnel manager operates, but clearly there are still problems for him in a situation where the plant bargaining which takes place is carried on by the works council, although the trade union may be strong in the plant, and if it is in any way strong, will certainly dominate the council. The concept of the 'works community' is very relevant to these concerns, and is not simply a misty ideal but an operative idea which has shaped the work of the personnel manager. But it is a very difficult concept to work with. Faced with a works council and union representatives inside the plant and outside to which he must relate, the personnel manager hangs on to the concept of personnel work for the individual, based on the existence of individual and personal needs and expectations which must be recognised and which he must attempt to meet. Friedrichs believes that it is precisely through success in this area that the more individually orientated personnel department will be able to be more effective in collective and conflict situations.[46] The kind of practical difficulty which arises from all this can be seen in the current problems at Volkswagen while this is being written.[47] Here the modern concern of personnel management to move away from its traditional problems to a direct concern for the satisfaction of the worker through changes in the content and organisation of his job fell foul of the complex situation described. In an experiment with group assembly of complete engines there was going to be a thorough test of the idea that workers are more effective and achieve more personal satisfaction in 'semi-autonomous groups'. The works council was not satisfied with the way the project was being organised, and objected to the group spokesmen emerging from these working groups, complaining that representatives for them should rather be the union stewards. The works council was soon limiting the 'autonomy' of these groups, but the full time officials of the union who now came on the scene to aid the works council also proceeded to ensure further limitation. Now the groups cannot choose their own members or representatives, nor can they decide their own work pace nor their own rest breaks. While the problems in this case are yet to be resolved, it illustrates the complexity of the personnel manager's job in attempting to deal with various individuals and types of institutions along the lines of his current personnel philosophy.

Despite its obvious problems, German personnel management has worked effectively so far. To appreciate all the reasons for this would take us too far into the social history and social structure of Germany. Let it only be said here that if the history of French trade unionism is a history of permanent combat, the history of German unionism might be called the history of permanent bourgeoisification. While there is truth in the popular British stereotype of a rigid, authoritarian German entrepeneur who is and intends to remain boss in his own house, and in the stereotype of the bureaucratic German manager, deferring to the boss and lacking or fearing initiative,[48] these stereotypes plainly fail to account for all the facts. Whatever the preconceptions which tell us that German industry by now should be either a sea of grey mediocrity with little enterprise or initiative, or if not this, then the scene of grave disorder caused by the too long repression of conflicting interests through various ill-considered institutional and social devices, there can be little doubt that it is our preconceptions which need re-examination. It may, of course, be argued that industrial peace and progress can be achieved at too high a price for the long run health of the whole society, but this is to take us very much too far afield now.

German, like French, personnel management is then only to be fully understood against a particular social and cultural background, even though a British personnel manager feels at home in discussing a wide range of personnel problems with colleagues from both countries. In the section which follows some tentative and general remarks will be made about personnel management in contemporary Europe. While it will not be possible to sketch in the background for other countries, as has been done so briefly for France and Germany, it will be understood that such an examination would inevitably change some of the impressions the British manager gains from such comparisons.

Some European developments and comparisons

When the classic international study of Harbison and Myers, *Management in the Industrial World*, appeared in 1959, it was still possible for them to paint such a gloomy picture of

European management in general and of France and Germany in particular that the reader could only be astonished to see the industrial progress these countries achieved in the event over the next decade, despite their supposed authoritarian and paternalistic management and lack of adequate personnel administration. The view from America was still jaundiced next year. F. T. Malm[49] found that the shortcomings of European personnel management sprang from their basic business objectives. The European objectives were to maintain existing market shares, limit output, control existing organisations in a centralised way with a familial and paternalistic approach. The American objectives were to expand markets, increase output, build organisations on a delegation principle and with a consultative and participative approach. While Malm was far too sweeping in his generalisations, it is nevertheless interesting that he found that the basic lack in European personnel management was the absence of a 'policy' approach to management, which seems to have arisen from too much emphasis on the key *personal* role of the top manager or owner manager, from the lack of what he calls an *organisational* view of decision-making, whereby policies could be seen as means for developing decision-making at lower levels, and from the prevalence of governmental regulations affecting industry in Europe.

While the 1960 ILO study on personnel management earlier discussed is to some extent a corrective to the broad criticisms of Malm, it is noteworthy that the next major study of European personnel management to appear concludes that it is now time for them to be 'more concerned with formulating policy'. Rubenowitz[50] found a high level of formal academic education amongst personnel managers, with lawyers making up the largest proportion of the graduates in Germany, Austria, France and Spain, with lawyers and economists in more or less equal numbers in Belgium and Switzerland. Lawyers were infrequent in personnel management in England, Italy and Portugal. Over sixty per cent of the respondents in his survey had worked in personnel for over nine years, and the bigger the country the higher the figure – France, Germany and England all had approximately seventy per cent. A very high proportion (seventy-five per cent) reported to the top management of their concerns.

There was a high degree of similarity between the functions of the personnel departments studied. These functions seem to have fallen into four groups. The first group concerned the training and development of managers. This was generally rated the greatest problem area, and the one least satisfactorily handled. The second group concerned personnel planning, training, organisation and communication, in which fields great problems were seen but moderately satisfactory methods for handling them were in use. The third group consisted of procurement and selection, promotion and transfer and conditions of pay and employment. These were thought of as comparatively large problems being satisfactorily handled. Finally the fourth group, comprising records, working conditions, social measures etc. were felt to involve comparatively minor problems being satisfactorily handled. No doubt nowadays these same personnel managers might see different priorities in the problem areas, but it is noteworthy that so many saw problems in the management and management development field where their influence was least. Of the larger countries it was in France that this was most apparent. On a comparison of the extent to which particular personnel departments concerned themselves with the whole range of functions covered by personnel departments in general throughout Europe, the German departments seemed consistently to have the widest coverage, followed by Sweden, Norway and then England. France and the Netherlands were about average or a little below for the sample, Austria, Belgium and Switzerland a little further below, with Italy, Spain and Portugal tending to have the least coverage.

A further analysis of the time spent by individual personnel managers on different functions brought home the extent to which in Sweden and Norway work on personnel records and statistics have been delegated, unlike the position in France where nothing like so much delegation had been achieved. The English personnel manager was distinguished by a greater involvement in training, as was to be expected, since the English training tradition is very much a company based phenomenon in contrast to the continental tradition of greater reliance on external educational bodies. (There has, of course, been a considerable convergence of English and continental approaches over the last decade.)

The most recent study of European personnel managers was reported by the de Bettignies brothers in *European Business* in 1973.[51] While Germany is missing from this study, there is a high degree of correspondence with previous studies, particularly with regard to the educational background of personnel managers. The prevalence of social science qualifications in Holland and Sweden and their noticeable absence in France and Italy raise interesting questions about how personnel work is seen in these countries. The average age of the personnel managers studied was Spain (thirty-eight), Portugal (forty), Italy (forty-one), Netherlands (forty-two), Britain (forty-three), Sweden (forty-five), France (forty-six). European personnel managers are comparatively mobile, particularly the Swedes and the British, the Spanish and the Portugese are the least so, while French personnel managers have the most seniority in their present companies.

The personnel managers show a wary attitude to sophisticated personnel techniques. No more than half use psychological tests in selection, and even where techniques are in more general use their limitations seem well understood. Nearly all those in the survey saw themselves as change agents (ninety per cent), needing to set up new management systems more congruent with the changing environment (eighty-six per cent) and needing to make special efforts in the field of participation (ninety-four per cent). The role of the personnel manager vis a vis the unions is everywhere expected to increase, but while the Dutch (seventy-five per cent), British (sixty-three per cent) and Swedes (fifty-four per cent) see the unions as an aid to participation, as many as forty-eight per cent of the French and Italians see the unions as hampering its development.

Perhaps the most interesting findings of the de Bettignies' study concern the perceptions of European personnel managers about their own role. They are most aware of their need for diagnostic skills, and the skills of administration are not seen as crucial. They increasingly wish to hold advisory, staff roles as against using line or functional authority, and to aid this they wish to build up more harmonious relationships with management colleagues. But when forced to a decision the personnel managers rely on their own personal values to a far larger extent than those of anyone else, least of all those of any professional body to which they belong. They see the need for looking more closely at problems of organisational functioning and for developing appropriate strategies and policies. All of this needs not only representation at the top of the hierarchy but actual and substantial influence at this level, which experience repeatedly shows can be a very different thing. The personnel man's previous administrative and technique oriented behaviour acts as a constraint to this development. Either the service he has offered will be poor, in which case he will lose credibility, and if he is too successful he runs the risk of being 'bound by his technical image'. In any case, much of the traditional concern for the internal resources of the firm can never be lost, – someone has to have this concern, so the de Bettignies brothers see European personnel managers as caught in a paradox, 'caught in a myriad of orientations which mean virtual explosion of his role accompanied by a painful feeling of deprivation and a search for his status'.[52] This view is strengthened by a study of Geert Hofstede, based on managers attending the IMEDE management development programmes in Switzerland.[53] Here personnel managers saw themselves as other managers saw them, carrying out the personnel function as a predominantly static role, while not succeeding in enabling their departments to make successfully creative contributions to their organisations.

If personnel managers share a common frustration, the

reference in the previous paragraph to the values of European personnel managers reminds us that there will be many differences in the way the personnel manager approaches this frustration point. We return to the opening considerations of national and cultural variables. These will be seen in the variety of national, broad approaches to current problems. For instance, there is an enormous interest amongst European personnel managers and their national governments in questions of the quality of human life. In Germany a very thoroughgoing approach to these problems has been attempted on the basis of 'scientific dirigism',[54] in France there has been much activity principally in the first place through collective bargaining, while in England the government have set up on the cheap a small work research unit offering advice to companies who come to hear of it and wish to receive some help. If we look more closely at the detailed differences between personnel practices in various countries,[55] we begin to have difficulties in disentangling those which are a result of cross cultural variables and those which are contingent on size, technology and other factors earlier mentioned. Only recently have the kind of studies been undertaken which will help us eventually to sort out such problems.[56]

But it remains true that European personnel managers see themselves as having a great deal in common. For some years now the Institute of Personnel Management in London has been holding bi-lateral meetings with personnel managers from Europe, and the author can add his personal testimony to the fact that these meetings have proved conclusively enough to those involved that there is enough similarity in their problems for discussions to be highly valued. The divergencies are also valuable, since these tend to be frequently between the members of the same national delegation as well as between nationalities, and throw light on what is fundamental and relatively permanent in a problem and what is more transient and relative to circumstances. Even if Russia were to be added to the list of bi-lateral discussions it is by no means certain that British personnel managers might not find familiar echoes from   current   Russian   experience   of   personnel management![57]

The term 'industrial relations' covers a wide range of relationships of a non-trade union and of a trade union character. With the trend to single channel representation in Europe the character of some of the problems changes, but through all this change European managements of companies of over about 1000 employees have found that these relationships cannot be handled effectively except through a process of organisational differentiation which gives rise to a personnel department. Great problems are inherent in the organisation and functioning of these departments. In no European country are the personnel organisations content with the present position and look forward to the general establishment of a more satisfactory kind of personnel function. While much anguish has been expressed over the years about trade union shortcomings in the field of industrial relations reform, it seems clear that European managements cannot afford to shrug off their own responsibilities in the need to rethink the organisation of management within the company for industrial relations. That means, in the first place, that they need to re-consider the organisation, staffing and functions of their personnel departments. In so far as some aspects of this problem necessarily go beyond the immediate horizons or competence of any management, there is even greater need for clear thinking and new approaches from European personnel managers themselves.

References

1. 'BL abroad', *New Society*, 20 November 1975, p. 411.
2. See, e.g., a recent EEC Euro-barometer survey first reported in 'The European Citizen and Social Change', *Euroforum* No 7, 1977 p. 3.
3. Ferrari, S., 'The Italian Personnel Manager', *International Management Review* No 1, 1975 pp. 67–74. See also his

'Cross Cultural Management Literature in France, Italy and Spain', *Management International Review* No. 4–5, 1974 pp. 17–26.

4. 'Can a Peasant Become a Personnel Manager', *Behavioural Science Report International*, July 1975 No. 41.

5. See on these points Negandhi, A. R., 'Cross Cultural Management Studies: Too Many Conclusions, Not Enough Conceptualisations', *Management International Review* No. 6, 1974 pp. 59–67.

6. Lyons, T. P., *The Personnel Function in a Changing Environment*, Pitman (London 1971).

7. Lawrence, P. R. and Lorsch, J., *Organisation and Environment*, Cambridge (Mass. 1967). For a study almost totally ignoring such problems, see Weinshall, T. D. and Twiss, B. C., *Organisational Problems in European Manufacture*, 2 vols., Longman (Harlow 1973).

8. For a start towards a sounder basis for comparisons, see Child, J. and Kieser, A., *Organisation and Managerial Roles in British and West German Companies*, University of Aston Working Papers, No. 39–1975.

9. As some early definitions of management in the Oxford English Dictionary have caused amusement by defining it in terms of trickery or deceit, so it is interesting to note that the first English use of the word recorded by the OED is in relation to a gang of robbers. There are many examples in the middle of the last century of the use of the term 'personnel' to distinguish the human from the *matériel* or material equipment of an institution. All the examples quoted in the OED are of a naval and military character, but an interesting early use of the term in an industrial context is to be found in a letter of 1867 about technical education abroad published in *British Parliamentary Papers* (see Pollock & Holmes, *Documents in European Economic History* vol. 2, p. 89). The terms 'personnel administration' and 'personnel management' were well established in the USA in the 1920s and were gradually coming into use in England before the Second World War. With the renaming in 1946 of the 'Institute of Labour

Management' as the 'Institute of Personnel Management' the latter term has become the norm.

10. Malm, F. T., 'The Development of Personnel Administration in Western Europe', *California Management Review*, Fall 1960, vol. 3, No 1, p. 69.

11. Wolff, P. and Mauro, F. 'L'Age de l'Artisanat' Ve-XVIIIe Siècles vol.II, *Histoire General du Travail*, ed. L. H. Parias, Nouvelle Librarie de France (Paris 1959).

12. Kulstein, D. I., *Napoleon III and the Working Class*, California State Colleges, 1969, p. 85.

13. Kulstein, *op.cit.*, p. 165.

14. Bron, J., *Histoire du Mouvement Ouvrier Francais* vol.II, (Paris 1970) p. 50.

15. Caire, Guy., *Les Syndicats Ouvriers*, Press Universitaires de France (Paris 1971).

16. Maurel, E., *L'Ingénieure Social dans l'Industrie*, (Paris 1929) p. 6.

17. Eggens, J. B., 'La Fonction Personnel Face à son Avenir' *Personnel* March-April 1976, No. 186, pp. 20–39. Roche, M. 'Les Trois Ages de la Fonction "Personnel" in *L'Usine Nouvelle'*, March 1971, pp. 196–219. For an account of the traditional *service du personnel* in a contemporary company see 'Un service du Personnel dans une Entreprise Traditionelle', *Personnel* No. 184, 1976, pp. 21–26.

18. Clegg, Hugh, *Trade Unionism under Collective Bargaining: A Theory Based on Comparisons of Six Countries*, Blackwells (Oxford 1976) p. 65.

19. Cottave, Robert (FNIC-FO), *Personnel*, No. 186, p. 46. NB Where the journal *Personnel* is quoted in this chapter it refers to the journal of that name published by the ANDCP in Paris.

20. Crozier, M., *The Bureaucratic Phenomenon*, Tavistock, 1964. For 'unity of command' see Fayol, H., *General and Industrial Management*, Pitman (London 1949) p. 24.

21. Leblanc, J., 'The Position and Responsibilities of the Personnel Department within the Undertaking. Some French examples in *The Position and Responsibilities of the Personnel Department inside undertakings*, Labour-

Management Relations Series, No 7, ILO (Geneva 1960).

22. Papers on the organisation of the personnel function at Rhône Poulenc from J. Catherine, Personnel Director, to the author in 1973.

23. See for further evidence of the thinking of M. Catherine and his colleagues their paper on Organisational Planning at the 12th Anglo-French Personnel Managers Meeting in Paris, 1973 held by IPM, London.

24. See Eggens *op.cit.* p. 32 for some simple illustrations of the differences between the three ages. If a new factory is being set up the first stage personnel man comes in after everything has been decided in order to recruit workers, the second stage man becomes involved in the detailed plans to do with training new recruits for the factory, arranging canteens for it and the like; the third stage personnel manager is involved before the decision to set up the company is even taken. Further, taking the example, of the necessary recruitment of labour for this new factory, the first stage personnel manager would recruit according to a profile of the kind of labour needed drawn up by others. The second stage manager would be involved at least a year in advance on deciding the type of labour needed, and would consider this in terms of age structure, turn-over and manpower planning problems generally. At the third stage the personnel manager would consider the recruitment against the background of a social and economic employment policy which guides the decisions of the firm, taking into account any implications for the structure of the organisation, its system of management, and any other consequences for personnel problems within the firm, (since changes in one part of the personnel system affect other not so obviously related parts).

25. ANDCP, *Personnel*, Mar-April 1976, No. 180.

26. Bosquet, R., 'Gestion ou Administration du Personnel?'. *Management France*, April 1972, pp. 25–32.

27. *Enquête sur l'Evolution de la Fonction Personnel dans 50 Grandes Enterprises Francaises*, Enterprise et Personnel (Paris 1972).

28. Friedrichs, H., *Moderne Personalführung*, Verlag Moderne Industrie, 1973, pp. 9–40.
29. Grebing, H., *The History of the German Labour Movement*, London, 1969, p. 53.
30. *Op.cit.* p. 151.
31. See, especially, Jankte, C., *Der Vierte Stand*, Freibung 1955 pp. 174–181. Geck, L. H. Ad., *Die Sozialen Arbeitsverhältnisse im Wandel der Zeit*, Berlin 1931, *passim*.
32. Boettiger, L., *Employee Welfare Work*, New York, 1923.
33. Beckerath, P. G. von, 'Personalwesen' in *Beiträge zur Hundertjährigen Firmengeschichte, 1863–1963*, pp. 393–444, Farbenfabriken Bayer AG (n.d.).
34. Pollock & Holmes, *Documents of European Economic History*, vol. III, p. 85.
35. Grunberger, R., *A Social History of the Third Reich*. Penguin (Harmondsworth 1974) p. 254.
36. Sorge, A., 'The evolution of industrial democracy in the countries of the European community', *British Journal of Industrial Relations*, vol. XIV, No 3, p. 280.
37. Arbeitskammer des Saarlandes: *Betriebsräte und Personalplanung: Probleme und Perspektiven*, Saarbrucken, 1974, pp. 29 f.
38. 'Der Personalleiter', *Arbeitsberichte* No. 19, Dec. 1962 Bundesvereinigung der deutschen Arbeitgeberverbände.
39. Arbeitskreis Dr Krahe der Schmalenbach – Gesellschaft, *Die Organisation der Geschäftführung – Leitungs – organisation*. 2nd ed. Opladen, 1971.
40. Deutsche Gesellschaft fur Personalführung, *Die Organisation des Personalwesens in einem modernen Unternehmen*, Luchterhand Verlag, 1973. NB. The work on which this was based belongs to earlier years.
41. Friedrichs, *op.cit.*, p. 35.
42. Clegg, *op.cit.*, p. 60.
43. Esser, O., 'The Position and Responsibilities of the Personnel Department in a German Undertaking', in ILO Labour Management Series 7, p. 22.
44. Bärsch, H. G., *Grundsatzfragen der Personal und Sozialarbeit*. Referat bei der Betriebsräteversammlung der Fried Krupp Gm BH Villa Hügel, 19 Okt 1972.

45. 'Is Germany's Famous Efficiency Making the Workers Lose Heart', *Times*, 19 August 1975.
46. Friedrichs, *op.cit.* pp. 35–36.
47. 'Union Versus Worker', *Economist*, 19 March 1977, pp. 91–92. This kind of difficulty was warned about at a recent ILO seminar. See *Workers' Participation in decisions within undertakings*, Labour Management Series No. 48, p. 34, ILO 1976.
48. Hartmann, H., *Authority and Organisation in German Management*, Princeton, N. J., 1959. Childs & Kieser, *op.cit.*
49. Malm, F. T., 'The Development of Personnel Administration in Western Europe', *California Management Review*, Fall 1960, vol. 3, No. 1. See also the same author's 'Personnel Policies & European Management', Management International 1961 (3), pp. 102–113.
50. Rubenowitz, S., 'Personnel Management Organisation in some European societies', *Management International Review* 4–5, 1968, p. 92.
51. Bettignies, H. C. & L. de, 'Men at the Cross-roads: Europes Personnel Managers', *European Business* No. 38, Summer 1973.
52. Bettignies, *op.cit.*
53. Hofstede, G. H., 'Frustrations of Personnel Managers', *Management International Review*, vol. 13, 4–5, 1973, pp. 127–132.
54. Delamotte, Y., 'Working Conditions and Government Policy, Some Western European Approaches', *International Labour Review*, vol. 114, No. 2, Sept-Oct, 1976.
55. See, e.g., Cruden, H. J., & Sherman, A. W., *Personnel Practices of American Companies in Europe*, American Management Association, 1972.
56. E.g. Child & Kieser *op.cit.* See also Child *et.al.*, *Growth of Firms as a Field of Research*, Aston Working Paper No. 30, 1975.
57. Poliakov, V. & Silin, A., 'Personnel Management in Russia', *International Labour Review*, vol. 106, No. 6, 1972, pp. 537–542.

8 Dismissals and the law: Britain and Europe

MICHAEL RUBENSTEIN

Staggering under the weight of the avalanche of legislation since 1971 conferring individual rights in employment, the personnel manager might be forgiven for thinking that the British worker must have more legal protection than any of his European counterparts. This chapter will show that in the key areas of individual labour law, the UK is well behind the norm for Western Europe. If we presume that the medium-term effect of European Community membership will be a levelling-up of standards amongst the Nine, to put it in a nutshell, 'you ain't seen nothing yet!'

In analysing the likely future shape of British labour law in so far as it relates to individual rights on termination of employment, it must be remembered that the traditional British approach involved no statutory regulation at all, save for the exceptional circumstances relating to health and safety at work in which protective legislation was deemed necessary. As recently as 1965, Professor Wedderburn could begin his classic treatise, *The Worker and the Law*,[1] by remarking: 'Most workers want nothing more of the law than that it should leave them alone. In this they can be said to display an instinct that is fundamental to British industrial relations. So marked is the characteristic that on some occasions the foreign observer looks in vain for what he would recognise as "Labour Law" in Britain.' Since 1965, there has been a quiet revolution in employment law. A Redundancy Payments Act; two sets of amendments to the Contracts of Employment Act; unfair dismissal under the Industrial Relations Act strengthened by virtue of the Trade Union and Labour Relations Act and supplemented again by the Employment Protection Act; the Equal Pay, Sex Discrimination, Race Relations and Rehabilitation of Offenders Acts and the Employment Protection Act itself, with its panapoly of individual rights all giving rights of action before Industrial Tribunals.

This radical change from a system where freedom of contract was paramount and statutory intervention negligible to a wide-ranging (though, as we shall see, far from comprehensive) structure of legal protections did not come about in a vacuum. The new legislation has been accompanied by a marked change in attitude by the TUC and by the increasing acceptance throughout Western Europe of the notion of an employee's job property right.

Trade union attitudes

British trade unions traditionally opposed a legal framework for individual employment rights, preferring to rely instead upon collective bargaining – and if necessary industrial action – to protect their members. The classic trade union rationale of the 1960s went something like this: workers will always be exploited unless they organise into trade unions; anything which hinders trade union growth must be opposed; a legal remedy for individual employment grievances means that the employee achieves satisfaction through the operation of the law rather than through the efforts of trade unions so that there is less incentive to become or remain a union member; *ergo*, the law should not do the job of the trade union. There are still today remnants of this attitude visible in the trade union movement. In large part, it accounts for the continued opposition of the TUC to a statutory national minimum wage. It certainly is the motive force behind the ambivalence of the far left to the statutory procedures established to remedy sex discrimination and ensure equal pay. The extent to which trade union officials actually hoped these Acts would fail is open to question. Many important unions have made considerable efforts to use the Industrial Tribunals and Employment Appeal Tribunal effectively. But there were others who all-too-readily leapt on the first decisions of Industrial Tribunals to reinforce their long-held thesis that only effective trade union organisation rather than statutory machinery can rectify grievances satisfactorily.

During the middle and late 1960s, however, official TUC policy towards employment legislation began to change. In 1963, the British delegation to the International Labour Conference voted in favour of ILO Recommendation 119 on 'Termination of Employment by the Employer' which recommended that dismissal should not take place unless there is a 'valid reason' connected with the conduct or capacity of the worker or based on the operational requirements of the firm – and that there should be a right of appeal against dismissal.

The ILO Recommendation was accepted by the British Government in December 1964 and led to the establishment by the Minister of Labour's National Joint Advisory Council of a committee to examine dismissals and dismissal procedures. Whilst the Committee's 1967 report, *Dismissals Procedures*,[2] did not favour early legislation to establish statutory machinery, preferring instead the development of voluntary procedures – it was at this point that the gradual transformation in the TUC's attitude reached its watershed. In 1966, the TUC's evidence to the Donovan Commission had been carefully neutral about a statutory right of appeal against unfair dismissal. But the TUC's representatives on the National Joint Advisory Council in 1967, whilst accepting the Committee's recommendations for improving voluntary procedures, considered that there should be legislation to give a right of appeal against dismissal with provision for exemption for satisfactory voluntary procedures.

The Donovan Commission itself made a strong recommendation in favour of unfair dismissal legislation and it was notable that the TUC did not oppose the proposals for statutory machinery to deal with unfair dismissal in the Labour Government's ill-fated White Paper, *In Place of Strife*.[3]

Then came the Conservative Government's Industrial Relations Act of 1971 establishing a right to bring complaints before Industrial Tribunals relating to alleged unfair dismissals. The TUC opposition to the Industrial Relations Act extended to a boycott of Industrial Tribunal membership but no clear line was laid down as to whether unions could take claims before Tribunals on behalf of their members.

Since the advent of unfair dismissal legislation in February 1972 and particularly since the repeal in 1974 under the Trade Union and Labour Relations Act of the parts of the Industrial Relations Act to which the unions objected, representation by trade unions of their members before Industrial Tribunals has become an important function of most unions. Union legal departments have expanded greatly and full-time officials have acquired considerable expertise in arguing unfair dismissal cases on behalf of their members before Tribunals.

In short, rather than proving a disincentive to trade union membership, the statutory protection against unfair dismissal and the skill developed by the more sophisticated trade unions in representing their members has provided a further and increasingly important string to the trade union bow. This new role has proved particularly important at a time when the role of full-time officers has been diminished through successive phases of incomes policy limiting the scope for collective bargaining and through the continued devolution of power to shop-stewards and lay officials. As a result, far from opposing the development of legislation promoting individual employment rights, the TUC in recent years has been largely responsible for the enactment of the new structure of statutory regulation which culminated with the Employment Protection Act. Official British trade union policy is now very much geared to strengthening and extending employment rights for individuals through law.

The influence of Europe

Western Europe has been a vital influence in determining the direction and shape of laws providing individual employment rights and there is every reason to suppose that it will continue to be so in the future. The importance of European developments can be seen at three levels.

Most Western European countries' economic performance since the war has far outstripped that of Britain. It is also a fact that perceived inadequacies in British industrial relations are seen as playing a major part in Britain's relatively poor economic record. This has led to a widespread view, particularly prevalent amongst sections of the Conservative Party, that the answer to British industrial relations difficulties lies in emulating the industrial relations institutions adopted in Western Europe – particularly in West Germany and Holland. Having failed to transplant the American system of legally-enforceable collective agreements via the Industrial Relations Act, the new fashion calls for adopting a participation structure based on the European concept of works councils. However misconceived is this simplistic search for panaceas, its general effect on public opinion should not be minimised. Nowhere is this better illustrated than in the current debate in worker participation. The call for workers on the board came initially not from the trade unions but from those admirers of the European system who saw participation as a device for promoting greater worker identification with corporate interests rather than as a means of enhancing trade union power.

Given the unsophisticated nature of their initial analysis, it is not surprising that proposals to adopt other attributes of the Western European legal structure for regulating industrial relations have met with less resistance from such quarters than might have been anticipated had they been viewed on the basis of Britain in isolation. 'If the Germans do it, it can't be all that bad' seems to be the way the reasoning goes. The importance of this for future developments is that it serves greatly to reduce the intensity of opposition to adopting further legal improvements to individual employment rights based on the European model.

The second and far more significant influence of Europe on British labour law has been in developing the concept of the job property-right which has and will continue to provide the intellectual underpinning for much of the UK structure of individual employment rights. As we noted above, the traditional legal basis of the employment relationship in Britain rested on the assumption that the employer and employee were free and equal parties to the contract of employment. Given this assumption, the contract of employment could be terminated by either side at will. Post-war legislation in Holland, Germany and France was based on an entirely different premise: the notion that through his labour an employee invests his 'asset' in a particular job, that when he is deprived of that 'asset' through no fault of his own he should be compensated and that he should not lose his 'asset' arbitrarily. This is the principle of an employee's property-right in his job.

In Britain, this concept was first reflected in the Contracts of Employment Act 1963 providing minimum periods of notice (one week after twenty-six weeks' service, two weeks after two years, four weeks after five years). The Redundancy Payments Act of 1965, however, was the first UK law based firmly on the property-right concept, with severance payments varying according to service, age and pay – i.e. the employee's investment in the job and the effect of his losing his asset. The extended notice periods in the Contracts of Employment Act 1972 and, more importantly, the greatly increased minimum notice as a result of the Employment Protection Act changes (one week after four weeks' service, two weeks after two years, rising to twelve weeks after twelve years) are tantamount to increased compensation for loss of job, since it is common for pay in lieu of notice to be given, particularly in redundancy situations. The change in the principles relating to unfair dismissal compensation made by the Employment

Protection Act providing for a basic award calculated like redundancy payment according to age, service and pay is another manifestation of this trend.

The second strand of the property-right principle regulates the circumstances in which a worker can be deprived of his job. Protection against unfair dismissal is the central pillar of the UK structure in this respect and it is noteworthy that both the amendments to the original statute made by the Trade Union and Labour Relations Act of 1974 and the 1975 Employment Protection Act have contained provisions to facilitate reinstatement or re-engagement – i.e. that the employee does not actually lose his job. Loss of employment on grounds of sex, married status, pregnancy, trade union membership; certain past criminal convictions, and colour, race, nationality or ethnic or national origin are now all rendered unlawful in the UK by a succession of statutes passed during the 1974–6 period.

Consideration of the ways in which the job property-right concept has thus far achieved recognition in British labour laws leads to the third influence of European developments. These are the specific statutory devices which have been employed in Western Europe to translate the property-right principle into practice. ILO Recommendation 119, itself an amalgam of Western European good practice when it was drawn up, formed the starting point for the Department of Employment in drafting the unfair dismissal provisions of the Industrial Relations Act. Concepts such as the legal right to a written reason for dismissal, an obligation to consult in advance with trade unions on redundancies, a right to time off to look for work in a redundancy situation, extra protection against dismissal on grounds of trade union membership or activities which have long formed part of the labour codes of most of our EC counterparts have found their way on to the UK statute book in recent years, whilst other European statutory devices – such as an obligation on the employer to look for alternative work before making employees redundant, and the need to consider re-training before dismissing for lack of capability – have been embodied in case law and in the Code of Practice.

Why UK law will change

Britain has moved far in a very short time in providing legal protection when employment is ended. But it is virtually a certainty that the 1980s will see further and dramatic improvements to the statutory scheme of employment protections. There are a number of reasons why.

First, it is a feature of 'reforming' legislation such as that relating to dismissals that it is never repealed and that if any changes are made to it, they are to strengthen it.

Second, there is a natural tendency amongst civil servants periodically to review reforming legislation – generally between five and ten years after its introduction – and strengthen it in light of changing attitudes, to close loopholes which have emerged and to take account of case law under the statute.

Third, with the exception of fringe areas such as the closed shop, dismissals legislation in Britain is in political terms non-partisan. All the main political parties support it. No Government would repeal it. But all parties have their own pet schemes for improvement. If returned to office, they would seek to implement their changes and because of the general support for legislation in this area would find little difficulty in doing so.

Fourth, it can be suggested that attitudes to legislation amongst the interest groups concerned change over time as a result of changes in behaviour. Prior to 1972, the right to dismiss was a cornerstone of managerial prerogative (albeit circumscribed by trade unions where organisation was strong) and the principle of unfair dismissal compensation met with considerable opposition. After five years of the law's operation, it is doubtful whether there are many managers who would not accept that legislation on unfair dismissal is morally correct, even if they are not always happy about the way the law works out in practice. And, of course, each year new managers who have never known another system enter industry. Behaviour can change attitudes. It seems reasonable to suppose that management will be prepared to accept a further strengthening of the law relating to dismissals in the not too distant future.

A further factor pointing towards further legislative change is the impact of collective bargaining. Statutory rights are generally based on existing best practice in industry at the time when they are proposed. Once enacted, they tend to become minima to be exceeded and improved upon by voluntary agreement. Overtime, the standard of good practice thus itself improves providing scope for further legislation.

Finally, there is the continued influence of European Community membership as a force for more job security legislation. In 1976, the European Commission produced a preliminary draft of a major report to the Council of Ministers on 'Protection Of Workers In The Event Of Individual Dismissals', the first stage in the preparation of a Community Directive to harmonise law relating to individual dismissals in Member States, following on from the Community Directive on Collective Redundancies (translated into UK law by the handling redundancy provisions of the Employment Protection Act). A final draft is expected to be sent to the Council in early 1978.

The shape of law to come

What changes to increase job security and enhance the employee's statutory rights are likely to find their way into a UK Employment Protection (Amendment) Act of (say) 1984?

Right not to be unfairly dismissed

The sections of the Trade Union and Labour Relations Act dealing with unfair dismissal are headed 'right not to be unfairly dismissed'. In a very real sense, this is a misnomer. The right embodied in UK legislation is a right to be compensated for unfair dismissal. There is no restriction on management's right to dismiss whomever it wants for whatever reason it wants. Under the revised unfair dismissal provisions of the Employment Protection Act, an 'order' for reinstatement or re-engagement is made the primary remedy. But here again the phrase used is a euphemism. The Industrial Tribunal cannot order an employer to take an employee back in the same sense as a court can make an order, contravention of which renders the offender liable for contempt of court. Where an employer fails to comply with an 'order' for reinstatement or re-engagement, the unfairly dismissed employee's only remedy is to seek an 'additional award' of compensation from the Industrial Tribunal.

Whilst it is unlikely that future legislation will force an employer to retain an employee whom he wishes to dismiss, a change in the law to stipulate that no dismissal has legal effect until it is declared fair seems possible. This would be in accord with practice in leading Western European countries. Thus the Swedish Employment Protections Act of 1974 stipulates that: 'Should there be a dispute over the validity of a dismissal with notice, the employment may not be terminated until the dispute is finally heard by a Labour Court.' In the Netherlands, the prior approval of the Director of the District Labour Office is required for individual dismissals. In Germany, the works council is empowered to object to individual dismissals and the employee in such circumstances is kept in employment until the Labour Court has ruled on the dismissal's fairness.

The first steps towards emulating this European practice in Britain were embodied in the 'interim relief' provisions of the Employment Protection Act. These sections allow an employee who thinks he has been victimised on grounds of his membership of a union or taking part in trade union activities to bring an interim claim before an Industrial Tribunal. The claim must be brought no later than seven days from the effective date of termination and must be supported by an authorised representative of the employee's union. If the Industrial Tribunal finds *prima facie* that it is likely that it will be held that the employee was dismissed on trade union grounds, it can require that the employee be treated as suspended on full pay (or reinstated) until the final determination of his complaint at a full Tribunal hearing.

Whilst a statutory procedure under which no dismissal would have effect until first declared fair by an impartial authority at first sight sounds quite radical, in practice most companies with agreed disciplinary procedures adopt such a policy. An employee whom it is proposed to dismiss will normally remain in employment or be suspended until the disciplinary procedure is exhausted. Were such a system adopted by law, it would almost certainly permit and encourage the development of voluntary procedures providing for independent arbitration on the fairness of dismissal through vehicles other than Industrial Tribunals.

Written notice In the UK, an employee can be dismissed either verbally or in writing. This contrasts with the position in Belgium, Denmark, France, Italy and Luxembourg where a dismissal is only effective in law if it is in writing. Indeed, in France, if an employer intends to dismiss an employee he must summon the employee by registered letter to an interview.

In its draft proposals to the Council of Ministers (published in full in *European Industrial Relations Review* Number 30)[4], the European Commission is unequivocal about the future shape of any Community Directive: 'As regards the form of dismissal, the worker must be completely clear about his position. Notice by the employer must be given in writing. Verbal dismissals should have no force in law.'

Information on legal remedies

Associated with any changes requiring dismissal notices to be in writing is likely to be a further reform requiring employers to inform employees of their statutory rights to contest the fairness of the dismissal. Such a proposal was considered by the UK Government but rejected at the time of the drafting of the Employment Protection Act. Since then, the European Commission's draft report recommends that: 'The written notice from the employer should include information on the legal remedies available to the worker. This should make special mention of time limits applicable. This will prevent an unjustified dismissal remaining in force because the worker, through ignorance of the law, did nothing to regain his job.' The case law which has developed in Britain as to the circumstances in which it can be said to have been 'not reasonably practicable' to have presented a claim in time is now extremely complex. It may well be that the advantages to employers and employees of ending the argument about whether the employee ought to have known of his rights by requiring that he be informed of his rights would outweigh any consequent increase in the volume of cases arising from such legal provision.

Longer minimum notice period

Notwithstanding the increased entitlement as a result of the Employment Protection Act, Britain – together with Ireland – is still at the bottom of the statutory minimum notice league table. Belgium, Denmark, France, Luxembourg and the Netherlands all provide for four weeks' minimum notice and this led the EEC Commission to recommend that: 'Bearing in mind the far-reaching effects of dismissal on the worker's existence and the need for him to find a new job or at least to adapt himself to the new situation, a period of thirty days' notice is considered the absolute minimum.'

Right to look for new job

The Employment Protection Act gives workers under notice of redundancy the right to reasonable time off to look for new employment to make arrangements for training. Belgium and Luxembourg both provide a general right to time off with pay to look for new work during a notice period, a right which is commonly reflected in collective agreements in other Common Market countries. According to the European Commission: 'A dismissed worker needs whenever possible to find a new job with a different employer before the expiry of his period of notice. For this reason, under the legislation of all Member States he should be given paid time off to look for a new job.'

Selection for redundancy

Decisions during late 1976 and early 1977 by the Employment Appeal Tribunal had the effect of conferring upon British management a very broad discretion as to the selection of redundancy candidates and limiting the grounds upon which a redundancy selection could be deemed unfair. According to the EAT in the case of *Vickers v Smith*[5] ([1977] *Industrial Relations Law Reports* 11), the proper test for an Industrial Tribunal to adopt in weighing the fairness of management's selection criteria is 'whether it was so wrong that no sensible or reasonable management could have arrived at the decision at which the management arrived'. The European Commission, in contrast, has stressed that dismissals should not be permitted unless the employer observes the rules of 'social selection'. 'In order to avoid discrimination and to respect the worker's interests as far as possible, the employer's decision must be examined from the social point of view; only those workers who are likely to be least affected by such a measure may be dismissed. It is difficult to draw up precise criteria, but importance is attached to the following points: age, length of service, employment prospects, size of family.' It is unlikely that any attempt to codify redundancy criteria according to factors such as family size would prove acceptable in Britain, but the EC's remarks do emphasise that the considerable discretion given to UK management in relation to redundancy dismissals is increasingly out of line with practice in other parts of Europe. A more likely model for the UK to follow is that provided in the Swedish Employment Protections Act which stipulates: 'In all cases of termination with notice owing to shortage of work and lay-offs, the employer shall apply the following rules of priority for rentention in employment. The employee's priority is determined initially by his cumulative period of service with the employer. An employee with a longer period of service has priority of retention in employment over one with a shorter period of service. In the event of equal length of service, the older employee shall be given priority.'

Alternative employment

Whilst the British Industrial Relations Code of Practice recommends that before making an employee redundant an attempt should be made to find him alternative employment, and the old National Industrial Relations Court endorsed this obligation in the case of *Vokes Ltd v Bear*[6] ([1973] *Industrial Relations Law Reports 363*), more recent interpretations of the law by the Employment Appeal Tribunal indicate that there is no obligation, as such, to search for alternative employment for redundant employees. Nor, the courts have held, will a dismissal on grounds of poor performance or ill health be held unreasonable, simply on the basis that the employer, before dismissing, did not try to fit the employee in elsewhere.

The British approach contrasts both with that in Sweden and with the proposed recommendations of the EC. The Swedish Act states definitively: 'Dismissal by the employer must be based on objectively valid grounds. Where it is reasonably practicable for the employer to provide other employment to the employee, the dismissal will not be objectively valid.' In relation to inadequate performance, the European Commission recommends: 'dismissal is only justified if there is no other job available where the worker can be employed in accordance with his skills and interests.' Similar legal provisions are suggested by the EC draft report where the ground for dismissal is redundancy.

Reinstatement for redundant workers

Sweden's Employment Protections Act provides that: 'An employee who has been dismissed owing to a shortage of work shall for one year after the dismissal retain a preferential right to be re-employed in the same work in which he has been employed.' Similarly, Luxembourg and Holland have statutory. provisions which give dismissed employees a priority claim on re-employment if vacancies arise. Such a right is sometimes embodied in UK redundancy agreements, but the EEC Commission would like to see legislation make it mandatory: 'Firms which have dismissed workers for technical or economic reasons are often able to increase their staff again after some months or a few years. In such cases it is only reasonable that employees dismissed earlier should be given preference. A period of two years after leaving the firm appears suitable.'

References

1. Wedderburn K. W., *The Worker and the Law*, Pelican (Harmondsworth 1965) p. 13.
2. Ministry of Labour, *Dismissals Procedures* HMSO (London 1967).
3. Department of Employment & Productivity, *In Place of Strife* HMSO (London 1969).
4. *European Industrial Relations Review*, no. 30, p. 21.
5. *Industrial Relations Law Reports*, vol. 6, no. 7, 1977, p. 11.
6. *Industrial Relations Law Reports*, vol. 2, no. 12, 1973, p. 363.

9 Incomes policy

JOHN GENNARD AND MICHAEL WRIGHT

Introduction

It is conventional to view an incomes policy as being characterised by some degree of direct interference by the government in the outcome of collective bargaining. This, however, is a narrow view of incomes policy since there are, and have been, countries in Western Europe where the government does not attempt to intervene directly in collective bargaining, but nevertheless clearly hopes to influence the behaviour of the collective bargainers, who are left to devise and enforce their own incomes policy. Incomes policies, however, have been seen by some writers as constituting an assortment of specialised measures designed to eliminate monopoly elements in labour and product markets as well as a series of imposed generalised guidelines governing the movement of money wages.[1] Under this definition an incomes policy would include things like, the reform of bargaining and trade union structures, changes in the policy of subsidising strikers' families through welfare payments to strikers, and the withdrawal of special legal or *de facto* privileges which unions enjoy. In addition there have been incomes policies which attempt to influence the growth of money incomes independently of the collective bargaining system, and which are seen as an integral part of long-term economic planning.

In this paper attention is given to the operation of incomes policies of the generalised guidelines type in five European countries. These five countries have been of general interest in incomes policy discussions and they have

Table 9.1 Price, wage and balance of payments changes
1970—76. Denmark (D), France (F),
Netherlands (N), Sweden (S), United Kingdom (K)

Base 1970 Quarter I = 100	Consumer prices					Hourly wage rates (i) Earnings (ii)				
1970	D	F	N	S	UK	D(ii)	F(i)	N(i)	S	UK
Q.4	103.0	101.6	102.0	102.3	102.7	107	102.4	102	102	103.9
1971										
Q.1	103.0	103.0	104.4	106.2	105.5	108	105.2	107	103	108.1
Q.2	105.0	104.6	107.1	106.1	109.3	114	108.6	110	106	110.3
Q.3	107.0	106.0	108.3	107.7	110.8	117	111.1	114	107	112.3
Q.4	108.0	107.5	110.4	109.6	112.2	121	114.0	116	113	114.9
1972										
Q.1	110.0	108.9	112.7	111.7	113.9	123	116.8	122	121	119.0
Q.2	112.0	110.4	115.5	113.0	116.0	128	120.5	124	125	122.1
Q.3	114.0	112.5	116.3	114.7	118.0	130	123.5	128	122	130.3
Q.4	116.0	114.9	119.3	116.1	120.8	135	127.2	129	125	134.2
1973										
Q.1	118.0	115.9	121.3	na	122.9	na	na	134	na	134.5
Q.2	121.6	117.3	124.9	114.7	126.9	151	136.4	na	135	140.8
Q.3	124.6	127.5	125.9	117.0	135.8	160	141.4	na	134	148.3
Q.4	129.4	142.1	128.8	120.4	145.3	170	146.8	na	137	152.2
1974										
Q.1	134.4	166.7	131.9	126.9	156.8	173	152.4	na	139	154.8
Q.2	140.0	176.2	135.9	130.5	161.0	184	160.7	167[2]	151	161.5
Q.3	143.6	166.6	138.3	133.8	165.6	189	170.4	173	151	175.9
Q.4	149.1	155.2	142.8	137.9	178.0	201	177.0	174	155	185.5
1975										
Q.1	152.2	143.0	145.8	139.8	192.5	210	184.2	184	158	195.8
Q.2	155.6	134.0	149.9	142.3	197.4	222	190.4	188	163	216.8
Q.3	158.3	136.0	152.9	145.9	201.3	226	200.0	196	178	227.8
Q.4	163.4	134.0	156.3	149.6	208.0	234	205.1	197	185	239.8
1976										
Q.1	166.6	140.0	159.0	153.3	215.2	239	210.7	206	193	254.3
Q.2	169.8	151.3	164.3	157.3	222.2	249	219.1	206	204	263.7
Q.3	171.4	162.9	165.4	160.5	233.8	252	227.9	209	204	268.1

Source: Organisation for Economic Co-operation and Development

Table 9.1 *continued*

				Balance of payments [1]					
	Current account					Net capital movement			
D	F	N	S	UK	D	F	N	S	UK
na	na	56	na	-102	+	+	487	+	347
na	na	70	na	177	+	+	543	+	973
na	na	1	na	22	+	+	278	+	634
na	na	586	na	-11	+	+	-92	+	668
na	na	165	na	-136	+	+	-610	+	953
na	na	614	na	-134	+	+	-589	+	57
na	na	296	na	-246	+	+	-379	+	-1045
na	na	-358	na	-159	+	+	-40	+	-79
na	na	-1061	na	-304	+	+	104	+	-198
na	na	na	na	-67	+	+	+	+	69
-1109	1244	1741	1840	-6	+	-447	-4628	-261	569
527	-2284	21	605	-182	+	720	120	-960	-267
-1273	-900	2490	1797	-308	+	2107	-597	698	531
-3325	na	957	-1159	-983	+	na	-1306	97	781
-1836	-9087	1375	188	-804	+	6144	-2622	-123	710
-571	-9229	1481	-1741	-808	+	8013	1283	5	513
115	-2531	1227	-1717	-794	+	849	-514	1748	-101
-470	-1531	280	-1639	-670	+	-4612	492	901	125
270	3847	1526	-1811	-335	+	2410	-2496	2511	127
-495	-566	471	-2329	-542	+	-153	48	2056	360
-2375	1985	1748	-803	-116	+	-2542	-1268	1929	-275
-3510	-5750	2312	-1857	-260	+	-4030	-1773	511	-269
-2475	-1940	426	-1816	-481	+	-1424	-4096	1152	-1267
-2275	na	1253	na	-508	+	na	na	na	-407

1 Expressed in millions of kroner, francs, guilders, krone and pounds respectively
2 Refers to hourly rates in manufacturing only.

certain similarities and differences. Since the end of the Second World War in the United Kingdom, Denmark and Holland the government has at various times intervened directly in the outcome of collective bargaining. In Sweden, on the other hand, since 1938[2] there has been no state machinery for incomes policy and the trade union and employers central federations have been responsible for the implementation and formulation of such policies, while in France an incomes policy has been seen as a necessary part of economic planning exclusive of collective bargaining.

The countries are all in relatively close geographical proximity and have experienced common economic problems, especially inflation and periodic balance of payments crises (see Table 9.1). In addition they are all dependent upon a favourable balance of payments performance if continuous economic growth is to be achieved. Britain and Holland lack raw materials and natural resources and are largely dependent upon the export of manufactured goods to achieve this objective. Sweden and Denmark lack a strong manufacturing sector and are principally dependent upon the export of primary products to obtain a favourable trade balance.

There are, however, differences between the countries with respect to the degree of representativeness of the trade union movement,[3] and the relationship between the trade unions and the major political parties. In Sweden and Denmark a very high proportion of the labour force is organised whilst in France it has been estimated that less than one-third of the workforce is in a trade union. In all the countries, except for France, there is a close working relationship between the unions and the social democratic political parties, and it is these parties that have tended, when in government, to favour incomes policies aimed at controlling the rate of change of money wage rates. When political parties of a right or centre persuasion have been in power the lack of a strong relationship with the trade union movement has often meant that when they are considering incomes policy they are attracted to price and money wages controls. This offers a potential means of gaining trade union support for some limitation on the rate of increase of money wages.

Why incomes policies?

An incomes policy is one of a number of anti-inflationary weapons in the hands of the government. Other policy instruments designed to achieve this end include fiscal policies (i.e. varying tax rates) and monetary policies (for example, changing interest rates, and hire purchase regulations). An incomes policy is not a substitute for these other weapons and in seeking to achieve their economic objectives the governments of the five countries under review have used a combination of all these policies. Using exchange rate policy as a substitute or in conjunction with an incomes policy is another way in which the effects of inflation on the balance of payments of a country may be alleviated. However, the distinction between these policy instruments is in practice not always clearcut. In 1973 the Swedish, and in 1976 the UK governments began using a policy of taxation variations as an incentive to modify labour force wage demands and wage levels. Is this fiscal policy or incomes policy?

The economic rationale behind an incomes policy is that rising prices are generated predominantly from increases in money wage costs.[4] Through moderating the rate of change of money wage rates an incomes policy is designed to lower the rate of inflation, improve the price competitiveness of domestic industry in home and foreign markets and thereby improve the balance of payments performance, raise the level of employment, and the rate of economic growth. In addition to the achievement of these broad macro-economic policy goals incomes policies have other objectives.[5] They are a means whereby the distribution of income between sections of the community can be changed, for example, from profits to wages and from the higher paid to the lower paid. This equity objective of an incomes policy has been important in attracting trade union support for such policies in Sweden, the United Kingdom, Denmark and Holland. There has been a third set of objectives which some proponents of incomes policy, particularly in the United Kingdom, consider to be the most important, namely to improve wage payment methods, industrial relations generally, and thereby make the internal labour market work more efficiently.

The giving by governments of the highest priority to an incomes policy in preference to other economic policy instruments has a number of advantages. Firstly, it enables a deflation in consumer demand without resorting to increasing unemployment, enabling a lower growth rate of money earnings than would otherwise be possible without higher unemployment. This may be preferred because unemployment (whether fiscally or monetarily induced) has economic, social and political costs; there are also obvious political advantages for any government in a policy which promises to reduce the rate of inflation but avoids the necessity to increase unemployment, raise taxation, and restrict credit. It is not surprising therefore to find that opponents of incomes policies have not only been critical of them in terms of their underlying diagnosis of inflation, but also because they offer a 'soft' political option to governments.[6]

A further attraction of incomes policies is that they are almost instantaneous in their impact. Unlike taxation and monetary changes the time interval between implementation and effect on the labour market is short. A third reason why governments are attracted to the use of some form of incomes policy is that they are potentially controllable by governments and, unlike taxation and monetary policies, can therefore be taken into account in forward planning. Monetary policy, for example, may be circumvented by firms in one country borrowing in another where interest rates are lower. Exchange rates policy as an alternative to incomes policy has the disadvantage that it may give rise to an internal inflation problem through its effects on the price of imported goods. In a country, like the United Kingdom, which imports nearly fifty per cent of its food requirements a downward movement in the exchange rate has a disproportionate effect on the price of food which in turn effects the cost of living and thereby expectations about the size of pay increases required to maintain real wages.*

As a policy instrument, incomes policies in themselves, are not usually introduced to tackle the underlying cause of an economic problem but are designed to hold the effects in suspension. Incomes policies are thus usually 'circuit breaking' policies behind which the structural defects underlying the current economic problem can be corrected. Therefore, a 'freeze' may break a seemingly endless cycle and offer a period of time in which workers' pay expectations can be adjusted and a more detailed policy developed. The period of the incomes policy enables manpower and industrial strategy policies to be adjusted to meet the re-allocation of economic resources necessary to solve the current economic problem. Incomes policies do not provide economic solutions in the way that monetary, fiscal or exchange rate changes do and they create their own distortions and problems, for example, how is the policy to be policed?

Obviously incomes policies will not be appropriate under all circumstances as their introduction implies something about organised labour's reaction to changes in real or money wage rates. If unions are prepared to accept real wage decreases but not decline in money wage rates the policy appropriate will probably be different to that if the preference was reversed. To introduce an incomes policy as a universal panacea ignores the fact that, as with other governmental economic policies, their effectiveness and the problems they create vary with the particular circumstances. An incomes policy is not sufficient on its own to enable macro-economic policy goals to be achieved, and it must be used in co-operation with other policies, for example, industrial re-structuring and manpower policies.

---

*It has been estimated for the United Kingdom that every seven cents fall in the value of the £1 relative to $ adds one percentage point to the general index of retail prices.

Up to now discussions has centred on the objectives of incomes policies and their attractions to governments as a tool of economic management. Before turning to the various forms that incomes policy has taken in the five countries under review it is worthwhile examining the economic circumstances in which the countries have introduced incomes policies. In the United Kingdom their introduction has been related to efforts to overcome balance of payments difficulties, following a deterioration in the international balance on current and long term capital account, stemming from a rapid increase in domestic price levels and money wage earnings.* The introduction of incomes policy in Denmark in 1963 was occasioned by an acute economic crisis, characterised by large increases of prices and wages, rising public expenditure and a shrinking currency reserve.[7] Again in Denmark in 1970 the government turned to incomes policies to deal with an economic situation of excess demand and increasing deficit in the balance of payments. Ulman and Flanagan report that the sensitivity of the Dutch economy and the response of Dutch planners to change in the balance of payments or balances on current account can be closely correlated with variations in the form of incomes policies introduced to control the rate of change of wages and prices, and their levels relative to international competitors.[8] The introduction of a wage freeze in Holland in December 1975 was also a response to a rapidly declining balance of payments situation.

In Sweden it has been the consensus that the collective bargaining partners should handle wage policy without intervention from the state, but in 1971 against the background of a very rapid increase in money wage rates and large scale strike activity in the public sector, Parliament enacted an emergency law that prolonged existing wage contracts for six weeks. This was the first unilateral intervention of the state in the history of Swedish industrial relations.[9] In France moves for a

*This was true of the introduction of all 'policy on' situations, i.e. 1948–50, 1956, 1961–2, 1966–70, 1972–4 and 1975 to date.

conscious, direct incomes policy emerged in October 1963 when a conference under the chairmanship of Pierre Massé met to explore the problems of planning incomes.[10] Massé explained that France had a permanent propensity to inflation which would threaten the maintenance of a steady and rapid rate of economic growth by causing balance of payments difficulties. By planning the growth of money incomes it was argued this 'problem' could be avoided; in the Fifth (1966–70) and Sixth (1971–5) National Plans guidelines were included with respect to money income movements if the overall objectives of the Plan were to be received. In the countries considered in this paper it is only in France that the introduction of an incomes 'policy-on' period has not been in response to a rapidly declining balance of payment situation. However in Holland incomes policy was introduced to maintain international competitiveness but changes in the details of the policy have been in response to balance of payments difficulties. On the basis of an examination of the economic situation in which incomes policies are introduced it is clear that the prime objective of such policies is the protection of international competitiveness and that the other objectives discussed earlier are in fact secondary.

Forms of incomes policy

It has been shown that the concept of an incomes policy can be defined in many ways and the form that such policies take is many and varied. However, from the countries reviewed in this paper at least four types of incomes policy can be identified, with the form used in any particular country at any particular time, determined by the industrial relations climate as much as by economic needs.

1) Exhortation

This type of policy consists of broad general recommendations to the collective bargaining partners, given usually by a Minister of Finance. The aim is to encourage trade unions and employers' associations to exercise restraint in wage and price setting by stating that large scale money wages increases will lead to an increase in prices whilst a large rise in consumer prices will simply spark off a demand for higher money wage increases to compensate for the reduction of real wages, i.e. the wage-prices spiral will continue. Exhortation is sometimes a preliminary to a more formal and detailed type of incomes policy. Exhortation about the size of money wage settlements in collective bargaining was adopted by the United Kingdom between 1948 and 1950. In 1948 the Government issued a statement on Personal Incomes, Costs and Prices[11] which called attention to the country's economic plight and said that there were no grounds for general increases in pay, although there might be exceptional circumstances where such an increase could be justified. Collective bargainers were expected to take this into account in the negotiation of new wage details.

2) Neutral expert reports

In this case the government appoints a neutral board of experts for the task of analysing the economic situation and providing information to the government and the collective bargainers on the economic consequences of an actual or an expected money income development. The expert group does not apply sanctions. It can only influence wage negotiations by means of raising the information level of the parties. This approach to incomes control has been applied in Denmark where in 1962 the Government established an Economic Council, composed of twenty members from all important organisations in the economy (e.g. labour, business and agriculture) and a steering group (called the Board of Chairmen) made up of three economists. The steering group presents a report on the economic situation and also has the power to advise government on policy between council meetings. The Economic Council makes recommendations to the

Government, the unions and employers' associations. The recommendations of the steering group can be used as arguments by the collective bargaining partners. However, influencing public opinion appears to be the most important role of the Council. The Neutral Experts report form of incomes policy operated in the United Kingdom between 1957 and 1962. In August 1957 the Government established the Council on Prices, Productivity and Incomes (colloquially known as 'The Three Wise Men') which was to keep under review changes in prices, productivity, and the level of incomes and report thereon from time to time. The then Chancellor of the Exchequer told Parliament that the council 'is not concerned with specific wage claims or disputes. Our hope is that the Council will create a fuller appreciation of the facts both in the public at large and amongst those more immediately concerned with prices and costs matters'.[12] In 1962 the Council's broad function of surveying the economic scene was transferred to the National Economic Development Council.

3) Money incomes control

Under this form of incomes policy with the help of an agency for supervision of money income movements the government tries to influence the outcome of collective bargaining. Such a policy is often backed by the Government having sanctions to prevent money income changes from taking place. In the Netherlands the Board of Mediators had legal responsibility for enforcing wages policy. It was expected to make decisions within the context of Government policy. The Minister of Social Affairs was responsible to Parliament for the Board's conduct.

In 1965 the UK government established the National Board for Prices and Incomes to supervise the movement of money incomes against criteria agreed voluntarily between the Government and the central bodies of the employers and the trade unions. However after July 1966 the three parties could not agree criteria which were thus laid down by Parliament in various Prices and Incomes Acts. Between 1965 and 1968 the Minister of Economic Affairs was responsible to Parliament for the work of the Prices and Incomes Board but after 1968 this function fell to the Secretary of State for Employment who was also responsible for the work of the Prices and Incomes Board. In April 1973 the UK Government established the Pay Board which was given two functions by Parliament. First to make sure that everyone concerned with the determination of pay followed the Pay Code, which laid down the criteria for pay movements and, secondly, to advise the Government about pay problems.

In France in 1966 the Government established a weaker version of the UK Prices and Incomes Board called *Centre d'Etude pour les Coûts et les Revenue* to help it in its task of keeping the growth of money incomes in line with its recommendations. It provides a periodic statistical commentary on trends in costs and incomes. Each autumn when preparing the annual economic budget the National Accounts Commission considers the compatability between trends in the various forms of incomes and the objective of the Government's economy policy. After consulting the interested parties the Government recommends increases in money incomes for the following year and announces the criteria which would justify deviations from the norm in particular circumstances.

4) Collective bargaining framework agreements

This involves the leaders of highly centralised employer and labour organisations agreeing criteria for the movement of money incomes in the light of the economic circumstances of the country. The bargaining parties themselves then exert the wage controls. This form of incomes control has operated in Sweden when the collective bargaining partners have established their own expert agency with the task of analysing the economic role of wages.

Differences in the relationship between the domestic social partners and the central government makes the form and practice of incomes policy vary internationally. In

Sweden the relationship between the Swedish Trade Union Federation (LO) and the Swedish Employers' Association (SAF) is such that the government only directly affects collective bargaining via the annual budget and the partners operate incomes policy. In France and the Netherlands such a 'loose' policy would not be recognised as an incomes policy because the relationships between the trade union centres, the employers' central organisation and the government requires a more decisive government role. In the United Kingdom such a policy would be unlikely because of the growth and importance of autonomous collective bargaining at the workplace. In addition the degree of control by the TUC and the CBI over their affiliated organisations is less than that of the LO and SAF respectively. However, at present in the UK it is only the close relationship between the trade union movement and the Labour Party that enables an incomes policy, of the form whereby unions agree to long-term restraint of money wage demands in return for certain fiscal, monetary, industrial and social policies being pursued.

European experience has shown that the details of incomes policies must be variable and adjust to changing economic and political circumstances. In those countries, like Denmark, the Netherlands and the United Kingdom where government direct interference is highest, governments have found themselves to be in periods of almost continuous 'policy-on'. In the UK several different and distinct types of incomes policy have made up the pattern (i.e. 1948–50, exhortation; 1957–61 neutral expert reports; 1964–70, 1972–4 direct income controls; 1975 to date, control by the central trade union organisation). In Denmark and the Netherlands the annual or biennial money income movement strategies have been internally modified rather than abolished. In Denmark, apart from the two year freeze (1963–5) the adjustment procedure has alternated between flat rate and percentage increases in wage rates while deliberate attempts have been made to avoid the problems arising from wage differential compression and the manufacturing/service wage leadership disruption by adopting a more flexible criteria for the movement of money incomes. In the Netherlands the policy has moved from uniform government control of wages by means of 'rounds of wages increases' (1945–58) to a 'differentuated wage policy' (1959–66) in which wage movements were related to productivity increases, to 'free wage determination' (1967–70), and finally to a policy of automatic wage indexation and a tripartite Central Agreement between the government, employers and the trade unions (1970 following). In France although the Fifth (1966–70) and Sixth (1971–5) plans have included guidelines for wage rises for differenct groups of workers allied to periodical increases in the national minimum wage, these guidelines have had to be modified in the light of political and economic changes. For example, after the events in Paris in May 1968 the government was forced to allow a wages explosion whilst in 1973 President d'Estang announced that a distinct policy wage restraint should be exercised with the public utilities industries, especially the railways being the model.

In the last decade the five countries reviewed in this paper have experienced few periods when some form of incomes policy has not been operating. In 1970 the Conservative Government in the United Kingdom dismantled the incomes policy controls that had existed since 1964, but operated an informal incomes policy (known as the 'n–1' policy) in the public sector of the economy. It was based on the assumption that there is a pecking order of wage claims in the public sector and that the level of wage settlement should be de-escalated by each group settling at a lower level than the previous group. In Denmark in 1970 a non socialist government attempted to persuade the trade union central organisation to accept an incomes policy based on a reduction of public expenditures, a temporary price freeze and the abolition of indexation of wages. When the unions refused the government turned to fiscal policies as a means of balancing the economy, but in 1974 incomes policy formally returned to Denmark. The 'policy off' period 1970–74 was not therefore because of a rejection of income policy as such – in fact such a policy was preferred – but because of an inability to gain the support of the trade unions.

5) Problems involved with incomes policies

Incomes policies give rise to a number of problems and in this section attention centres on the way the five countries have dealt with three such problems – pay differentials, the protection of real wages and the enforcement of the policy.

(a) Pay differentials The economic function of pay differentials is to reflect labour market demand and supply. Differentials allocate the labour force between occupations, industries and regions, and as there are those who argue that if the spread of pay is too wide adverse economic and social consequences will arise, to be generally acceptable an incomes policy must appear to be 'fair' and social justice seen to be done (e.g. giving special treatment to the lower paid workers). In the United Kingdom incomes policies have tried to balance the economic function and social justice considerations of differentials by exempting certain pay increases from having to conform with the criteria agreed for the general movement of money incomes. The economic efficiency aspect of pay differentials was recognised in the 1948–50 wage policy and the 1964–70 incomes policies. In 1948 it was recognised that pay increases above the general level of wage settlement envisaged 'were necessary to attract labour to undermanned industries' whilst between 1964 and 1970, apart from the period July 1966 to the end of June 1967, exceptional pay increases were permissable 'where it is essential to secure a change in the distribution of manpower and a pay increase would be both necessary and effective for this purpose'.

In the 1964–70 incomes policy-on period the need for social justice was recognised by allowing pay increases above that envisaged for the general level of pay settlements 'where there is general recognition that existing wage and salary levels are too low to maintain a reasonable standard of living'. Between April 1973 and February 1974 UK governments tried to reconcile the conflict between efficiency and equity considerations of differentials through the criteria laid down for the general level of pay movements. For example, between April and November 1973 the total amount of increases in pay for any group of employees was not to exceed the sum which would result from the payment of £1 per week per head plus four per cent of the current pay bill for the group, exclusive of overtime. The collective bargainers, therefore, could re-distribute the sum attempting to balance efficiency and equity considerations. In re-distributing this sum the Government indicated that the emphasis should be on the lower paid.[13] Against a background of inflation running at an annual rate of over twenty-six per cent an incomes policy was introduced on 1 August 1975 which concentrated on 'social justice' in determining the criteria for pay movements over the next twelve months. In adopting a flat rate approach (maximum payment was to be £6 per week) it was recognised that differentials would be compressed and that this would give rise to economic problems but that the policy was not to be seen as one for the permanent narrowing of differentials.[14] In August 1976 the policy attempted to reconcile economic efficiency and the compression of pay differentials by establishing a criteria for pay movements in terms of percentage but constrained between a minimum and maximum absolute amount of pay increase. It is recognised that in the phase of the policy to run from 1 August 1977 that in deciding the criteria for money wage movements greater weight will have to be given to re-establishing differentials rather than norming them.

Unlike the UK, Sweden and Denmark have concentrated their incomes policies mainly on a desire to narrow pay differentials to the exclusion of labour market forces. This deliberate attempt to narrow the spread of pay differentials has been achieved by the trade unions adopting 'solidaristic' wage policies. Under such policies the trade union central confederation and the employers' central confederation negotiate a central agreement which usually provides for equal general absolute wage increases and special additional supplements for lower wage earning groups. In Denmark, but not in Sweden, such agreements also generally include cost of living supplements expressed in absolute terms. The success or otherwise of the solidaristic wage policy was much debated but it is clear that this policy has been unable to isolate the pressures of the market on pay. In both Denmark and Sweden wage drift during contract periods had allowed the market forces to nullify the solidaristic minimums and have enabled certain workers, particularly skilled manual workers, to re-assert their differentials at the plant level. The Swedes have attempted to prevent the existence of wage drift from giving rise to feelings of unfairness amongst private sector non-manual workers and public sector workers by allowing larger nominal wage increases to be negotiated for these groups than for manual workers in the private sector. However this has not prevented tension between public and private employees.

Like the Danes and the Swedes, the Dutch have attempted to ignore the market efficiency aspects of pay differentials but have found this an impossible position to maintain. In Holland a national job evaluation scheme has been used to establish a structure of wage differentials considered to be more 'rational' than that provided by the market. It has been estimated that in 1950 about sixty per cent of industrial manual workers in the Netherlands were subject to job evaluation. By 1971 this figure had risen to seventy per cent whilst the figures for all employees and white-collar workers were sixty per cent and twenty per cent respectively.[15] Initially the Dutch attempt to control wage differentials in the interest of social justice led to 'wage co-ordinates' by which an effort was made to relate via job evaluation all workers' wages to the laid down statutory minimum through differentials based on skill and regional differences. Under market pressures 'black wages' appeared when it was realised that an excessively rigid wage structure might hinder economic growth. An attempt was made to accommodate this danger by the introduction of incentive schemes, as a result of which pay differentials began to open out. Under the pressure of market forces in 1967 the Dutch Government was forced to take steps towards fully market determined wages, but within a year found it necessary to pass a law which laid down a minimum level of wages and extended existing and collective agreements for twelve months.

In France incomes policies, as laid down in national economic plans, have included guidelines for wage rises for different types of workers related to the planned development of the economy. In doing this the market allocation function of pay differentials has been recognised, but the lower paid worker has not been neglected. As in Holland, Sweden and Denmark there is a statutory minimum rate of pay (SMIC) that must be paid to workers in employment. In Sweden and Denmark the floor of pay has been established by national pay negotiation between the central confederations of trade unions and employers.

Support for lower paid workers either through some form of minimum wage legislation or by exceptions to the criteria for the general level of pay increases has, in all five countries, been an integral part of any incomes policy. The narrowing of pay differentials through these processes has helped to produce possible disintegrative forces within an incomes policy. However, changed differentials can also be brought about by other aspects of the policy than discrimination in favour of the lower paid. Established pay links between groups of workers can be broken by the timing of the introduction of the policy, especially if it is imposed during the course of a wage round, for example, as in Britain in November 1972 or Denmark in 1963, and by the stricter application of the policy in one sector of the economy than in another, for example, in France in 1964 and in the UK between June 1970 and November 1972. Established relativities can also be broken because of the ability of some groups of workers rather than others to benefit from certain aspects of the policy. For example in the manufacturing sector of an economy workers may benefit from individual incentive payment schemes whilst those in the service sector may not. Then again within the manufacturing sector there are workers who are paid by the piece and those who are paid by the hour and in an incomes policy-on situation an employer may be unable to adjust the pay of time rate workers to fetch them back into line with those of piece rate workers.

The disturbance of pay differentials has often led to a break down in general support for incomes policy culminating in industrial action. In France in December 1964 the government's imposition of an incomes policy in the public sector widened the gap between private sector and public sector pay and resulted in a general strike in the public sector which was followed by further strikes in early 1965. In Sweden 1971 saw strikes by civil servants and other highly paid white collar workers who through TCO and SACO opposed the LO solidaristic policy. In the period 1969–70 total wage increases within the LO-SAF area amounted to more than twenty per cent whilst for civil servants it was only ten per cent and for the highly paid SACO union members it was even less. When bargaining started in 1971 the civil servants were relatively successful in raising their pay relative to the private sector, but the SACO met with little success and strikes broke out in February 1971. The conflict spread and at the height of the protest nearly 50,000 higher officials in state and municipal services were involved in strike action. The strikes ended at the end of March when the Swedish government was forced for the first time to intervene directly in the outcome of collective bargaining by passing an emergency law which extended existing contracts for six weeks. In the UK in January 1972 and February 1974 the National Union of Mineworkers called its membership out on strike in support of a wage claim considered necessary to re-establish the position of the coal miners at the top of the earnings league table. It was argued by the union that the operation of incomes policy had contributed to this situation, and the size of the claim in both strikes was outside the then existing limits of incomes policy. In 1977 there have also been stikes by groups of skilled manual workers in the UK against the narrowing of differentials caused by the imposition of incomes policy in the summer of 1975.

Differentials pressure, therefore, is one of the problems created by seeking an incomes policy 'solution' to economic problems. Pressures resulting from discontent with changes in pay relativities resulting from the operations of incomes policy mean that such policies have to be amended if general support for such policies is to be maintained. In all the countries reviewed changes in differentials have been a potential disintegrative force within the policy. In an attempt to overcome this problem in the UK the Pay Board in its report on *Relativities*[16] suggested principles and procedures for dealing with relative pay levels in times of incomes policy. The Board considered that flexibility for relativity movements should be built into incomes policies to help mitigate inequalities and increase acceptance of such policies. The Board advised that procedures should allow for preliminary selection via certain principles and consultation with the TUC and the CBI, followed by an extensive, wide-ranging enquiry by an examining authority (the Relativities Board) after which recommendations would be passed to the Secretary of State for the final decision on the issue. However the policy collapsed before this procedure could properly be introduced and the idea has not been resurrected again since.

b) Protection of real wages Another source of discontent with a deliberate wages restraint incomes policy, when long-term support is required, is that prices should not outstrip money incomes by too much, i.e. it is expected that current living standards should be maintained or only fall for a very short period of time. The power to control prices in countries heavily dependent on trade, like the UK, Denmark and Holland is difficult because in the UK, for example, the country has to import over fifty per cent of its food needs as well as most of its fuel and raw material needs and pricing policies are outside its direct control. How then have the five countries attempted to protect living standards?

In Denmark, France, Holland and for a short period of time the United Kingdom, attempts were made to protect wages by relating them to price changes via cost of living or threshold agreements. In Denmark index linked wages have operated unbroken since 1945 and collective agreements have on average lasted for two years. Attempts by Danish governments to end indexation in 1970 and 1973 met severe opposition from the trade union movement and the only initiative allowed to the government was in 1973, when the government managed to overcome union opposition by substituting a tax free allowance for the first three cost of living rises of 1974. However in March 1975 the government gave statutory support to its incomes policy which, *inter alia*, gave legal backing to flat rate cost of living increases in wages whilst in September 1975 the Government agreed that if index linking of salaries led to more than two adjustments in 1976 then financial assistance would be given to industry. In 1970 and 1971 the government actually agreed to reimburse industry for large cost of living increases in an attempt to limit cost-push pressures on prices.

In France the indexing of wages to price increases was introduced just before the beginning of the Second World War, but in 1958 indexation of wages and salaries was outlawed except for the statutory minimum wage. However, in 1969–70 the indexation of wages to prices was re-introduced, and since 1970 a number of agreements have been introduced which guaranteed an increase in real purchasing power to workers. The Dutch have traditionally been against direct indexation* but introduced it in 1970–1. After two years the government decided to try and abolish it but failed. Indexation was introduced into British incomes policies in November 1973. The government announced that one of the aims of its policy would be to protect living standards against a high rate of increase in prices,[17] by allowing provision for the negotiation of threshold

*Immediately after World War II the only acceptable wage increase was a cost of living adjustment.

agreements. These would enable pay to be increased by up to 40p a week if the increase in the Retail Price Index reached seven per cent above its October 1973 level, and by up to another 40p per week for every one per cent rise above that level. With the lapsing of the Counter-Inflation Act (1973) in November 1974 this experimentation in indexation ceased. Sweden recently began indexing wage changes to price movements as part of the 1977-9 collectively bargained incomes policy.

There is a mixture of views on the merits of indexation of money wages. The supporters of indexation argue that its merit is that workers will not project their future expectation of price inflation into their wage demands, and therefore costs will only increase at the actual rate of inflation and not the expected rate. It is also argued that indexation is essential if unions are to be persuaded of the merits of long-term fixed contracts. They must be reasonably sure that their members' real wages will be protected during the life of the contract. The opponents of indexation argue that such wage increases perpetuate inflation because they are pay increases not financed by an equivalent increase in output. Indexation has also been opposed on the grounds that because payments are received after the price increases have taken place, real wages never catch up, and that if the index to which wages are linked includes indirect taxes then fiscal policies designed to supplement incomes policies will make the objectives of incomes policy more difficult to achieve. In an attempt to overcome this problem the Danes, who have most experience with the policy, adapted their indices by deciding at certain times to omit indirect taxes, or break out of indexation by offering flat rate compensation, none of which have been very successful.

c) The enforcement of the policy In Sweden and Denmark, except for special circumstances, the responsibility for ensuring that the incomes policy is adhered to has rested with the collective bargaining partners. In Denmark the government in February 1963 carried out the so-called 'totality solution'

by which *inter alia* existing collective agreements were
extended for three years. At the end of this freeze period in
1965 things returned to normal. In December 1976, against
an economic background of deteriorating balance of
payments, the government introduced a statutory incomes
policy to limit wage increases between December 1976 and
March 1977 following a failure of the collective bargaining
partners to reach agreement over pay. In Sweden the
government has only intervened with statutory powers in
1971 when Parliament prolonged existing contracts for six
weeks.

The approach of leaving the policing of incomes policies
to the collective bargaining partners has been the approach
in Britain, except for occasions when the Government,
unions and employers have been unable to reach
agreement on the terms of an incomes policy. However,
between July 1966 and 1970 and between November 1972
and July 1974 a statutory incomes policy existed. Under
various Prices and Incomes Acts and Counter-Inflation Act
the onus of the responsibility for insuring that the pay limit
was observed was placed firmly on the trade union, and to
breach the policy was a relatively costless exercise to the
employer. Under the Prices and Incomes Acts it was a
criminal offence for a trade union to undertake industrial
action to force an employer to pay a wage increase that had
been vetoed by the Government following an adverse
report from the Prices and Incomes Board. Under the
Counter-Inflation Act (1973) it was also a criminal offence
for a union to strike or threaten to do so to force an
employer to contravene a notice or order issued by the Pay
Board.

In the incomes policy introduced in August 1975 and its
modifications in August 1976 the responsibility for
observing the pay limit was shifted to the employer. With
respect to the nationalised industries the government will
not finance breaches of the policy through the provision of
subsidies, or extra borrowing, or by allowing them to
reflect such pay settlements in higher prices to the
consumer. While in the case of local authorities the

government restricted that rate support grant payable so that if there are any national pay settlements in excess of the limit no grant is payable on the excess. In the private sector the policy was to be policed by not allowing firms which made excessive pay settlements to relfect these settlements in higher prices to the consumer. In addition to enforcing the policy through the prices side the Government will not give financial assistance under the Industry Act (1975) to companies that have breached the pay limit nor will it award government contracts to firms that so behave.

This enforcement of an incomes policy via the employer rather than the trade union has been central to incomes policy in France. From 1966 there have been a series of agreements between governments, trade unions and employers (*Contract du Program*) designed to achieve effective price controls. Under these agreements any firm introducing excessive price increases would forfeit the financial incentives available to employers under the Fifth and Sixth plans. There is thus some implicit control of wages embodied in the system, since a firm granting wage increases above the national norm cannot pass these on via price rises and can only seek to offset them by productivity improvements.

In the Netherlands, except for very short periods of time, a compulsory incomes policy has operated. Between 1950 and 1958 the policy was simple. A national job evaluation scheme established a national minimum and fixed weighting for semi-skilled and skilled workers. One basic single percentage increase with no exceptions was permissible for everybody. The policy was enforced by the Board of Mediators and prosecutions were taken against employers who breached the policy. However, as market forces made it more difficult to hold the policy the resort to prosecution stopped. In 1959 a new government favoured 'greater responsibility for separate sectors of industry' in wage matters. Pay in a sector was to reflect the productivity of that sector, but by 1966 the spectacle of different rates of increase in productivity and therefore in pay, placed too great a strain on people's notion of what was fair and at the end of 1967 a 'free' wage policy was adopted whereby the contracting parties were primarily responsible for collective agreements conforming with national economic interests. However, in 1970 the law on the Determination of Wages was introduced. Under this the Minister of Social Affairs after consulting the Foundation of Labour (a body containing representatives of employers' associations and trade unions) and the Social and Economic Council, which advises government on the wider problems of social and economic policy, could decree that wages and other conditions of labour operative at the time should remain valid for six months after the date of expiry, and that employers who did not comply with such ministerial measures are liable to prosecution. The Government has the powers to enforce an incomes policy but has lacked the confidence to resort to legal sanctions, and this has been the case in the UK and France, although it should be said that the number and importance of challenges to the government's policy have been few.

Conclusions

From the review of the operation of incomes policy in five countries the following conclusions can be drawn:

1) The number of policies which can be considered to be incomes policies are many and varied. It appears that there is an evolutionary process in the development of incomes policies and that to talk of *an* incomes policy is to be dangerously restrictive.

2) As a means of achieving macro-economic objectives an incomes policy is a necessary policy weapon but is insufficient in itself. Such policies are generally 'circuit breaking' behind which the structural defects underlying an economic problem can be tackled.

3) The distinction between incomes policy, fiscal policy and monetary policy is not clearcut. In the UK, Holland and Sweden there have been attempts to influence the size of increases in real disposable income by trading tax

reductions against lower wage demands.

4) Countries tend to introduce incomes policies at times of declining balance of payments following rapid increases in wages and domestic price levels.

5) European experience has shown that the details of incomes policies must be variable and adjust to changing economic and political circumstances. As the relationships between the social partners and the partners and the government change, differing features of policies are emphasised.

6) With respect to pay differentials the UK incomes policies have attempted to balance the economic function of pay differentials with narrowing pay differences in the interest of 'social justice' (e.g. improving the relative position of low paid workers). In Sweden and Denmark the collective bargaining partners have deliberately set out to narrow the spread of pay differential through a 'solidaristic' wage policy. The Dutch have attempted to tackle pay differential questions by a national job evaluation scheme, but like the Swedes and the Danes they have been unable to isolate the influence of market forces. In all the countries reviewed changes in differentials resulting from the operation of the policy are a potential disintegrative force within the policy.

7) Great Britain is the only country in which no minimum floor for pay has been established by legislation (France and Holland) or centralised collective bargaining (Sweden and Holland).

8) In Denmark, France and Holland, and for a short period of time in the UK and recently in Sweden, attempts have been made to protect real wages during periods of restraint by relating pay movements to cost of living changes or threshold agreements. Apart from the UK attempts by governments to abolish indexation have met strong opposition from the trade union movement.

9) In Sweden and Denmark the enforcement of the policy has rested with the collective bargaining partners. In the UK and Holland the method of enforcement of the policy has varied. Between 1966 and 1970 and 1972 and 1974 the onus

for the responsibility of holding the pay limit was imposed on trade unions through the availability of criminal sanctions against them. In the Netherlands the policy is enforceable against employers who breach the policy. Since August 1975 the burden of enforcing the policy in Britain has been transferred to the employer through the amount of price increase allowable as a result of an increase in wage costs, and the withdrawal of a right to government assistance and contracts. In France the policy has also been enforced through the prices side and not against labour. However in the UK, Holland and France the government has rarely been put in a position where it has had to use these powers against employers or trade unions.

10) Incomes policies as an economic weapon have become an essential part of a country's economic strategy. Their directness and controllability has attracted governments at times when either economic or political conditions required short term action. They have become so much a part of European economies that the prospect of a long period of policy-off during which time problems will surface is a long time off. Every European country reviewed in this paper has been unable to function without resorting to some form of incomes policy in recent years.

Appendix

Chronicle of incomes policy developments: United Kingdom; the Netherlands; Denmark; Sweden and France

The United Kingdom
1948 Government issued a statement on Personal Incomes, Costs and Prices which said there was no justification for any general increase in money incomes. Voluntary Wage Restraint introduced.
1949 £1 devalued.
1950 Collapse of voluntary wage restraint.

1956 Prices plateau policy – confined to public sector prices.

1957 Council on Prices, Productivity and Incomes (The 'Three Wise Men') established.

1961 Government announced 'Pay Pause' to be enforced in the public sector and Wage Council industries. Hoped 'Pause' would lead to long-term policy.

1962 'Guiding light' of 2–2¹/₂ per cent per annum for general pay increases. National Incomes Commission established to consider on reference to it by the Government specific wage claims or settlements.

1964 Productivity, Prices and Incomes Policy established.

1965 National Board for Prices and Incomes established to references on prices and incomes referred to it by the Government. 3–3¹/₂ per cent increase per annum in money incomes.

1966 Incomes freeze imposed – norm for income movements Act of Parliament to enforce the policy. policy.

1968 £1 devalued – norm for income movements modified.

1970 Conservative Government comes to power. Rejects formal incomes policy.

1971 National Board for Prices and Incomes abolished. 'N – 1' informal incomes policy operates.

1972 Government imposes six months pay freeze – backed by Parliamentary powers.

1973 Government establishes Pay Board and Parliament approves a Pay Code in Counter-Inflation Act.

1974 Labour Government dismantles the Pay Board. Social Contract introduced – Government to pursue certain fiscal, monetary, industrial and social policies in return for which unions will restrict pay claims to guidelines set out by the TUC.

1975 *The Attack on Inflation* White Paper. Social Contract amended. Pay increases to be restricted to a maximum of £6 per week.

1976 Social Contract further modified. Pay movement criteria amended – pay increases to be restricted to five per cent per annum with a minimum of £2.50 and a maximum of £4 per week.

The Netherlands

1939 Government granted the power to impose 'price stops'.

1943 Foundation of Labour established. Enabled union-employer-co-operation on collective wage setting and policing.

1945 Extraordinary decree on Labour Relations; giving the government power over wage determination. Also created the Board of Government Mediators, who were empowered to review and adjust collective contracts.

1951 Following several Balance of Payments deficits, the unions agreed to a 'wage stop' which meant a five per cent cut in real wages.
The government initiated an inter-industrial programme of job evaluation.

1954 Foundation of Labour requested that the 'wage stop' be abandoned. Government guidelines introduced to maintain labour's share of national income.

1955 Union leadership accepted a three per cent wage increase under urgings from the government to avoid balance of payment pressures.

1956 Following large wage drift, the Government resorted to arbitration on wage levels.
Wage increases beyond three per cent were not allowed.

1957 Unions accepted a further policy of extreme restraint, under deteriorating Balance of Payments conditions.

1959 Productivity wage increases encouraged by the government as well as price cuts.

1961 The 1939 Law on Prices amended, setting new criteria for pricing decisions:
a) only non wage cost rises can be passed on,
b) absolute profit margins to be maintained.

1963 The productivity criteria for wage increases dropped. Replaced by econometric projections made by the Central Planning Bureau.

1965 July; all Unions supported the removal of the 1963 conditions.

Minimum wage law introduced.

Wage indexation agreements appeared.

1966 Unions unable to reach agreement over wage levels for the 1966–7 period. Government unilaterally set a wage norm of $7^1/_2$ per cent. The unions and employers refused to co-operate.

The 1961 price controls lapsed.

1967 Foundation of Labour opposition to the 1963 wage controls.

A general price freeze introduced.

1968 May: Government proposed that all collective agreements be frozen through 1969 (union opposition forced its withdrawal).

September: New legislation to give Government greater power over wages (unions and the Social Democrats opposed).

November: Government accepted union calls for minimum wage standards to replace the previous maximum norms. The new minimum levels were open to decentralised bargaining.

1969 April: Price freeze announced.

Government announced a deflationary policy following several agreements which set wage levels above the government guideline of four per cent.

Wage indexation extended to short term contracts.

1970 Agreement reached on wage norms for 1970.

Following disagreement over wages both the NVV and the NKV withdrew from central bargaining procedures.

1971 Indexation extended to many industries.

1973 December; Government intervened following a break down of collective bargaining to set an interim wage increase.

1974 March; Government offers tax cuts to enable a new *Centraal akkoord* to be reached. The *akkoord* covered (a) flat rate wage increase and (b) threshold agreement of indexation.

1975 January; wage negotiations collapse and unlike 1974 the government refused to mediate.

February; following a collapse of wage agreement procedures, Government issues a wage decree and sets a limit on dividends and fees.

June; Government issues 'White Paper on Incomes Policy'.

1976 March; a consultation board on incomes policy established.

May; Government introduced a Bill on Income Distribution giving workers a share in excess profits, an incentive to encourage unions to keep wage demands low.

July; Statutory Incomes policy again introduced following a further breakdown in the collective agreement process.

November; Government announced a flat rate cost of living adjustment.

Denmark

1918 Wage indexation introduced. Abandoned in 1930.

1945 Indexation re-introduced based on semi annual cost of living adjustments. This encouraged the L.O. to accept two and three year contracts. Adjustments on a flat rate basis, based on a threshold level of price change.

1950 A period of very high wage drift.

1956 First public recommendations for a move towards an organised incomes policy.

1962 Parliament legislated for an incomes policy.
The Economic Council established, also Board of Chairman comprising academic economists.

1963 March; legislation for:
a) Two year freeze on contractual incomes,
b) A 'kitty' to be distributed to the low paid,
c) Retention of the escalator clause,
d) Regulations for profit and price margins.

1965 March; freeze ended.
Government awarded large pay increases and attempted to rectify inequities.

1967 Board published the 1967–9 guideposts as two

components; (a) per capita income growth component, (b) a central negotiated component. The Danish Krone devalued by 7.9 per cent in late 1967. Government proposed a one year suspension of the wage escalator. The LO objected.

Government imposed a freeze on profit margins.

1968 New Government (centre-right coalition), being unable to persuade the LO to accept suspension of the accelerator, raised taxation as a deflationary measure.

1969 Board called for a three per cent increase in per capita income for the period 1969–71.

1970 Government re-introduced a partial freeze on service prices.

Government agreed to subsidise employers for wage increments generated by the wage escalator.

1971 Government allowed higher paid public servants only one-third of cost of living change.

1973 New Liberal Government suggested replacing the wage escalator with a flate rate payment. The trade unions objected.

1974 Eight weeks price and profit freeze introduced.

Tax free allowance substituted for the first three cost of living rises in 1974.

February; Parliament approved the payment of a subsidy to employers as a reimbursement for rising costs.

An Enabling Act introduced, giving the government power to determine the amount of inflation/oil price rise wage increases.

1975 January; the Danish Trade Union Federation (LO) and the Danish Employers Federation (DAF) agreed to new negotiation guidelines.

March; following a breakdown in DAF-LO negotiations, the Government legislated an incomes policy: (a) extending the existing collective agreement for two years, (b) introducing a flat rate cost of living adjustment, (c) imposing a price and profits freeze.

September; the Government compromised over its

indexation, but began setting public sector wages as an example for wage increases.

1976 September; Government introduced an 'Economic package' incorporating an incomes policy: (a) 1977–8 wage increases to be limited to six per cent, (b) indexation again adjusted, (c) Government legislated its intervention on pay discussion if wage increases were too high, (d) spending cuts and indirect tax increases were also included to help reduce the balance of payments deficit.

December; again, following a breakdown in LO-DAF negotiations, the Government legislated a short-term statutory incomes policy to March 1977.

Sweden

1938 First 'Basic Framework Agreement' between the LO and the SAF. Covered an agreement over joint wage guidelines and incorporated the LO's 'solidaristic wage' policy.

1939 LO and SAF accepted a period of voluntary wage policy for the duration of World War II.

1949–50 The LO accepted a period of voluntary wage restraint.

1950 Devaluation of the Krone.

1952 Government continued to exhort the unions to accept wage restraint set within limits of a norm laid down by the Government.

SAF proposed a return to centralised bargaining between the social partners, and the LO accepted, as a temporary measure.

1956 Centralised wage determination was formally re-introduced.

1964 A wage 'kitty' system was adopted the LO and the SAF.

1966–70 The 'kitty' system was modified so that each sector's wages should be adjusted on the basis of the proportion of low paid workers in the sector, plus for every year of the three year agreement, a wage drift component would be added.

1967 SAF proposed identifying a negotiable wage level by removing for the 'scope for wage increases', a component which would 'drift' over the period of the agreement. The LO rejected the formular as a denying of collective bargaining.
The SAF made further moves towards creating a more explicit incomes policy.

1969 A joint report prepared by the LO and the SAF presented. Considered the pattern of wage and price formation in Sweden. Recommended wage increases of between eight and $8^{1}/_{2}$ per cent per year other the period 1969 to 1970.

1970 The Government introduced a price freeze.

1974 February; the LO and SAF agreement was for only one year (the first time since the 1950s) and agreed on a 3.3 per cent wage increase.

1975 May; the Basic Agreement arranged for wages to increase by 13p per hour. For the first time ever, re-negotiation during the contract period was agreed.

France

1937 Wage indexation introduced.

1945 Price Control legislation introduced.

1958 1945 price controls were removed. Substituted a deflationary policy for 1958–9.

1959 Finance law outlawed wage indexation except for SMIC (minimum wage earners).

1963 Price freeze introduced. Also a wage and salary 'stabilisation programme'. The freeze was then adjusted to price controls.

1963–64 Massé Conference attempted to gain voluntary restraint over wages.

1964 Government adopted a three stage procedure for determining public sector wages in which the unions would negotiate for the distribution of a 'global' wage offer between their workers.

1965 Government introduced the *contracts du programme*, to cover the period of the Fifth Development Plan (1966 to 1970). Permitted industries freedom in price determination if they accepted a compulsory price review procedure.

1966 Fifth Development Plan included income guidelines to achieve stable unit labour costs; *indicative norms*. The unions began to dispute the extent of the 1966 'global' offer.

1968 The wage explosion followed May and June strikes; did not provoke a price freeze, but pressures on the Balance of Payments grew.

1969 August; The Franc devalued; a temporary price freeze imposed. Pompidou Government made moves to create a wage restraint environment:
a) encouraged union participation in management,
b) encouraged cost of living adjustments to wage rates,
c) revised the minimum wage level,
d) introduced government sponsorship of *mensualisation* (i.e. reclassification of weekly paid workers to monthly paid).

1970 The minimum wage procedure re-adjusted (SMIC) to improve the speed of indexation.
A form of indirect indexation for all wages and salaries reintroduced.

1973 President d'Estang reasserted desire to avoid a full incomes policy, preferring to use public utilities, especially the railways, as a guiding sector.

1975 Government planned a purchasing power increase of only a half per cent per quarter.

1976 August; Premier Chirac called for some form of social contract. Rejected compulsory profit and price freeze.
October; Premier placed a freeze on prices to the end of 1976.
Wage indexation equal to price increases introduced.

References

1. See G. Haberler, 'Incomes Policies and Inflation: an analysis of basic principles' in *Inflation and the Unions*, The

Institute of Economic Affairs (London 1972) p. 4.

2. In 1971 the government interferred to extend a 'Basic Agreement'.

3. For more detail see W. Kendall, *The Labour Movement in Europe*, London, 1975.

4. A discussion of the causes of inflation is outside this paper as is the underlying mechanism by which wage cost increases are seen as fuelling inflation. For a discussion of these two questions see M. Parkin, 'Where is Britain's Inflation Going', *Lloyds Bank Review*, July 1975.

5. See F. Blackaby, 'Incomes Policy: a background paper' in F. Blackaby (editor), *An Incomes Policy for Britain*, Heinemann Educational Books (London 1972) p. 217.

6. See F. W. Paish, *Rise and Fall of Incomes Policy*, The Institute of Economic Affairs (London 1969) p. 3.

7. See N. Elvander, 'Collective Bargaining and Incomes Policy in the Nordic Countries: a comparative analysis', *British Journal of Industrial Relations*, Vol. 711, No. 3, November 1974.

8. L. Ulman and R. J. Flanagan, *Wage Restraint, a Study of Incomes Policies in Western Europe*, University of California Press (Berkeley 1971).

9. N. Elvander, *op.cit.*

10. Haywood, 'Interest groups and incomes policy in France', *British Journal of Industrial Relations*, Vol. IV, No 2, July 1966.

11. Statement on Personal Incomes, Costs and Prices, Cmnd. 7321, HMSO (London 1948).

12. See A. Jones, *The New Inflation*, Penguin Books (Harmondsworth 1973) chapter 3, p. 49.

13. *The Programme for Controlling Inflation: the Second Stage*, Cmnd 5205, p. 8, para 26, HMSO, (London 1973).

14. *The Attack on Inflation*, Cmnd. 615, annex, para 2, p. 13, HMSO, (London 1975).

15. See John R. de Jong, 'National Wage and Job Evaluation in the Netherlands', in F. Blockaby (ed), *An*

Incomes Policy for Britain, Heinemann Educational Books (London 1972).

16. See Pay Board Advisory Report No 2. *Relativities*, HMSO, (London 1974).

17. See *The Price and Pay Code for Stage 3: A Consultative document*, Cmnd. 5444, para 14, p. 7, HMSO (London 1973).

10   Women and work

JENNY DORLING

Inevitably this chapter is largely about inequality and how this problem is being tackled – through legislation and the provision of amenities and services – within the European Community. Of course, women are not the only disadvantaged group: there are probably also unequal employment opportunities for men over forty, immigrants, people in certain geographical regions etc. Women are particularly significant here because they constitute more than one third of the working population of Europe.

Does the unequal treatment of women matter? There is growing pressure within the western world for equal treatment of women on both economic and social grounds. Sexual discrimination does not affect women alone: it has a negative influence, direct and indirect, on children and other members of the family, and through them on society as a whole. The Council of Europe has resolved[1]:
- to take action to ensure equality between men and women regarding access to employment, to vocational guidance and training and in respect of work conditions and pay
- to strive to reconcile family responsibilities with the work aspirations of the people concerned.

But what is equality in this context? The concept has undergone a subtle change over the years. It has developed from the principle – still explicit in legislation – that working women should have the right to be treated on the same basis as men to the view that genuine equality of opportunity in employment demands broad social adaptation and change. Hence the Economic and Social

Committee of the Council of Europe has stated its opinion that 'efforts to eliminate discrimination in employment will only achieve lasting success when the traditional allocation of family responsibilities and ideas about the respective roles of men and women change'.[2]

The present position of women at work, the main obstacles to equality and selected current measures to assist women – legislation, maternity leave and benefits, child care, more flexible working arrangements, training – are considered here in the light of this philosophy.

Some basic facts

The most striking feature about women and work in Europe is the degree of similarity in their position and in the character of their employment. First, there is a general increase in the numbers of women working, particularly amongst married women working part-time.

Women's present share of total employment ranges from thirty-five to forty per cent in most of the member states with slightly lower representation – about twenty-six – in Ireland, Italy and the Netherlands. The most significant recent phenomenon is the growth in the activity rate of married women. In all but three of the member states – Ireland, Luxembourg and the Netherlands – married women make up over fifty per cent of the female work force.

In the present social climate, it must be assumed that many of the married women will face, or will already have experienced, a break in employment. This is obviously a critical factor in women's employment but should not be exaggerated in view of the current trend. The length of the break for child bearing and rearing is getting shorter and it is estimated[3] that the average is now about eight years for the Community as a whole and as little as three years in Germany.

Part-time work is the principle factor in the growth in the employment of married women within the Community, particularly in Denmark, Ireland and the Netherlands. It is, for example, estimated that twenty-nine per cent of all women in employment in the UK and thirty-six per cent in Denmark work part-time. Few men work part-time and part-time work generally is associated with limited opportunities for advancement and even in some cases legal disabilities.

Whilst women's employment is growing, it is also very sensitive to economic variations. The rate of female unemployment within most of Europe has increased more rapidly than male unemployment until, for the Community as a whole, women's share of total unemployment exceeds by ten per cent their share of total employment. Differences between male and female unemployment rates are partly attributed to structural problems of women's employment, for example, decline in some of the industries and occupations in which women predominate, and also to the fact that many of the women seeking employment are trying to return to work after a break.

The nature of women's employment within Europe has three common characteristics: it is relatively concentrated; it is lower paid than men's; and it involves less training. The majority of women within the European Community are employed in a narrow range of industrial and occupational sectors in which there are relatively few men. Large numbers of women are employed on assembly lines in electronic factories and as machinists in the textile and clothing industries. Women dominate office work but as clerks, typists and receptionists rather than office supervisors and managers. More than sixty per cent of working women within the Community are in the tertiary sector – compared with only forty per cent of men – where they predominate as sales assistants, waitresses and cooks, nurses and paraprofessionals in health and child care. Where highly qualified women work in large numbers they are almost certain to be teachers, librarians or social workers. Conversely, women are a distinct minority in employment in the professions and the crafts and in executive and administrative posts. Perhaps the key features of women's employment are its segregation, its relatively low skill content and its low status. It is not, therefore, surprising that women throughout the Community earn less than men. For example, the average gross hourly earnings of women manual workers in manufacturing industries within the Community in 1975 ranged from only sixty-one per cent of men's (Luxembourg) to eighty per cent (Italy).

Apart from the obvious effect of skill levels on earnings, a recent study for the European Community[3] found that job segregation by sex was a major influence on men's and women's earnings. For women of equal qualifications, wages were higher in mixed sectors, where neither male nor female workers predominated, than in exclusively female industries or occupations.

As might be expected from the preceeding paragraphs, there are significant differences in the training which men and women receive. Women throughout the Community are generally at a disadvantage in relation to men in terms of the numbers who receive formal training; the average duration of training; the range of occupations for which training is received; the skill level of the training. Despite the wide variety of training opportunities, the greatest concentration of women continues to be in preparation for jobs traditionally held by women.

The main obstacles to equality

This and other evidence amply demonstrates women's inequality at work. The basic causes of this inequality are an inter-related complex of cultural, social and economic factors. There are many publications on this subject (e.g. Reference 4) and the problems, once again, are much the same in different countries.

The main obstacles and problems which restrict women's access to training and employment are a function of women's current roles in society. The majority of women cannot conform to what is regarded as the normal pattern of working life: an uninterrupted span from the end of education to compulsory retirement, structured to fill something like eight hours a day, five days a week, forty-eight weeks a year.

There is evidence that women's work aspirations are greatly influenced by their, and others', expectations of women's roles in society. Many girls select jobs and careers which in their opinion will be compatible with a future married life. Scientific careers, particularly engineering, do not appear to meet this requirement.

Employers' attitudes towards women at work are conditioned by assumptions about women in general which may not apply to individual women. Hence many employers see no point in providing girls with lengthy training because they assume that the majority will get married and leave employment. They generally prefer employing men because they assume that men's job performance will be better in terms of labour turnover and absenteeism.

On average, such assumptions may be justified on economic grounds. Women do have a shorter average working life than men: there is obviously a lower return to employers in general for training the average woman than for training the average man. Statistical evidence on comparative labour turnover is inconclusive but it is obviously significant that a large part of women's turnover involves leaving the labour market whilst men's normally involves only a change of employer. On average, absenteeism is more frequent for women than for men, the difference being mainly attributable to different domestic circumstances. However, these generalisations mask enormous variations between industries, occupations and individual women. In practice, too, the economic disadvantages in employing women must be offset against the potential legal costs of ignoring sex discrimination legislation and the advantage to employers, despite legislation, of lower levels of women's pay.

There are also less rational arguments for a preference

for employing men. These relate to alleged physical and personality differences and differences in ability between men and women. Thus, for example, it is often asserted that women are less suitable for particular kinds of work because they lack the necessary physical strength or are too submissive and conversely that they are more suitable for jobs involving manual dexterity. These arguments are losing ground, at least in theory, as it is realised that the differences within each sex far outweigh the differences between the sexes.

The attitudes and expectations of people in general in their roles as parents, teachers, friends, husbands, wives, employers, fellow workers etc. constitute the biggest single obstacle to equality of opportunity for women. This factor in itself creates other obstacles. For example, vocational guidance throughout the Community is based on present vocational structures and qualifications which can only produce previous models. Legislation protects only 'the weaker sex' from adverse employment conditions.

There are also more general obstacles to women's equality at work. A number of predominantly female occupations, for example, junior non-manual and certain occupations in services, are growth areas of employment and have recruitment problems. This is an obstacle which discourages women from widening their horizons: it could – but for various reasons probably will not – be seen as an opportunity to reduce job segregation by encouraging more men into these occupations. Conversely, there is a general decline in skilled manual employment which is one of the main sources of long-term training for men: increased competition for fewer training places must increase women's disadvantage. In addition, as already noted, the current unemployment crisis affects women disproportionately.

What is being done

The problems are formidable. They are being tackled at

Community level in three ways: through legislation and through the provision of finance and information.

Legislation is discussed in more detail in later paragraphs. There are three legal instruments which refer specifically to the employment of women: Article 119 of the Treaty of Rome calls for the abolition of all discrimination concerning pay based on the sex of the worker: this is supported by a Directive which is binding on all member states and there is also a Directive on equality of treatment for men and women workers. Legislation is so far the only significant tangible area of achievement.

As for finance, the European Social Fund[5] provides grants for approved ventures by member states of up to fifty per cent of costs incurred. The promotion of employment for women is included among the objectives of the Fund. The main provision of relevance to women is Article 5 which covers grants to remedy the causes of imbalance affecting employment. Women over thirty-five are included among the categories who may benefit from grants, as well as young workers of either sex under the age of twenty-five. However, few requests have been submitted which are aimed specifically at the promotion of women's employment. Article 7 which empowers the European Commission to promote, carry out or financially aid projects or pilot studies involving a maximum of thirty workers, is also of interest here.

The Economic and Social Committee has recommended that the conditions governing aid from the European Social Fund should be amended to assist in providing women with better opportunities for employment, vocational training and promotion.[2] The Committee also feels that an examination should be made of how nursery schools, day nurseries etc. could be wholly or partially financed by the ESF.

The European Vocational Training Centre is seen as the main source of information to the general public about the 'educational' neglect of the female half of Europe's population. It is proposed that the Centre should make European comparisons and studies of vocational guidance, training and retraining and should analyse the factors in discrimination. It is also proposed that the European Foundation for the Improvement of Living and Working Conditions should study men's and women's working conditions, particularly in terms of flexible working hours, and the material and social working conditions and the physical demands in predominantly female jobs. Information of this kind could form the basis for a Community campaign aimed at changing outlooks and attitudes to women's work.

At national level, action centres around legislation, public services, and research and exploration. The emphasis is on women's rights and the provision of services to help them to achieve those rights. All the member states have legislation on equal pay and most on equal treatment. Most also have specialist committees or advisers on women's employment. For example, Denmark has a Commission on the Position of Women in Society which has produced reports on such issues as educational problems and the position of women in the labour market. Great Britain has an Equal Opportunities Commission which is working on guidelines for employers to help them develop equal opportunity personnel policies as a first step towards a statutory code of good practice. The scale of operation of such national Committees/Commissions is fairly small. However, they could play a crucial part in the development of active policies and programmes to implement national philosophies.

Legislation

As already noted, attention within the Community to promote equality of opportunity for men and women in employment has tended to focus on legislation to prevent discriminatory practice. Council of Europe Directives provide the minimum basis for national practice.

There is a *Directive on Equal Pay*[6] which requires member states to abolish all discrimination concerning all aspects and conditions of remuneration based on the sex of the worker. The principle of equal pay applies to 'the same work or work to which equal value is attributed'. Job classification systems for determining pay must be based on the same criteria for men and women. There is also a *Directive on Equal Treatment*[7], to be enforced by August 1978, which requires member states to abolish all discrimination, either direct or indirect, based on sex, marital or family status through the adoption of measures to provide women with equal opportunities in employment, vocational training and working conditions.

However, the impact of legislation in this area, whilst important, is likely to be marginal for a number of reasons. As with many kinds of legislation, there are difficulties in interpretation and enforcement. More important in this case, legislation has the disadvantage of compelling changes in behaviour or practice without encouraging changes in attitude. Unwilling compliance with regulations in any area is often based on adjusting as little as possible and seeking opportunities for evasion. Legislation directed to an area such as women's employment where the principle constraint is attitudes does nothing to attack the basic problem and may even discourage action in excess of the minimum required.

The specific legal instruments have obvious disadvantages. Equal pay legislation can do little to eliminate differences between the earnings of men and women when, for example, there are essentially separate labour markets for men and women; when the alleged typical qualities of women, such as dexterity, are undervalued in relation to those of men, such as physical strength; and when payment systems so often reward the seniority in employment which many women lack. Similarly, equal treatment legislation establishes a right of access to employment and training but does nothing to counteract the social and cultural pressures which prevent the majority of women from applying for consideration or to provide the facilities which will enable them to take up employment.

Nevertheless, anti-discrimination legislation provides a basis for equal opportunity programmes. As long as it is seen as a means of enabling change and not as the agent of change it can serve a useful purpose.

It is less easy to make positive comments about protective legislation which safeguards women only in relation to general problems in employment. Most of the member states impose restrictions on the employment of women at least in relation to occupations which are considered dangerous or unhealthy. Some, including Great Britain, retain legislation restricting women's working hours and overtime and their ability to undertake night work.

Protective legislation, introduced with the best intentions, creates artificial barriers to women's employment in certain occupations. The Economic and Social Committee of the Council of Europe[2] has called for a review of the provisions protecting women and an investigation into the effect of night and heavy work on workers' health. There seems to be growing support for the view that the same standards of protection should apply to men and women alike. This is now a generally accepted principle in the United States. Within the European Community, Denmark at least has abolished protective legislation for women only. Pressures from trade unions amongst others mean that application of the same standards is likely to lead to an increase in protective measures covering men rather than a decrease in those covering women.

The other significant area of legislation specifically directed at women in employment – maternity leave – is both a protective measure and a means of assisting women in employment.

Maternity leave and benefits

Arrangements for maternity leave and benefits vary but are generally incorporated into some form of national system with set minima and provisions protecting the mother's rights to work during her pregnancy and her right to return to work following a period of maternity leave. Great Britain generally compares favourably with the rest of the European Community and is more generous in terms of length of leave.

The British Employment Protection Act 1975 protects women from dismissal on grounds of pregnancy and, for those with at least two years' service with their employer, permits maternity leave of up to eleven weeks before the expected date of confinement and twenty-nine weeks after the baby is born; the Act also provides for six weeks' maternity pay in addition to the State Maternity Allowance. Belgium, Denmark and France, for example, each permit a total of fourteen weeks' maternity leave but with allowances for the whole period amounting to sixty per cent of earnings plus supplement in Belgium and ninety per cent of earnings in Denmark and France.

Laws relating to maternity leave again express a narrow concern with mothers and therefore tend to reinforce traditional assumptions about parental roles. This new legal protection may also be seen as increasing the costs associated with employing women and thus discourage managers from recruiting and promoting women – where they have a choice – despite the provisions of equal treatment legislation. The potential discriminatory effects of maternity leave might have been lessened if statutory rights to paternity leave had been included.

There appears, however, to be a growing recognition that paternity leave may be as appropriate as maternity leave. So far, only Sweden has taken action on these lines. On 1 January 1974 the Swedish system of maternity assurance was converted into a parental insurance scheme. Fathers are entitled to stay at home during the immediate pre and post natal period to care for other children. Following the birth of the child, parents are free to decide which will remain at home after the twenty-nineth day of post natal leave for the remainder of the 180 days allowed. In addition, either parent can take ten days paid leave per year to take care of a sick child.

It must be emphasised that the legislation confers a right

on pregnant women. Take up rates can vary enormously depending not only on the availability of child care facilities, but also on such factors as type of employment, state of the labour market and geographical location. However, given the availability of employment opportunities and suitable child care facilities, it seems likely that increasing numbers of women may take maternity leave. For example, a national survey of fifth form girls in Great Britain found that fourteen per cent intended to work continuously while their children were young.

Child care

If it is intended, as it presumably is, that maternity leave should allow time for a socially desirable function without prejudice to employment, legislation must be accompanied by facilities for child rearing. Lack of adequate provision for the care of children means that many women have no choice between working or staying at home or at least no choice in the kind of work which suits them. Child care need not mean exclusively the provision of facilities but this is at least a starting point.

The demand for places in publicly approved day nurseries in all member states greatly exceeds the supply. It is, for example, estimated that there are 800,000 children under three of working mothers in Germany and 79,000 in Belgium and that the number of places in day nurseries are 20,428 and 13,568 respectively. In most member states the provision of nursery schools or classes for children between two or three years and the age of compulsory school attendance is distinctly better but still inadequate. There are also problems in all member states in the supervision of children of all ages outside school hours and of care for ill and elderly members of the family.

On the other hand, there are widespread doubts about the desirability of encouraging mothers of young children to work outside the home. Many employers doubt the ability of such mothers to attach sufficient priority to their work and there is also an unresolved debate on the effects of child care on young children.

Nonetheless, the European Community and some individual member states – notably France, Germany, Italy, Luxembourg and the Netherlands – are committed to measures to improve child care facilities. The problems are family problems and in a broader sense problems of society: their solution usually devolves on the mother. The European Commission has proposed[8] that the community (with a small 'c') should take a greater responsibility through the provision of facilities and also that paid leave should be available, as it is in Sweden, for either the mother or the father to care for sick children. As already noted, the European Social Fund may be of assistance in this area.

More flexible working arrangements

Mention has been made of the growing realisation that the issues raised by women's employment demand broad social adaptation and change. Professor Alistair Heron, who has been conducting an international study of pre-school services for OECD[9] has suggested that '... it is beginning to be realised that the problem of day care might eventually solve itself, so to speak, if the working hours and conditions of employment for both men and women could be made equally flexible and interchangeable: the "liberation" of women from the home may in the long run depend, for essentially practical reasons, on the "liberation" of men from the work place. Just as the full health of the individual can be promoted by a judicious balancing of work, play and sleep, so could it also be promoted within the family unit by a balancing of the time spent by children with their mother, their father, and the care and education resources of the community.'

There has been an increasing focus of attention within the Community to greater flexibility in the working life of people generally. However, the main developments to date have been confined to the introduction of flexible working hours which require the worker to be at work during a core time each day and only provide freedom to choose working hours outside the core time. Any form of flexible working hours can give working parents better opportunities to fulfil their family responsibilities. However, the fact that such a high proportion of women with family responsibilities work part-time suggests that the current trend does not provide them with the desired, or necessary, degree of flexibility.

Many women, and men with family responsibilities, need the ability to adjust their working lives over months or even years, rather than days to accommodate education, training, family duties, employment and spare time activities. The standard working arrangements of teachers have been shown to suit many married women. If such standards, or the flexibility to adjust working hours to similar patterns, existed for other occupations, highly qualified women could undoubtedly be attracted to a wider range of occupations. Why confine flexibility to working hours? Many jobs could as readily be undertaken at home and at the workplace as the work and personal circumstances dictated. Such developments, however, will almost certainly await periods of manpower shortage when it is necessary to seek new sources of the required labour.

Training

Training is seen as a vital measure in enabling women to take up employment in a wider range of jobs. In principle, equal treatment is guaranteed by law; as has been seen, women's actual share of training throughout the Community is both small and narrow.

The limited extent of women's training is particularly disquieting in the face of evidence[8] that access to educational and training opportunities is cumulative. Those who have received substantial education and training are more likely to recognise the need for further development and to have the initiative to seek out and/or take advantage of opportunities than those who have not. Similarly, research has shown that participation in employment increases in relation to education and training received. The more education and training a woman has received, the more likely she is, for example, to continue working or to return to work after having a family and the less likely she is to be absent from work or to change her job frequently.

Progress within the Community is largely confined to a recognition of the needs and problems and the adoption of principles, *viz.* that women should be treated equally with regard to access to all types and levels of vocational training. The keynote within Europe is equality: securing for women a greater share in the training opportunities which men enjoy so widely. Since a more even distribution of opportunities depends more on the changing of attitudes than on the process of training, the emphasis is on improved vocational information and guidance.

There are, however, some specific provisions for the general training of women. Germany's programme is probably the most comprehensive within the Community. The Federal Institute of Labour has a special section which designs training programmes for women re-entering employment. Several kinds of training are available including refresher and upgrading training, conversion courses and new career programmes. Generous credit is provided for earlier work experience (including housework) to shorten the training period normally required and trainees receive approximately eighty per cent of the wage for the training occupation. The Institute operates an alternative scheme under which employers receive a subsidy for providing on-the-job training for women returners.

Great Britain is also notable within the Community for promoting measures which exceed the principle of equality. Apart from expanding women's training opportunities, the Training Services Agency, which is responsible for public training services in Great Britain, attaches particular importance to improvements in the actual training for many of the occupations in which women predominate.[10]

This is intended to help them in attaining promotion into senior posts normally occupied by men and in being able to move into other jobs with higher skill profiles.

In addition, British legislation in this area goes beyond the provision of equal opportunities. The Sex Discrimination Act 1975 permits positive discrimination in the provision of training both to encourage members of one sex (usually women) to take up jobs traditionally held by members of the other sex and to assist those who have interrupted their employment to discharge domestic or family responsibilities. Current response to this provision is mainly in terms of special grants or awards by industrial training boards for the training of girls/women in traditionally male occupations, for example as engineering technicians and managers, and short re-orientation courses for women contemplating a return to employment.

That then is the general pattern of women's training within Europe. There has in addition been a growing recognition that women wishing to return to employment need special help in assessing their capabilities in relation to employment and/or training opportunities; in gaining confidence in their abilities; in refreshing, or acquiring new, knowledge and skills.

It seems likely that there will be a growth in the provision at national level throughout the Community of short-term assistance to married women wishing to return to employment which will enable and encourage them to participate with men in standard programmes of vocational training. For example, the Ministry of Labour in Denmark organises a two week induction course for older women. German employment offices provide specialist counselling services from women officers. The French Ministry of Education funds a five week, part-time day re-orientation and adjustment programme. A large number of colleges in Great Britain offer, independently, a variety of re-orientation courses for potential women returners and consideration is being given to the possibility of public support. The intended and likely influence of developments on these lines is that women will have the opportunity to reevaluate their vocational choice in a wider context than hitherto.

Conclusions

This chapter has described, in brief, a quite formidable range of disadvantageous circumstances and difficulties relating to women's employment: the limited job opportunities and earnings of the growing number of women working, particularly married women; the problems of returning to employment after a break; the difficult reconciliation of many women's domestic role with standard patterns of employment; drawbacks to part-time work; the shortage of child care; the discriminatory effect of protective legislation. The most notable omission is social security where evidence of discrimination in terms of pensions, sickness benefits and unemployment benefits would fill another chapter.[8]

It must be obvious from the magnitude and interdependence of the problems that it is not enough to take action to prevent discrimination: active measures are needed to tackle the differences in men's and women's circumstances which underlie equality. Women have become accustomed to being treated as a reserve labour force which provides a buffer for the male core against economic fluctuations. Because of their expectations – of work and life in general – women do not take advantage of the opportunities which exist now: it seems unlikely in the short term that they will respond in force to legislation and minimal increases in public services.

So what is being done? It is generally recognised by those who determine policy within Europe that genuine equality for women in employment is not possible without some fundamental changes in society. In practice, current policies and programmes tend to seek to enforce the treatment of women -on their merits and to ease the burden of their social function. The emphasis is on helping women to reach male standards, thus extending male roles to all society and leaving the majority of women still at a disadvantage in competing with men.

Active measures so far have tended to concentrate more on the special problems of the mature woman returning to employment than on expanding opportunities for girls leaving school. In the absence of an overall expansion in employment opportunities, there is evidence that this policy is creating opportunities for women at the expense of girls. Hence, for example, in Great Britain, the increase in training for adult women through the publicly funded Training Opportunities Scheme has been accompanied in some areas by a decrease in initial training by employers of girl school leavers. It must be assumed that as this displacement effect becomes more obvious, there will be more positive counter-activity to at least recover, if not increase, opportunities for girls.

I have made frequent references to pronouncements of the Economic and Social Committee of the Council of Europe because these considered judgments are indicators of likely future trends. They point to legislation in the area of social security; further extension of public services to assist women; special grants towards the cost of training women for selected occupations; innovatory and demonstration projects in the field of women's employment. Measures such as these are prescribed to advance the 'fundamental principle' that men and women should enjoy a right, but not a duty, to work in equal measure and under the same conditions.

At the same time, other more general measures may also assist women. For example, the likely development within the Community of greater opportunities for workers to obtain educational leave could be of particular benefit to women in making up earlier deficiencies. On the other hand, many activities primarily directed at women, such as flexible working arrangements, will also benefit men who share their employment.

What could have been done? Many proponents of women's rights suggest that it is wrong for governments to concentrate almost exclusively on changing women's circumstances; if they must, national policy addressed to women's problems on, for example, industry, employment, health, child care, social security, should be co-ordinated. The Swedish system provides a helpful contrast with its integrated labour market-training-social welfare programme. Sweden's programme also includes measures seemingly undreamt of within Europe such as industrial development loans dependent on the employment of at least forty per cent of the minority sex in that industry.

The likely effects of present policies and programmes within Europe are difficult to gauge. In numerical terms, a growing demand is projected from women for employment. However, the rate of growth of women's employment will obviously depend both on the availability of jobs and the alleviation of some of the problems which women face. In qualitative terms, substantial change is likely to be long-term as society accommodates to new definitions of sex roles and the equalisation of parental roles. For example, daughters (and sons) of working mothers will have their expectations, aspirations and values shaped by a completely different social environment than their forebears.

Two final points. First, despite my negative comments about current policies and programmes, it is highly significant, and encouraging, that action is being taken within the Community at a time of great anxiety about the employment crisis. Second, we are all guilty of generalisations which very often do not apply to individual women: for some women, current action will provide the means and the spur to achieve genuine equality in employment.

References

1. Official Journal of the European Communities No C 13, 12 February 1974.
2. Official Journal of the European Communities No C 286, 15 December 1975.

3. Sullerot, E., *The Employment of Women and the Problems it Raises in the Member States of the European Community*, Commission of the European Communities (Luxembourg 1970).
4. DE Manpower Paper No 11, *Women and Work: A Review*, HMSO (London 1975).
5. *The New European Social Fund*, Commission of the European Communities (Brussels 1973).
6. Official Journal of the European Communities No L 45, 19 February 1975.
7. Official Journal of the European Communities No L 39, 14 February 1976.
8. *Equality of Treatment between Men and Women Workers (Communication of the Commission to the Council)*, Commission of the European Communities (Brussels 1975).
9. Working Document in preparation for OECD: reference taken from *Mothers in Employment*, ed. Nickie Fonda and Peter Moss, Brunel University Management Programme (Usebridge 1976).
10. *Training Opportunities for Women*, Manpower Services Commission/Training Services Agency (London 1975).

11 Industrial training

PETER LONG

In a society in a state of complete equilibrium the need for training is confined to the function of replacement: that is, training the young to enter working life; and developing those already working to acquire additional skills or knowledge.

Our society, however, is not in a state of equilibrium in that sense, and it is necessary to provide training to deal with the situations produced by changes stemming from technological and economic developments.

The consequences of technological changes may be limited to individual firms; to complete industries; or they may extend to the nation as a whole. They may flow from the introduction of new machinery or new processes; or they may originate from the opening of an entirely new industry by a discovery such as that of the transistor. Whatever the cause may be, it is virtually certain that the changes will involve the need for training.

Economic changes also have their effects. These may be localised, by such events as the opening or closing of collieries, or the extension or decline in demand for ship-building; or they may be more widespread in their consequences, resulting from boom or – at the other end of the spectrum – recession.

Additionally, there are those trends which have been present to a greater or lesser degree in all advanced societies, such as those of Western Europe, for many years past. They are based upon the steady decline in the numbers employed in agriculture; the effects of the re-structuring of industry, with reductions in the numbers working in the traditional industries such as mining and textiles, and the growth of new ones, such as the automobile industry; and the great growth in the numbers engaged in the public services of one sort or another.

The following table[1] demonstrates this trend quite clearly. Although the figures are for the EEC in general, they are equally representative of the general situation in the UK.

Table 11.1   *Distribution of civil employment between major sectors* (in percentages)

Sector	1955	1960	1965	1970
Agriculture	24.3	19.6	15.9	13.4
Industry	40.0	42.4	43.5	43.9
Services (inc. public bodies)	35.7	38.0	40.6	42.7

From all these factors in combination it is evident that there is a situation necessitating the movement of people whether from one type of industry to another, or from one type of occupation to another: in either case there will be a need for training.

On top of the needs that have existed in the past, there will be a greater need in the future to meet the requirements of industrial legislation, such as the Health and Safety at Work etc. Act, and the Employment Protection Act. Furthermore, although it is impossible to forecast at this moment the precise form in which worker participation will develop, there is no doubt that there will be more shop-floor involvement in the running of industrial organisations, and this will produce accompanying training needs for the participants, to enable them to play a significant role.

The extension of the need for training is clearly established, and thus it is necessary to look at the way in which it is fulfilled at present, and more particularly, how it may be fulfilled in the future.

Until the last twenty years it was left almost entirely to industry itself. However, this has been proved to be inadequate for the ever-increasing task, and so there have been drastic changes in the organisation of training in this time.

The most significant of all was without question the passing of the Industrial Training Act in 1964. This gave the Secretary of State for Employment the power to set up training boards covering different 'activities of industry or commerce' with the following main functions:

(i)   to ensure an adequate supply of properly trained men and women at all levels of industry;
(ii) to secure an improvement in the quality and efficiency of industrial training;
(iii) to share the cost of training more evenly between firms.

Summarised briefly, therefore, the general purpose of the Act was to leave the responsibility for training with industry itself, but to encourage it to take place by the payment of grants, which, in turn, were produced by a system of levying throughout the industry in question.

The structure of training boards consisted of equal members of representatives of employers and trade unionists from the industry concerned, together with a small number of educationists.

Each training board was required to gain approval from the Secretary of State for the plans it had formulated to fulfill its obligation to see that satisfactory training – in terms of quantity and quality – would be carried out; and specifically for the purpose of raising a training levy amongst the firms within its scope.

The creation of the individual training boards began in 1964 and continued throughout the following years, until by the end of 1971, there were 27 boards covering industries employing fifteen million people.

The training boards undoubtedly made an impact, in large part perhaps because of the effect upon firms faced with a levy which might amount – as in the case of the firms within scope of the Engineering Industry Training Board in its early days – to 2.5 per cent of their annual payroll. There was much to support the view, widely quoted at the time, that it had put the subject of training into the board rooms of Britain.

The immediate benefits of the new systems were an increase in the quality and quantity of training, with more careful analysis of training needs, and the acceptance of more systematic methods of training, particularly in the field of apprenticeship training. A measure of the increased importance attached to training was the sharp increase in the number of training officers and instructors; the number of off-the-job training places; and of group apprenticeship schemes embracing the smaller firms.

However, there were criticisms of the system. Whilst the principle of grant versus levy was simple in concept, it might not be fair to all firms within an industry: for example, those with a low labour turnover would have no need to do the amount of training done within the firms with a high turnover. Furthermore, it was often felt that there was too much administrative work entailed in the process of claiming grants: time which could more advantageously be spent in carrying out the process of training.

In 1972 Robert Carr, who was then Secretary of State for Employment, produced a document, *Training for the Future*[2]. This looked at the whole subject in the light of the need for economic growth 'in the context both of regional policy and of our forthcoming entry into Europe'. In particular the report dealt with the need for an increase in the number of training places provided under the Government Vocational Training Scheme; and it examined the effectiveness of the industrial training boards.

It stated the government's intention to introduce a massive increase in training to meet the needs of individuals who would not otherwise be given the chance to train within industry: in fact it proposed an extension to a target figure of 100,000 men and women under what would be called the Training Opportunities Scheme. As a step towards this figure – which compares sharply with the total of 16,650 people trained in 1970 – it was recommended that there should be not less than 60–70,000 trainees by 1975.

The report then proposed a general phasing out of the levy/grant system within the industrial training boards, leaving the boards with their advisory role.

In the event, most – though not all – of the recommendations were incorporated in the Employment and Training Act, 1973. This brought into being the Training Services Agency, as recommended in the report, as the executive arm of the newly created Manpower Services Commission.

It also amended the Industrial Training Act, enabling training boards to submit for approval their proposals for the issue of certificates of exemption from levy, which could then be issued to employers whose training arrangements were regarded as satisfactory. This has had the effect of maintaining the controlling influence of the levy system in a much simplified manner.

The new Training Services Agency has three broad aims, quoted in its leaflet, *A Five Year Plan*:[3]

1. To improve the efficiency and effective performance of manpower.
2. To help people to fulfill their needs and aspirations in their jobs.
3. To increase the effectiveness and efficiency of training.

It carries out these aims in particular through its co-ordinating role with the industrial training boards; its requirement to oversee the state of training in those concerns, such as the nationalised industries, which fall outside the ITB coverage; by its provision of the various 'training within industry' courses either for industrial supervisors or training officers; and through its administration of the Training Opportunities Scheme.

The impact made by the TSA has been quite considerable. Since the implementation of the Employment and Training Act there has been a general introduction of levy exemption schemes by the industrial training boards. There is no doubt that the boards have thus been given the freedom to extend their activities to contend with the longer-term training needs of the firms within their scope.

The use of 'training within industry' schemes has developed over the years from the original job instruction, job relations and job methods courses for supervisors, introduced in the war years. Now more than 20,000 people are trained each year in the wider range of courses, including those for supervisors in offices and retail distribution.

Probably its greatest impact – certainly in numerical terms – has been achieved by the results of the Training Opportunities Scheme. In meeting its objective of providing training in skills for those who wish – or need – to develop them as a means of improving their job potentiality, there has been a considerable growth in training places. These have been provided by an expansion of the places available in the system of Government Training Centres, now re-named Skillcentres; by the use of places within colleges of education, polytechnics and universities; and by way of training places within industrial firms. It should be added, of course, that the TOPS incorporates the availability of allowances for the trainees, to make the offer of training a reality.

In spite of all these positive developments, however, there are still clearly identifiable problems which remain to be solved.

The TSA produced a discussion paper, *Vocational Preparation for Young People*[4] in 1975, drawing attention to the failings of the present training system as a means of meeting the long-term economic needs of the country; and to the lack of proper preparation of a vocational nature for great numbers of young people entering employment each year.

The former subject was re-stated in a consultative document *Training for Vital Skills*,[5] produced jointly by the Department of Employment and the Manpower Services Commission in the following year.

The report put forward for consideration the concept of *collective funding* – which had also been suggested in the earlier paper – as a possible way of helping to alleviate persistent shortages of workers with skills vital to economic growth. It made the point that the economy needs a supply of people with *transferable skills* – that is, those which can be used by different firms or even industries –- in order to take advantage of periods of rapid expansion. It accepted that the present system gives no encouragement to individual firms to carry out lengthy apprenticeship training over and above that designed specifically to meet their own requirements. Indeed, it is the absence of attention to the *overall* manning needs of the country that is a major criticism of the system produced by the Industrial Training Act; and this situation has been exacerbated by the Employment and Training Act's introduction of the right to exemption from training levy.

The suggested principle of collective funding is designed to provide, out of money raised either solely or jointly from industry or from public funds, all or part of the cost of initial training for selected occupations. The training would be entered into by individual firms on a contractual basis, which would be agreed in order to meet the *total* needs for those occupations. The report contained a list of jobs that might be covered by the scheme: this included a variety of skilled trades, particularly in the engineering industry, as well as draughtsmen and work study officers. It was not, of course, put forward as a definitive list but it included the occupations that their researchers had shown to be in short supply persistently over many years: Table 11.2 shows the ratio between vacancies and the unemployed in certain jobs.

This analysis, in so far as the engineering industry is concerned, is further supported by a very recent report[6] produced jointly by the National Economic Development Office and the MSC. The report establishes that not only has there been a sharp reduction in the number of craftsmen in engineering, but additionally it is estimated that there will be a fall of about a third in the average number of apprentices completing their training in the years immediately ahead. The reductions in numbers are largely a consequence of recession, but the effects will reach into the period of economic recovery.

It is too early to know whether the idea of collective funding will be adopted. It is clear that there is a pressing problem, but it does not necessarily follow that this concept presents a practicable solution. It would operate as an addition to the present ITB system, and therefore it would

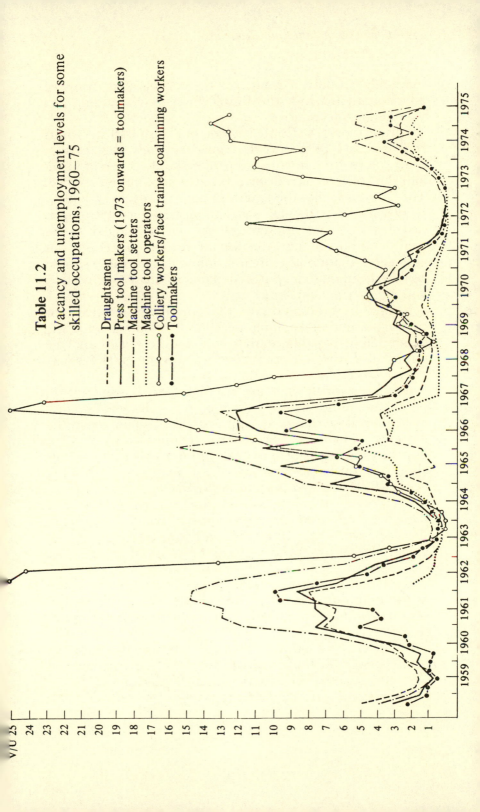

Table 11.2
Vacancy and unemployment levels for some skilled occupations, 1960–75

- – – – Draughtsmen
- ——— Press tool makers (1973 onwards = toolmakers)
- –·–·– Machine tool setters
- ········· Machine tool operators
- —○—○— Colliery workers/face trained coalmining workers
- —●—●— Toolmakers

inevitably produce a return to the complicated forms of administration which the Employment and Training Act was designed to remove.

Furthermore, the Confederation of British Industry, in its response[7] to the proposal, argued strongly that certain other more fundamental remedies should be examined, and the concept of collective funding should be dropped. The CBI stated that the length of apprenticeship should be related to the particular occupation for which training is being given; and apprentices should be judged to be proficient by the introduction of testing procedures. It considered that the age of entry into apprenticeship should be raised, although it appreciated that this had a connection with the payment system.

It also drew attention to the present disincentive for people to undertake long periods of training, with the steady fall in pay differentials between the skilled and the semi-skilled: this is a point also made in the NEDO report referred to earlier.

It is noteworthy that the training boards were by no means unanimously in favour of the collective funding principle: those that were opposed were usually so on the grounds either of opposition to the setting up of bureaucratic procedures to deal with it; or they had doubts about the probable accuracy of the manpower planning upon which it would have to be based.

The other part of the discussion paper *Vocational Preparation for Young People*, was only mentioned in passing in *Training for Vital Skills*. Nonetheless, details of an experimental programme have been given in another Government document, *Unified Vocational Preparation*. In its concern with the problems of young people leaving school at the minimum age, it deals with an area in which this country compares unfavourably with some other European countries.

It is inevitable that in reviewing the short-comings of our own system, we should look further afield, particularly at our more successful partners within the EEC.

The system of training which has most in common with

that in the UK is probably that in West Germany. State involvement has been a comparatively recent departure, and was stimulated by a continuing shortage of labour. It is built on a more rigidly separated educational system than is now generally in operation in the UK; and with a minimum school leaving age of fifteen.

The three specific interlocking items of Federal legislation were:

1. The Employment Promotion Act (*Arbeitsförderungsgesetz*) – June, 1969[8]
2. The Vocational Training Act (*Berufsbildungsgesetz*) – August, 1969[9]
3. Federal Training Promotion Act (*Bundesausbildungs-förderungsgesetz*) August 1971[10]

The Employment Promotion Act in its preamble stated 'The measures under this Act are to aim, within the framework of the Federal Government's social and economic policy, at the achievement and maintenance of a high level of employment, at a steady improvement of the employment pattern and thus at the promotion of economic growth'.[11] Apart from the general responsibilities for vocational guidance and placement conferred upon the Federal Institute for Labour (*Bundesanstalt für Arbeit*) specific responsibility for the occupational integration of certain groups of people was included: mainly the handicapped; women wishing to return to employment; and older people. It also referred to vocational training, the subject of the second Act.

The Vocational Training Act laid down clear standards to be followed in training for each of the separate occupational trades: there were about 500 of these at the time that the Act was implemented, but it was the intention that the number should be reduced to more manageable proportions.

The Act stated that written training programmes must be issued at the beginning of training, and certificates of proficiency at the end; that trainees shall attend a part-time vocational school – usually on one day a week – in addition to their industrial training; that the trainers who instruct them must be properly qualified; and that the industrial training premises must be suitable.

It also included provision for further training and re-training, a theme returned to in the Vocational Promotion Act. This gave individuals a statutory right to take appropriate courses, with the assistance of generous grants raised by equal contributions from employers and employees.

Whilst there are clear similarities between the systems operating in Germany and the UK, there are also very real differences, such as the practice in Germany of employing large numbers of foreign workers, reaching a peak in September 1971, when they constituted 10.3 per cent of the total labour force. This presents a buffer against rising unemployment; and it provides a pool of labour for the less skilled jobs.

The differences of greater significance in so far as training is concerned include the fact that the length of training for craft apprentices is shorter than in the UK, and there are standards of proficiency to be demonstrated for the successful completion of training.

In France, as opposed to either the UK or Germany, there has long been a much greater degree of state involvement in the training system. Craft training has for many years been carried out in large part 'off-the-job' in training centres throughout the country. It has been financed by a special tax, first introduced in 1925 – the *Taxe d'Apprentissage* – which much later prompted the concept of a levy in our own Industrial Training Act.

Whilst this method of apprenticeship training has been undoubtedly highly successful in producing skilled workers, it was not capable of providing the extent or the flexibility of training that has subsequently become necessary to meet either the needs of the economy or the social aspirations of individuals.

There has consequently been a succession of laws in recent years, most notably of 16 July 1971, which also brought together parts of the earlier legislation. Under this law there were four separate acts on vocational training.

These – as cited in the OECD report 'Manpower Policy in France'[12] were:

No. 71–575 on the organisation of permanent vocational training in the context of permanent education

No. 71–576 on apprenticeship

No. 71–577, guidance law on technical training

No. 71–578 on employer participation on the financing of initial technical and vocational training

Although the legislation is wide ranging, it is possible to concentrate on certain features which are of particular importance. It is based upon the acceptance of a *right* to continuous vocational training, and covers the following distinct type of training:

1. *Conversion.* For those who are not in employment, such as women wishing to return to work; and those wishing to change their occupation.
2. *Prévention.* For those who need re-training because of impending redundancy.
3. *Adaptation.* Training for a first or new job.
4. *Promotion professionelle.* For those wishing to move from one level of job to another.
5. *Entretien et perfectionement des connaissances.* For those in employment who need to keep abreast of changes.

Workers have the right to leave to take a course of training up to one year for a full time course or 1200 hours for a course which is either part-time or discontinuous. This right is subject to certain limitations: for example, workers must have two years' service with their firms; and the proportion attending courses from any firm is restricted to two per cent. It does not extend to those who possess a degree of occupational qualification which was gained within the previous three years. There is provision for payment to those who are granted leave to attend a course.

Every employer – other than central and local authorities – with 10 or more workers has to allocate a proportion of the wage bill to training activities. At the outset – in 1972 – the figure was 0.8 per cent of the payroll, but with the intention that it would be raised to two per cent in 1976. The firm is able to finance its *own* training activities from the allocation, including the right to make payments of up to ten per cent to approved external training organisations. They must then pay to the Treasury the balance not spent.

The Government also allocates a very substantial sum to the cost of training: for example it proposed to spend £150 million in 1972, as against the employers' commitment to allocate about £140 million.[13]

One of the longer-term effects of the EEC will undoubtedly be a movement towards harmonisation of training, since this must be achieved if there is to be full labour mobility between the member countries. As K.-H Massoth stated at the BACIE Annual Conference in 1972, shortly before Britain's entry into the community, 'if we succeed, in the future, in organising a systematic exchange of information on national policies and reforms, as well as in having closer co-operation between, above all, the governments of the member countries, then the result might be a gradual harmonisation of the education and training systems in the 70s and 80s. Even if greater differences in the organisational details remained, there should at least be the possibility of some comparability in the levels of training and qualifications. This would mean that a degree of harmonisation could be pursued and achieved in vocational training strategy rather than through standardisation of the present systems.'[14]

If this, then is the aim and the method of improving standards by training, one of the means of achieving this is the EEC Social Fund.

At the outset the Fund was designed to provide a source of money to help with the effects upon employment of the integration of the member countries. Between 1960 and 1971 a total of $421 million was spent on schemes involving 1,436,000 people.

It was considered, however, that more money was required; and the training needs changed as time went on: 'Whereas in 1958 a major problem facing the six had been fairly large-scale unemployment, by the mid-1960's the problem was no longer unemployment as such, but the inability of many workers to perform the technologically-advanced jobs that were being created. Thus retraining on a much wider scale, both occupationally and geographically, had become necessary.'[15]

As a result of the limitations of the Fund in its first stage, it was reformed. The second phase came into operation in 1972, to run until 1977. Its scope under Article 4 allowed for contributions to be made from the Fund in circumstances where continuing integration places jobs at risk, and in 1974 the scope was further widened to take account of some of the special needs of handicapped people, and of migrant workers. Under Article 5, help is possible in dealing with more basic problems of unemployment and underemployment, which whilst not directly stemming from integration, would otherwise impede the progress of the Community. The same Article also allows for help for specific groups, such as handicapped, elderly and young people. Financial help is given by way of grants of half the cost of approved projects.

To give some understanding of the scale of the help available from the Social Fund, Britain in 1974 was allocated about £26 million, made up in the following way:[16]

	£
Agriculture	64,000
Textiles	240,000
Handicapped	350,000
Migrants	2,640,000
Development Regions*	18,400,000
Technical Progress	160,000
Handicapped Workers	4,000,000
	£25,900,000 approx.

This amount came from a total allocation by the Commission of £106.1 million: a sum, of course, contributed by the Community members themselves.

Help from the Social Fund is additional to that provided from the Regional Development Fund

Amongst the projects within the UK, quoted in an article in *Training* in January, 1976 were[17]:

i   language courses for immigrant workers relating to employment.

ii   training and resettlement of agricultural workers, and of workers in, and leaving the textile industry.

iii   women returning to work.

iv   training school in oil technology.

v   Footwear, Leather and Fur Skin Industry Training Board to recruit unemployed young people under 25, and unemployed and under-privileged young and handicapped people to train as surgical shoemakers mostly from priority areas.

It must be considered probable that there will be a growing use of the Fund as a means of helping with the costs of training and retraining to meet the changes in the pattern of employment within the country, although this will clearly depend upon the terms of reference of the Fund in its next phase.

Summary

It is impossible in the course of a single chapter to cover fully what is demonstrably a vast, complex subject. It is only possible to point to the circumstances – such as the speeding-up of technological change and the rises and falls in the state of the economy – which have extended the needs for training and retraining; and to describe briefly the systems developed to meet those needs.

At this stage certain conclusions can be stated, and future probable trends established:

1.   There is a need for manpower planning across the entire spectrum of industry and commerce, and not just within *parts* of it, to provide the basis for the anticipation of future changes in employment patterns.

2.   Because individual firms tend to plan their training programmes on their own requirements, which will in turn often be influenced by short-term considerations,

there must inevitably be increasing intervention on the part of the government – and of the EEC – to encourage and support, particularly in times of economic stagnation, the training that is necessary for the economy as a whole.

3. It is clearly established that no longer is it realistic to set out to train people on the assumption that they will spend a life-time in the same industry or even occupation. It follows, therefore, that apart from the training and retraining needed to fit them into new jobs, there is an obvious case for the provision of initial broadly-based training as a contribution towards later mobility.

4. Additionally, with the growing influence of the EEC, it is reasonable to expect that there will be acceptance of the individual's *right* to training, not only at the outset but throughout the entire span of working life.

5. Standards have improved greatly in recent years, with a much higher degree of professionalism amongst those responsible for training. There will undoubtedly continue to be improvements both in training methods and techniques, as the knowledge of human behaviour and motivation is increased; and the demands of industrial society become increasingly complex.

6. There has been an awareness recently of the need to prepare young people more adequately for their working lives. This is a subject which has, as stated earlier, received greater attention in certain other European countries than in the UK, but no doubt it will extend to influence the British educational system. Linked with this there will almost certainly be a movement to align more clearly the requirements of industry with the production of graduates from the places of higher education.

7. In looking at the relationship between the nature of training in the UK and in other countries it is all too easy to give the impression that it is we who have everything to learn and little to teach. The reality is different: the development of training in Europe in

recent years has shown that each country is prepared to adopt those policies or practices from elsewhere which are most likely to meet its own circumstances. An eclectic approach of this nature will inevitably continue because of the much greater awareness of the activities of other countries, particularly those within the EEC.

Finally, to put the entire subject into context, F. C. Hayes[18] wrote in 1972: 'Training cannot be regarded as a solution to general economic problems but, without it, other solutions become impossible.' This statement is manifestly as true to-day, but just as the problems have intensified during the intervening years, so the role of training must become more important.

References

1. Preliminary Guidelines for a Community Social Policy Programme, 1971.
2. Department of Employment, *Training for the Future*, HMSO, 1972.
3. Training Services Agency, *A Five Year Plan*, HMSO, 1974.
4. Training Services Agency, *Vocation Preparation for Young People*, HMSO, 1975.
5. Training Services Agency, *Training for Vital Skills*, HMSO, 1976.
6. NEDO, *Engineering Craftsmen: Shortages & Related Problems*.
7. CBI, *Education and Training Bulletin Supplement*, 1976.
8. Employment Promotion Act, 1969.
9. Vocational Training Act, 1969.
10. Federal Training Promotion Act, 1971.
11. Employment Promotion Act, 1969.
12. OECD, *Manpower Policy in France*, 1973.
13. Hayes, F. C. 'Manpower Policies in Europe', *Personnel Review*, Vol. 1, No. 4, 1972.
14. Head of the Department for Vocational Guidance and Vocational Training, Directorate-General for Social Affairs, EEC.

15. COI Reference Pamphlet 136, *Britain in the European Community: Social Policy*, 1975.
16. *op. cit.*, (page 19).
17. Elliott Ruth, 'Training Opportunities in the EEC Social Funds', *Training*, January 1976.
18. Hayes, F. C., 'Manpower Policies in Europe', *Personnel Review*, Vol. 1, No. 4, Autumn 1972.

Bibliography

Barber, J. W., (ed.) *Industrial Training Handbook*, Iliffe Books (1968).

Manpower Policy in the UK, OECD (Paris 1970).

Manpower Policy in Germany, OECD (Paris 1974).

Manpower Policy in France, OECD (Paris 1973).

Training for the Future: A Plan for Discussion, Department of Employment (London 1972).

Training for Vital Skills: A Consultative Document, Department of Employment (London 1976).

Industrial Training Act, 1964.

Employment Training Act, 1973.

Training, Incomes Data Services, Study 135, 1976.

Baer and Morris, 'Human Resources Development in West Germany: Some Trends', *Industrial Training International*, October 1974.

Dyer, Nadine, 'Vocational Education and Training in the FDR', *Industrial and Commercial Training*, February 1977.

Hayes, F. C., 'Manpower and Training Policies in Europe', *Personnel Review*, Autumn 1972.

Vocational Training in the EEC, BACIE/IPM/ITO, 1972.

Bacie Journal, BACIE, December 1972.

Britain in the European Community: Social Policy, COI Reference Pamphlet 136, 1975.

Hallstein, Walter, *Europe in the Making*, Allen and Unwin (London 1976).

Charnley, A., *Paid Educational Leave*, Hart-Davis Educational, (London 1975).

Developments in Educational Leave of Absence, OECD (Paris 1976).

Elliott, Ruth, 'Training Opportunities in the EEC Social Fund', *Training*, January 1976.

12 The United States collective bargaining system

SOL BARKIN

Contracting union sector and power; ascending management sophistication and influence.

Enthusiasm for the American industrial relations system flourished among academics, government officials and trade unionists in the first postwar decade. Viewing it as a countervailing force to business, liberals supported union penetration of industrial society. Union growth would produce greater balance in our economy and constitute a powerful force in support of ongoing New Deal programmes. Unionism spread; collective bargaining penetrated key industries; constructive and stable relations, developing during the war period, assured relative industrial peace. Little thought was given to the context from which unionism had emerged. Nor could its supporters foresee that traditional proposals for the correction of social-economic injustices and for industrial democracy would be subordinated to the role of a protective force for group interests, primarily for organised employees. Nor could they forecast the rehabilitation of management's position in society or its renewed ascendency in industrial relations and in restraining trade union penetration and power.

The trade union movement is currently faced by the challenge to redefine goals and methods. Should it abandon recent gestures toward greater collaboration with management as well as government and take a more militant stance? The questions arise at a time when the government returns to Democratic control and when new union leaders are taking over presidential posts at the AFL-CIO and at several national unions. Many serious questions confront the industrial relations system. Should the nation reaffirm its encouragement of unionism, bilateral decision-making and a countervailing system of private economic decision-making? How shall collective bargaining be articulated with the expanding role of Federal governmental economic and social direction? Shall unionism in the public sector be encouraged and how shall it be conducted in this area?

I. Characteristics of the United States industrial relations system

A. *System conditioned by law, administrative agencies and the judiciary*

In the thirties trade unions and collective bargaining were stimulated and protected by law, by the decisions of administrative agencies and by the judiciary; and it is understandable that these forces should play a central role in shaping the new industrial relations system. They have channelled developments within specific confines, imposing restraints, providing directions, distributing rights and obligations in response to questions posed by conflicts in the labour markets and by the changing public moods. Executive directives and laws reinforced the spontaneous surge toward unionisation among public employees. But the courts as well as administrative agencies are redefining the rights of individual employees and procedures for collective bargaining. Political executives and legislative bodies are seeking to retract the locus of final decision-making back to themselves suggesting for the future novel bargaining relationships in the public sector.

The significant legal instruments underlying the system include the National Labor Relations Act and its amendments, the state and local labour relations laws, the National War Labor Board, the Civil Rights Act (title VII), Age Discrimination in Employment Act, Occupational Safety and Health Act and Employee Retirement Income Security Act.

Labor relations laws initially dealt with the protection of the employees' rights to organise into unions, and to engage in bargaining through exclusive agents. Later amendments broadened the jurisdiction reaching into new industries. They also laid down rules for the conduct of union government and placed other restrictions on unions and managements. The National War Labor Board helped to mature bargaining procedures as well as the structure and contents of the agreements following from them. Other statutes prescribed specific terms of employment or personnel policy. The principle of voluntarism inherent in the system sanctioned governmental neutrality in unionisation drives and collective bargaining but did not block the detailed regulation of union operations or the enactment of individual terms of employment.

B. Decentralisation, fragmentation and uneven penetration

These forces moulded an industrial relations system characterised by a high degree of decentralisation, fragmentation and uneven penetration. Managements continually resisted and only grudgingly accepted unionism, and union leadership has had to battle for the rights of exclusive agent in each business separately. The result has been industrial tensions and combative attitudes but not any sense of class identification. With unions competing for bargaining rights in the same business, much inter-union conflict ensued, generating additional uneasiness and a sense of alienation among unions and their rank and file membership. Appeals had to build on local resentments and expectations.

The degree of penetration of trade unionism and collective bargaining has varied over time, sector, geography and occupation. National unions and employee associations in 1974 reported a membership of 23.4 million, with the associations accounting for 2.8 million or twelve per cent or 29.9 per cent of the employment in non-agricultural establishments. According to the 1970 household population survey 17.2 million employees or 20.4

per cent were identified as union members. The differences in numbers may be attributed to a rise in union and association membership of 1.6 million between these two dates, the reluctance of association members to record themselves as union members, and differences in data-collection methods.

Union membership in the non-governmental sector remained static and may have even declined during the last two decades despite the rise in the labour force. But the growth of unionism and collective bargaining in the public sector more than offset such trends, producing a net increase in union membership. Surveys of these in non-governmental enterprises with collective bargaining agreements covering a majority of the employees in both offices and plants in metropolitan areas showed a drop in the rate of coverage from seventy-three in 1960 to sixty-three in 1972–4, the shrinkage occuring in all regions and industrial sectors. Public sector unions and associations disclosed 5.3 million members in 1974 or 37.7 per cent of the employment. Federal employee membership was 52.6 and state and local government, 34.2 per cent, making the public sector one of the most extensively organised.

The uneveness of union organisation is disclosed in the 1970 households survey. The percentage of union members of different categories were as follows: men – 27.6 per cent; women – 10.3 per cent; white – 20.2 per cent; negro and others – 21.85 per cent; blue-collar workers – 39.3 per cent; service workers – 10.8 per cent; white-collar workers – 9.8 per cent; sales workers – 4.7 per cent. Percentages for major industries were: transportation and public utilities – 44.2 per cent; construction – 39.2 per cent; durable goods manufacturing – 28.7 per cent; public administration – 22.2 per cent; wholesale and retail – 10.2 per cent; services and finance – 7.8 per cent. And the rates for union members in the four national regions were: north central states – 25.6 per cent; north west – 25.0 per cent; west – 20.8 per cent; and the south – 11.4 per cent.

Public support for unionism and collective bargaining has significantly eroded. The Gallup poll noted that public approval declined from seventy-one per cent in the thirties to sixty per cent in the seventies with most of this change occuring when corruption was disclosed and more recently. Particularly significant is the shrinkage of support among liberals and youth, essential elements in any pro-labour coalition. Such polls and surveys, to be sure, are somewhat deceptive. Often those who are lukewarm in their response to inquiries about unions respond favorably to union efforts to improve their own conditions of employment.

The decentralisation of the industrial relations system is further reflected in the trade union and employer bargaining structures. National trade unions remain independent of the central body, the AFL-CIO, which has no authority to intervene into union collective bargaining. Nor can it help co-ordinate collective bargaining demands, strategy or achievements. Such activities remain the province of the individual unions. Those bargaining patterns as evolve tend to be set by the major industrial and building unions. Moreover, national unions often follow legislative objectives which promote their own special interests. Unions in the low-wage industries began the battle for federal minimum wage legislation long before the AFL-CIO concerned itself with this issue. The central body takes few initiatives in presenting the 'union case' to the public except for occasional statements by staff people.

The autonomous position of national unions is further illustrated by the abstention of three important national trade unions and some minor ones from the central body. These unions and employee associations are equal to half of the membership of the AFL-CIO.

Local union autonomy is a revered principle and particularly visible today in the local services and building trade unions. Locals in favourable bargaining situations repeatedly disregard pleas from national headquarters for moderate wage settlements. Hence the nationals have been favourably disposed to legislation curbing local unions, finding their own power too limited to pursue such a course.

As for management, there is no American equivalent to

the national employer-industrial relations spokesmen found in most European industrial nations. Large companies prefer to pursue their own individual policies. In the absence of a strong centralised trade union institution, with formidable economic or political power, there is no pressure to create comparable countervailing employer organisations. Local or industrial employer associations exist for highly unionised multi-employer bargaining units or are occasionally formed, as in the case of the local Constructions Users' councils and the Contractors Mutual Association, to promote a hardened and united attitude to union demands or to discourage leapfrogging of concessions.

C. Types of collective bargaining relations

Four basic types of management-union relations may be found in the USA. The first antedating the thirties is characterised by joint regulation and is the traditional one in which collective bargaining is customarily carried on by unions and employer associations. It is in local or dense industrial areas with many small companies.

The second, industrial government, evolved in the new era in places where the relationship has been tested over time and management has accomodated itself to labour's belief in unions and reliance on collective bargaining for the attainment of parity and protection. The classic cases of 'industrial peace' evolved from this type of relations. So too, do experiments seeking to improve the grievance system or productivity, or to deal with specific plant problems. There are even a few experiments in new styles of 'industrial democracy' though attempts are more frequently made to improve the quality of life at the workplace.

Unions in this setting become increasingly knowledgeable about the specific operating and economic problems of management. When external job threats develop, they may at times join the company in seeking protective public support, particularly in the field of imports. In recent recession years unions occasionally passed up gains or even agreed upon concessions to maintain an operation. Building trades locals, for instance, granted wage reductions or lifted restrictive work rules on a project or city-wide basis so that unionised contractors could bid competitively against non-union contractors, (who now perform forty per cent of commercial and industrial construction), or could undertake residential building or rehabilitation projects. Similar actions appear in other industries.

There have been two major structural changes involving large companies in the bargaining system. One is centralised bargaining with the larger company unit replacing individual plant negotiations. The second is co-ordinated bargaining in which separate national unions representing locals negotiating with a company join in a bargaining coalition. Managements at first resisted this approach but almost one hundred such arrangements now exist.

The third group of enterprises includes those seeking to discourage organisation and they maintain an adversary relation with unions after contracts are signed. Bilateral decision-making is repugnant to these managements. They stay within the law or at times judicially test decisions by administrative agencies, so as to minimise concessions made in the collective bargaining process.

The fourth group consists of enterprises deliberately and overtly resisting union penetration. An eminent electronics products manufacturer clearly expressed this approval declaring 'we shall spend a lot of money to fight a union tooth and nail'. To avoid unionisation management will shift operations to regions where unionism is not well established such as in rural areas or in the South, with the latter being a traditional haven for employers seeking protection against unions. Other states with right-to-work laws prohibiting union-employer agreements requiring employees to become union members or give financial support to the bargaining agent belong in this grouping.

Instead of declining over the years, as many had expected, the volume of cases handled by the National Labor Relations Board has recently risen sharply which

suggests mounting tension. Unfair labour charges (section 8
(a) (3) peaked at 15,090 in fiscal year 1976 or two and a half
times the number in 1961. More than sixty-four per cent of
these charges dealt with alleged discrimination and illegal
discharge of employees due to union activities. Equally
suggestive of the heightened tension is the large number of
charges alleging refusal to bargain, 6,729 in 1976. The
growing number of decertification elections, jumping from
124 in 1964 to 611 in 1976, provides another index of this
union-management conflict. The AFL-CIO Industrial
Union Department, in a study of 1970 NLRB union election
victories, found that five years after these elections unions
had secured and maintained contracts in only two out of
three cases.

Management representatives have become most artful in
using NLRB procedures to delay elections or contract
consummation. These factors, some employers realised,
produced higher costs and instability and were being
utilised by a minority of businesses to the disadvantage of
the remainder. They feared the consequence – namely,
changes in labour laws which would favour trade unions,
and they joined in proposing restraints on such abuses. But
the minority continued to violate the National Labor
Relations Act despite reprimands and penalities.
Apparently they prefer any costs to the acceptance of
unions and collective bargaining. The classic prototype in
this category has become the J. P. Stevens Co., a Southern
textile company which has effectively fought off unions.
The success of these anti-union employers stems in part
from the propaganda and conflicts which the campaigns
for the enactment and support of state right to work laws,
(permitted by section 7 (B) of the 1947 Taft-Hartley Act) have
prompted.

The trade union reaction to these attacks has been largely
formal and legalistic rather than the direct response that
might encourage public support. Investments in new
organisational drives, while thought significant for
individual unions, remain modest on balance. Though an
Organisational Department was established after the

merger in 1955 its resources are limited. It has helped initiate selected co-operative community campaigns and unlike the CIO, assumes that organisational efforts remain the responsibility of individual unions. Criticisms of NLRB procedures are more important; so too, the concerted efforts to secure amendments of the labour laws and to repeal section 7 (B) of the NLRA. Recently the AFL-CIO proposed penalties for companies failing to bargain, including the imposition of a check-off system for union contributions. But it has been reluctant to urge that a skeleton contract, including arbitration of grievances, be ordered for repeated violators of the law.

D. Concentration on wages, hours and working conditions

Much has been made of the singular preoccupation of our industrial relations with wages, hours and working conditions to the neglect of social and economic policies. But this outlook is not unique. Comparisons with employee attitudes abroad indicate a similar focus. What is distinctive, however, is the willingness of trade union leaders to be responsive to these attitudes and to avoid demands for enlarging the review and bargain over rights with management. But it was not always so. For example, CIO leaders well into the early fifties articulated and actively supported larger social programs. The reversion to 'bread and butter unionism' of an earlier era and the erosion of social idealism particularly among CIO unions have varying sources including the decline of social criticism and of attacks on corporate power among liberals, the pyramiding of such immediate problems as displacement from automation, low rates of economic growth, high unemployment, and the rising claims and growing protests of large ethnic groups and of young workers, as well as the economic instability of the organized industries, prodding key unions to greater co-operation with management.

In the early post-war decade unions did move to expand the area of mandatory bargaining, a goal which gained considerable support from the NLRB and from the courts.

They obtained various gains to bargain, involving incentive systems changes in methods of payment, as well as employee benefits and pensions, subcontracting, closure or contraction of plants, and the right to bargain on the workloads. But in their effort to limit management's 'reserved rights,' they encountered increasing vehemence, the companies insisted upon broader and clearer definitions of their protected areas for unilateral action. 'Management prerogative' clauses became increasingly common and the list of company rights, seeking to confine union jurisdiction to wages, hours and working conditions became more extensive. One UAW-management agreement includes a catalogue of decision-making liberties for the company which runs to more than a dozen pages. Furthermore, management undertook to pursuade union leadership, and often succeeded, on the merit of preserving its flexibility in plant operations so as to assure optimum profits, and its ability to finance improvements in employee benefits and better working conditions.

E.Legalistic rather than joint problem solving system

Many earlier pronouncements on collective bargaining regularly described it as a step toward or the very essence of industrial democracy, a new system of industrial government. And, in fact, the early agreements for highly competitive industries had indeed created joint industry-union, problem solving institutions to promote interests. Management sought competitive stability and unions, a system of standard rates and rules. The agreement became the basis for understandings which would promote these objectives rather than a rigid code of rules dictating behavior. Invariably joint agencies headed by impartial umpires helped to resolve differences.

With the thirties, the collective agreement became a formal legal instrument. Its terms defined management-union obligations and responsibilities. Unspecified rights were successfully co-opted by management as an area reserved for its unilateral discretion. Under the older system of bargaining unions assumed considerable if not the primary responsibility for the administration of agreements. Under the new arrangement management took this initiative, relegating employees and union officials to the role of the complainant. The agreement itself grew in size as it included the actual instrument, the arbitrator's interpretations and supplemental instruments. It became the artifact of the labour law coming under careful scrutiny of counsel for both parties. Vagueness of phrase promoted new conflicts, rather than opportunities for working out new understandings, thus the administrative process provided further occasions for haggling and the adversary relationship hardened.

Complaints are relevant only if they charge violations of specific contract terms. Procedures for handling grievances are carefully spelt out, the underlying assumption being that issues would be resolved at the lowest level by the foreman and shop-steward. But actual practice forced appeals to higher levels, cluttering up the pipeline, leaving grievances festering and creating frustration and disillusionment. In a few celebrated cases as International Harvester, the steel industry, and arrangements sponsored by the United States Federal Mediation and Conciliation Service efforts have been made to strengthen the machinery at the lowest procedural levels. Such efforts, however, requiring specific agreements and considerable investment of personnel and time have not generally been taken.

Many difficulties in handling grievances have developed other than this tendency to funnel them to the top appeals officials. The amount of training of the first level officials falls below that of earlier years. Management's representatives have become more sophisticated and the subject matter, more technical as increasingly advanced company control practices and employee benefits, pensions and safety are introduced. Local union shop officials find it necessary to obtain more technical assistance, but few national trade unions have adequate personnel for local needs. Trade union views respecting the limitations of techniques or goals remain at best vaguely defined;

members and local officials react to irritants rather than bargain for the establishment of a system more consistent with their interests. Strangely enough only isolated academic studies of the grievance process and the technical issues have been made.

The mounting requests for arbitration panels dramatise the limitations of the system. But the system itself, increasingly legalistic, protracted and costly has also produced bitterness. The arbitrators tend to be conservative. Unions have called for expedited and less expensive procedures and several have instituted shortcuts as in the steel and postal industries, and the American Arbitration Association as well as the Federal Mediation and Conciliation Service. These include pre-selection of arbitrators, elimination of lawyers, briefs and transcripts, discontinuance of costly additions such as meeting halls, and the substitution of bench awards for long opinions. But these ventures are still unusual. Legalistic rather than problem solving approaches continue to dominate the administrative process.

With the introduction of new anti-discrimination laws and the organisation of administrative agencies to enforce them, grieved employees now have an external channel for securing remedies. Employees may file charges of discrimination in employment. Voluntary settlements and court decision have produced significant changes in personnel policy affecting seniority and lay-offs, thereby further subordinating the voluntaristic and problem-solving character of the collective bargaining process.

F. Public sector bargaining increasingly politicised

With the spread of unionism and collective bargaining in the public sector, and of agencies financed by public and philanthropic funds, begins a new chapter in the history of our industrial relations system. The growing significance of these trends for the larger union movement is apparent but the ultimate impact is difficult to project. They will doubtlessly and profoundly affect its outlook and activities much as did earlier groups, such as the mass production worker.

Low rewards, capricious and unformulated personnel practices, and unilateral decision-making provided the original impetus for public unionism. Collective bargaining has substantially improved employment conditions in many areas, considerably narrowing the gap with the private sector. But the latter bargaining procedure is being found inadequate and often inappropriate for the public sector. The multiplicity of employee organisations with different philosophies for public employee representation and degrees of commitment to collective bargaining within the same governmental unit are proving troublesome, if not unworkable. And the financial crunch, especially in local and state governments, has thrown the unions back to defensive positions, calling for moderation of demands, agreements to cutbacks in employment and to budgetary reallocation to the different services, and consent to limitations upon salary increases and to savings derived from higher productivity. Public employees have become scapegoats for local difficulties and the target of structural governmental reforms. Advanced managerial techniques are being introduced to secure higher production quotas, tighter staff schedules, and more intimate controls. Citizen resistance to tax increases has made it popular for elected chief executives and legislators to resist union demands and at times unilaterally to modify or cancel agreements, basing their decisions on the ultimate sovereignty of government. Unions have therefore been forced to supplement their bargaining activities with more intensive lobbying, appeals to the public for support, and advocacy of new methods of financing community services including federal aid and at times re-allocation of funds, thereby emphasising the political nature of the bargaining process in the public sector.

II. United States system highly prone to industrial action

Though the nation's industrial relations system is among

the least prone to political strikes and labour generally lacks a sense of class identity, the rate of industrial action is among the highest of industrial countries. Since 1963 its rate of days lost from industrial stoppages per 1000 employees was exceeded frequently only by countries like Canada, Ireland and Italy. There is little support for the thesis that strike activity is declining here or in other industrial nations. In the United States, it continued at a high rate even during recent periods of wage control, with the annual rate of days lost standing on the average of 36 million for 1971–75. The number of strikes actually climbed from the 5,000 level in the sixties to 6,000 in the mid 1970's.

No doubt the highly fragmented nature of the industrial relations patterns accounts for the high frequency of walkouts. Over ninety per cent of the days lost are associated with negotiations of new agreements or demands for union recognition clauses. The concentration is particularly high in specific industries and areas. About a third of the actual strikes, a slightly lower proportion of those involved, and a minor part of the work days lost occur during the term of the agreement, usually in the form of wildcat and unauthorised strikes. Other kinds of active protest also occur such as working to rules, lowered production and quality, and absenteeism, as well as rejection of negotiated contracts.

III. Management and unions cultivate political leadership

Neither management nor unions have since the thirties been associated with third, or minor parties. They have worked through the existing political system; the two dominant parties are in fact coalitions of state parties reflecting a wide range of political opinions. American labour, particularly the manual worker and low income groups, has maintained close ties with the Democratic parties for historical, ethnic, and leadership reasons and their political orientation.

Business and trade union political activity concentrates first on the election of officials favourable to their respective views and influencing legislators, executives and administrators through lobbying activities.

Trade unions maintain political action committees financed through the membership voluntary contributions, from which funds are granted to favoured candidates during election campaigns. Their members and officials also assist these candidates through programmes of voter registration, political communications, endorsements and aids for assuring actual voting. Business too, traditionally provided financial aid to candidates, bringing many to disrepute, as in the Watergate and subsequent scandals. Because of recent legislation, corporations have also set up political action committees for raising funds to influence the voting pattern of stockholders and management employees. Considerable interest is also now focused on congressional and local elections. Neither unions nor business can dictate or dominate the processes of candidate selection, except in some local areas, but each seeks to influence the choice. Though trade unions, with few exceptions, have remained closely allied with the Democratic parties, they do not control or overwhelmingly influence them even with respect to labour issues. The Democratic organisations operate independently through its party officials which include few active unionists.

Facing a roster of elected executive and legislative officers and administrators, both business and unions act through personal influence and lobbies to gain their political ends. Both groups offer statements at public hearings or privately circulate them to acquaint legislators and officials with their views. Lobbies represent the main channel for promoting desirable or discouraging, or modifying, unwanted legislation or administrative actions. Trade unions occasionally assemble their leaders in the state or national capitals to emphasise their position or engage in lobbying. Mass demonstrations are rarely employed. Lobbyists are usually full-time officials supported by occasional part-time recruits. The corporate community, for its part has recently constituted a Business Roundtable to co-ordinate its lobbying efforts.

IV. Recent improvements in earnings and benefits modest

Collective bargaining institutionalised the national trend toward high earnings and expanding benefits for labour. Unions negotiated substantial wage increases in the 1930s and labour and social legislation included a federal minimum wage, a forty-hour week, and unemployment insurance and social security laws. Consequently, earnings were now supplemented by extensive private and public 'social benefits.' A high base for world comparisons resulted. In the same decade unions also erased the traditional practice of cutting wages during recessions; they negotiated contracts which became the pace-setters for all industry.

The historic UAW-General Motors agreement set another landmark by providing for annual wage increases of three per cent and an automatically protected wage level which was adjusted to rising costs of living. Other industries either followed this formula or negotiated similar substantive packages. Out of these negotiations evolved the practice of the long-term contract, extending from two to five years, including provisions for deferred wage increases. The union demand for a guaranteed annual wage led in 1955 to a supplementary unemployment insurance benefit, granted primarily in the automobile and steel industries. The fifties also recorded major innovations and improvements in fringe benefits including pension systems, health and welfare programmes, more paid holidays as well as more weeks of paid vacation for long service employees. Powerful unions secured job guarantees, shares in profits or other bonuses as *quid pro quos* for the relaxation of restrictions on work assignments, the introduction of technical and job changes or accelerated retirements; weak unions received less or nothing. The differences in benefits grew among industries, and among plants in the same industry, with unionised companies usually enjoying the best terms.

Beginning with the early sixties, real improvements in

wages and benefits became more moderate. Agreements generally conformed to the guides negotiated in previous decades. The hourly earnings index annually rose on an average of 3.1 per cent in current and 1.6 per cent in real dollars (1960–6), with the latter hardly equalling the level of the 1948 UAW-GM contract. Spurred on by advances among construction workers and by resurgent rises in living costs, labour grew more militant and took on corporations which resisted union demands. Work days lost from industrial strife jumped from forty-eight million in 1967 to a peak of 66.4 million in 1970, with an annual average of fifty million (1967–71). The major settlements for this period (1966–70) netted on the average 6.6 per cent wage rise with a peak of 9.1 in 1970. The average annual increase in the hourly earnings index for the period (1966–70) was 5.7 per cent in current dollars and 1.3 per cent in real terms.

Contract improvements remained modest owing to wage controls prevailing through April 1974, to severe recessions, and to declining bargaining power in several key unionised industries. The improvements in major settlements averaged annually (1971–6) 7.3 per cent with a peak of 8.8 per cent in 1971. In real terms it was 0.6 per cent. Union industries and members fared better than non-union ones. The hourly earnings index rose at an average annual rate of 7.5 per cent and the real index, 0.6 per cent. But the real hourly earnings of many union and non-union employees actually declined.

Incremental improvements were made in fringe benefits. Health benefits were extended to optical, dental care and prescription drugs in some contracts. Major medical schemes became more common as did maternity benefits. The sixth-week vacation with pay was offered in selected cases to long-service employees. In 1976 the automobile workers negotiated a provision for additional twelve paid days of holidays in the third year of the contract. Unions in a few instances gained the right to inspect health and safety conditions in their plants and to examine health expert reports. Legal pre-paid services were obtained in some agreements.

Along with these improvements came gains in publicly provided benefits. Employer private benefits rose from 12.1 per cent of compensation for working time for production workers in manufacturing industries in 1959 to 18.8 per cent in 1972. Employer payments for public social insurance systems expanded in the same period from 4.8 to 7.8 per cents, which was double the rate of increased private benefits. Other public benefits are financed by general federal, state and local taxes.

During the sixties and thereafter earnings as well as private and public social benefits increased more rapidly in other industrial countries. The forty-hour week has become universal. The gap narrowed so that at present employee real earnings, private and public benefits, and job guarantees in these countries, particularly Sweden and West Germany, exceed those enjoyed by the American worker.

V. Is the reassessment of the United States trade union movement imminent?

Since the middle fifties critics have urged the AFL-CIO to reassess its future course. Such an examination has not occurred. But union leaders now more widely recognise the need for fresh thinking. Some favour a more ambitious organisational campaign and the elimination of multi-union efforts on the same target. Others urge new publicity campaigns and sweeping revisions of policies and the extension of activities.

In 1974 an *an hoc* government commission, including labour leaders, seriously considered limiting the rights of union members to facilitate the acceptance of negotiated agreements. But the sentiment has changed. It is reflected in the popular support for insurgent candidates for the high union offices. These candidates call for greater rank-and-file participation in decision-making, more local autonomy, and militant union behavior when dealing with large conglomerates and transnational corporations. Demands are being made for more aggressive support for government aid as well as legislation which would complement collective bargaining and universalise benefits and protection, extending them to the disadvantaged and minority groups. While the immediate successor for George Meaney as head of the AFL-CIO appears settled, there is talk that the new President's term would be cut short by union leaders demanding a more aggressive stance. The newly elected officers of national unions, though generally recruited from the current leadership ranks, seek new policies and programs to distinguish themselves. Their attitudes are likely to be strengthened by management's anti-union position, the growing proportion of unorganised workers and by the changes in industrial employment profiles which challenge existing unions.

Underlying the new movements is the assumption that union leaders will ultimately respond without past restraints to the call for greater aggressiveness, and that it will promote more innovative incremental changes to satisfy employee aspirations, broaden union appeals, limit management where necessary and expand its demands on government. Unions' appeal to blacks and women will have to increase since they constitute an ever expanding proportion of the work force. The direction will be away from an insistance on a special interest-oriented outlook to a broader class orientation, such as appears in current European unionism. The growing importance of public sector unions will undoubtedly reinforce the impulse to reassess and reorient.

VI. Managements are adaptative and sophisticated

American management successfully improved its image in the war and post-war periods discarding its image as scapegoat for all of the evils in society and in the shop. During the two eight-year terms of Republican presidents this rehabilitation was strongly reinforced as business values and policies have been increasingly entrenched. The Laboristic Age, a phrase coined to express management anxieties over union domination, turned into a period of Management Ascendancy.

During this post-war period corporate business became bigger and more pursuasive. Growth, mergers and conglomerates created corporate giants spanning diverse industries. After 1965, the nation's businesses penetrated Europe and other areas, and multiplied the number and importance of American-based transnational corporations, particularly in the manufacturing field. These immense financial and production structures with their varied sources of goods and huge financial reserves were better positioned to resist unions and their demands.

Management sophistication in the handling of industrial relations also grew. New arts for combatting unions appeared. Many assisted by academicians introduced newer personnel and management techniques, that diminished the possibilities for union penetration. 'Human relations' approaches gave way to new 'organisational behaviour' orientations which stressed personal job satisfaction, and higher productivity and stability at the workplace. Some innovations were made to meet the demands for improved quality of life but none toward satisfying the workers' total life goals. University trained personnel displaced factory promoted supervisors and facilitated the adoption and implementation of these new ideas and tools. Corporations negotiating with unions met union demands with counterdemands and asked for *quid pros quos* to protect their 'managerial rights'. Some companies deliberately co-operated with unions and engaged in collective bargaining, recognising the value of unions in securing greater group cohesion and discipline, a more productive work force, the sanctions useful for management's performance and in discouraging class orientation.

VII. Final observations

Public support has weakened for the three basic premises of the nation's industrial relations system; namely, encouragement to organise into collective bodies, trade unions; bilateral decision-making within the enterprise on matters affecting labour's interests; and privately organised countervailing forces to insure economic stability as well as equitable price and resource allocation decisions. Concurrently, the large conglomerate and transnational corporations gained greater sway over the economy and society and management focused on internal plant strategies to win the acquiesence of individual workers to their position. The result has been a wide diversity of labour-management patterns. The nation's executive and legislative branches became more central to the operation of the economy, imposing accomodations on the conflicting interests through political decisions as well as increased intervention, regulation, and directives. But business continued to preach the doctrine of free enterprise, denigrating the expansion of governmental action. Neo-classical economic theories and conservative philosophies enjoyed a revival completely unforeseen by their critics.

The trade-union movement remained a bastion of concentrated membership in selected areas. But it faced new problems in the private sector as key industries experienced serious competitive problems, and reduced their total employment, particularly of blue collar employees, thereby weakening union bargaining power. Unions in the public sector now are encountering legislative and executive opposition, as services are constricted, some contracts are cancelled, and others trimmed for reasons of economy.

Factors then, are planning the way for substantial changes in the procedures, practices and philosophies of the industrial relations system. Debates on the future developments have hardly begun as academics and the adversaries do not wish to face up to the realities. It is impossible to project the future course. There are many alternatives and controversy and actual events have yet to define the most likely roads.

13 The future of industrial relations in Europe

JACK A. PEEL.

The structure and background

Do we stand on the threshold of a new prosperity or on the brink of economic disaster and can the world's formidable technological armour co-exist peacefully with its ramshackle social machinery? The answer to these crucial questions will depend largely on whether industrial relations can be improved, though the prospects for improvement are linked to the swirling tide of social and economic changes induced by science, technology, education and communications. The trends suggest a bumpy ride ahead for industrial relations practitioners in Europe. If industrial relations are bad, they poison the social climate and impede economic progress. Conversely, there is a striking correlation between good industrial relations and economic success, with Germany, Switzerland, Sweden, Denmark and Norway being among the leaders, closely followed by Austria, Holland, Belgium and France.

Before gazing into the crystal ball, however, the main structural strands of trade union and employer organisations should be outlined. They mirror the diversities of the societies in which they exist. Britain, for instance, had a trade union movement before such basic state activities as compulsory education or universal male suffrage. On the Continent trade union development was on average fifty years behind that of Britain – a reflection of the British lead in industrialisation. On the Continent, however, egalitarian influences, frequently descended from French Revolutionary ideas, were at work far earlier.

Political and legal remedies for grievances tended to be used more on the Continent than in Britain and their industrial relations have retained this legal tone since that time.

Many European countries, for example, had laws regulating collective agreements long before Britain had laws dealing with trade union organisation. Works councils too, have evolved into powerful bodies with legal rights and do much to compensate for the fragmented nature of Continental trade unionism since they represent the workforce of whole plants, irrespective of individual union affiliations. Another variation is that in Ireland, Denmark, the UK and Germany, the unions group mainly into one national confederation, but in many other European countries there is more than one national trade union centre, each being distinguished by ideological commitments.

Running from left to right in political terms, they group as follows: Communist, Socialist and Social Democratic; Christian and Christian democratic. But not all these divisions are found in every state and not all the individual members share the same ideological views of their union or grouping. There are Social Democrats in Communist Unions and Communists in Social Democratic Unions. Moreover, the nature of the national organisations varies considerably. Some like the British TUC are loose advisory bodies, albeit with great influence, whilst others, like the French Communist Group (CGT) or the Italian Communists (CGIL) are tightly organised for concerted political action.

The three main ideological groups are as follows:

The Christian (confessional) and Christian Democrat The confessional unions are found in Belgium, Holland, France, Italy, Luxembourg and Germany and concentrate more on improving wages and working conditions than promoting radical social change or revolution. In the Netherlands, the division between rival Christian beliefs has led to the creation of separate groupings of Protestant and Roman Catholic Unions (the CNV and RKWV). Despite these divisions, these two groupings, together with the other national trade union centre, the socialist NVV, work well together. The attraction of common interests overcomes the pull of conflicting ideologies. The gap between the confessional and Social Democratic Unions is sometimes filled by Christian Democrats, who lay less emphasis on religious issues than some confessional unions.

Socialist/Social Democrat Most of the unions come in this category, though the dividing lines between the two above named groups are blurred. The Social Democrat unions are generally linked to the Social Democratic parties and this emphasises consensus rather than conflict, while some of the Socialist unions merge imperceptibly into the Communist unions.

Communists The two largest Communist union groups are found in Italy and France. In general they look to revolution rather than reform and look to political leadership from members of the Communist Party. The Italian CGIL, however, was recently allowed to affiliate to the ETUC and has pledged itself to work through the Italian constitutional system to achieve its ends.

The parent trade union organisation for Europe is the ETUC (European Trade Union Confederation) which held its first Congress in 1973. At the time of its second Congress in April 1976, it had thirty affiliated national trade union organisations with a total membership of thirty-seven millions, including the powerful British TUC and German DGB. Christian trade union confederations in Europe are also affiliated to the ETUC. The only major European trade union outside the ETUC at present is the French CGT, but it may make an application for affiliation in the future.

The main strength of the ETUC is in its relationships with the European Community and with the European Commission in particular, with which it has close and comprehensive links. The ETUC favours the creation of industrial committees and six have already been approved. They are the European Metalworkers' Federation (EMF), the

European Federation of Agricultural Workers' Unions in the Community (EFA), the Trade Union Committee of the PTTI for the EEC countries, the European Regional Organisation of the International Federation of Commercial, Clerical and Technical Employees (Euro-Fiet), the Metal Workers and Miners' International Committee and the European Committee of the International Secretariat of Entertainment Trade Unions.

The role of these industrial committees is still evolving, but already they have given certain industries a specific European dimension and are seen by the ETUC as a key element in the European structure of trade unionism. The ETUC has the same basic dilemma as the European Community in recognising diversity in national patterns of organisation, but striving for steady progress on a common front at the same time.

The Union of Industries in the European Community (UNICE) was set up in 1958. As its name implies, it covers the Community countries and brings together the central employers' federations in the Nine. Greece has also been associated with UNICE since 1962. Amongst its aims is that of 'encouraging the elaboration of an industrial policy in a European spirit'. Its work also includes studying the activities being pursued in the institutions of the European Community and making known the views of industry. Two important committees consisting of permanent delegates and experts facilitate these tasks. Like the ETUC, UNICE has close and continuous links with the relevant Directorates-General of the European Commission.

Multinational companies – their problems and opportunities

Most people roundly denounce or stoutly defend multinational companies which are in themselves a rueful commentary on modern democratic society – a sort of sad barometer of its strengths and weaknesses. They reflect man's technological ingenuity, the ruthlessness of the boardroom power game, the inability of national governments to cope adequately with international business problems and the need to relate the profit motive more closely to social responsibility.

To denounce multinationals in general is as unrealistic as presenting them as benign institutions devotedly working for the public good. The truth is probably between these two positions. They bring considerable benefits to society and create a plethora of problems. They are a pertinent example of the gap between man's technological brilliance and society's ramshackle social machinery. In a nutshell, multinationals have been trapped by the speed of their own advance. They have far outdistanced their running-mates, governments and trade unions, who have to work in a more ponderous, participative – some would say devious! – way. Multinationals now stand exposed to criticisms, often trenchant, based on a mixture of fact and misunderstanding.

In a wider sense too, industry and society are on a collision course, due to the inherent conflict between nationalism, which divides the world into smaller compartments and segregates the human race into smaller groups, and industrialism, which tends to embrace the whole globe. Raw materials are needed and markets sought in every corner of the earth. This incompatibility between political and economic life has produced two wars during this century and motivated bodies like the UN, the ILO, the OECD and the European Communities – organisations not just idealistically conceived, but rooted in a practical awareness of the problem. Multinational companies are the sensitive nerve-endings of this historical conflict.

It may seem arrogant, but someone has to try and assemble the pieces of this social jig-saw, a puzzle created by the cumulative effect on industry of science, war, education, poverty and technology. In the absence of a co-ordinated response from governments and trade unions to multinationals, the European Community is working hard to forge a new framework of social accountability within which such firms will operate. Putting it with absolute candour, there is no time to wait for codes of conduct to be meticulously devised by academics and politicians. In the nature of things they will argue about such a code for years, whereas the pressures on industrial relations systems are already beginning to look dangerous. Action is required now in the form of a 'holding operation'.

This does not mean that the Community is opposed to multinationals as such – indeed, they are an obvious and integral part of the drive to increase the wealth of the Community and ensure its fairer distribution. But it does mean reminding such organisations that more power means more responsibility. Unless this is forthcoming, then a blind and unyielding resistance to big firms as such will develop amongst workers, with a consequent deterioration in industrial relations. The European Community believes it can devise effective controls in this field, as unlike the UN, OECD and the ILO, which have no legal powers to implement policies in member countries, the Community is a political organisation with a system of laws and the institutional means to enforce them. There are Regulations, which are binding on member states – Decisions, which are also binding but with geographical selectivity – Directives, which are binding as to ends but with implementational flexibility and Recommendations and Opinions, which rely on the force of a moral commitment.

Despite the political sensitivity of the subject, the Commission has sent nine Directives to the Council of Ministers since the end of 1973, on matters directly concerning multinationals. Only two have been agreed so far – those which remove gross disparities between national laws on mass redundancies and protect workers' acquired rights when transfers of ownership take place. The other seven Directives being studied by the Council concern:

1. A Statute for European Companies.
2. The structure of limited companies, including worker participation.
3. Common tax arrangements applying to parent companies and their subsidiaries in different member states.

4. Common tax arrangements applying to mergers, hivings off and the transfer of assets between companies in different member states.
5. The harmonisation of national laws applying to mergers.
6. The compulsory prior notification of mergers.
7. The establishment of a Community guarantee system for private investment outside the Community.

The foregoing measures form a coherent network designed to give companies the autonomy and economic elbow-room they need to operate successfully, but within a new social and economic framework giving greater weight to the human aspects of business.

Take, for instance, the acquired rights Directive previously mentioned. This is designed to protect the basic rights and privileges which workers accrue after long service with a firm and which are all too often lost when transfers of ownership occur. It means that an acquiror firm will inherit liability for the acquired rights of workpeople in the firm being taken over. It will involve the automatic transfer of the employment relationship from the former employer to the new one and the protection of workers against dismissal solely on the grounds of the change in the structure of the firm.

Measures like this are made necessary by the rapidly rising number of transfers of ownership and control of companies in recent years. In some Community countries this trend has resulted in a situation where the share of industrial turnover of the hundred largest industrial undertakings has risen to fifty per cent of the total. These developments may be economically justifiable, but the problems they pose for workers are obvious and serious. Where such changes take place according to civil law rules of transfer, workpeople have no legal right to have their previous employment relationship passed on automatically to the new controlling undertaking. If the new owner refuses to take over the previous employment relationship, then the workers concerned lose their jobs. Even if the new owner is willing to preserve their jobs, he has the right to make further employment dependent on a change in the terms of employment, thereby abolishing the acquired rights of the workers concerned. This is a small segment of the problem area surrounding the activities of many large companies and makes it easy to see why multinational companies are becoming political punch-bags.

Adam Smith may not have been wholly wrong when he equated the pursuit of self-interest with the public good provided the pursuit is enlightened. It would be utterly naive, however, to assume that this entrepreneurial dictum can take European industrial society through its present trauma. I believe the role of multinational enterprises is fourfold:

(a) To maximise profit.
(b) Reward fairly those who create the profit.
(c) Involve workers closely in management decision taking.
(d) Meet wider social and communal responsibilities.

These aims are intrinsically right. They are civilised and a blend of the practical and idealistic. The concept of worker participation has a key role in the Commission's strategy on multinationals. I have not developed the arguments as they are being handled adequately in another part of this book and in the welter of documents and meetings on the subject. Suffice it to say that worker participation is morally justifiable, democratically desirable and almost certainly economically beneficial.

Similarly, the ways in which a co-ordinated trade union response to multinationals might be developed bristles with complications. Possible platforms on which to build such a response might be the ICFTU world trade union organisation, the International Trade Secretariats which cover individual industrial sectors and the Joint Committee structure within the European Commission, which already embraces seven industries with many others in prospect. These Joint Committees are voluntary, bipartite and sectoral and are gradually introducing a European dimension to industrial relations at a pace decided by the participants. Apart from the varied structures and political disposition of European Trade Unions, most of them are sorely pressed on their home fronts finding answers to inflation and unemployment. This stretches their leadership capacity to the limit and makes the longer-term but equally important task of a co-ordinated approach to multinational industrial relations seem a little academic. Trade unions are alive to this danger of the growing power of multinationals being rivalled only by the growing number of books, articles and conferences about them. The risk is that familiarity with the subject gleaned in this way, without a picture of what needs to be done, might induce cynicism or indifference. Trade unionists, however, are aware of the fact that an effective response to the challenge of multinational companies must be made on two fronts. One is within the companies themselves and the other is through co-operation with the community as a whole.

My theme is not to catalogue the sins or virtues of multinational companies, but to stress the need for them to assume a level of social responsibility consonant with their economic powers, which have tended to put them outside the normal instruments of control provided by governments and trade unions. Until such bodies can provide effective social counter-weights, the European Community is trying to devise minimum standards of social accountability in the form of new European laws. This legislation has started and will continue to develop. It should be accepted as a fact of industrial life, not only by multinational firms operating within the Community, but by the executives in multinational headquarters located outside the Community. There are also various ways of contributing to Community affairs and influencing the law-making process. There are over seventy consultative bodies which assist the Community, most of them containing representatives of employers' organisations. At ministerial level, trade union and employer representatives meet Employment Ministers in Tripartite Social Conferences from time to time. Moreover, the nine Council Ministers each represent a member Government, the actual Ministers depending on the subject under discussion.

Finally, it should be said that the Commission itself has to consult comprehensively governments, employers and trade unions, both formally and informally, on all aspects of its work. If multinational companies feel a persecution complex developing, they should remember this and make sure their views are expressed with vigour and cogency. Meanwhile, the Commission will no doubt seem like a referee with a piercing whistle and a gimlet eye for infringements in the rules of the industrial game.

Evolution towards European collective bargaining

Linked with the sensitive problems of multinational companies is the equally emotive and wider topic of Euro-bargaining. This must eventually come, if only because collective bargaining must generally reflect the scale of economic activities to be realistic. If company law is being harmonised between European countries to facilitate more trade and the barriers preventing the free flow of labour and capital are being loosened, then bargaining must at some stage adjust to this wider spectrum. Understandably, neither unions nor employers are enthusiastic about the concept at present. Employers see themselves being saddled with impossible commitments and punitive additions to labour costs, not to mention the threat of 'Euro-strikes', whilst unions are apprehensive about losing their hard won autonomy. So employers generally are afraid of 'levelling-up' agreements, whilst unions in the richer European countries do not enthuse about a possible 'levelling-down' process, which would erode their favoured position.

There are two other arguments in favour of giving a European dimension to collective bargaining. It is felt by many to be morally wrong for gross and continuous disparities to exist between the wages and conditions of workpeople doing the same work in different countries. Some variations will always exist and reflect the historical and economic background of the industries concerned, though blatant differences are hard to justify. Moreover, substantial differences in wages and conditions between the

same industries in different countries tend to make
industrial relations abrasive in the country with the adverse
comparison. The British miners, for example, were made
aware by the media and their participation in the
Consultative and Joint Committees of the European
Commission of the earlier retirement pension provisions of
miners in Germany, France and Belgium. They pressed
hard for the same facilities, obtaining a compromise which
reflected common sense and negotiating ingenuity, but the
seeds were sown by the Joint Committee contacts.

The Commission's Joint Committees are voluntary,
bipartite and sectoral. They have developed sporadically
since the 1950's and currently cover seven industries – coal,
steel, agriculture, sea-fishing, road transport, rail transport
and inland waterway navigation. Another dozen such
committees are in various stages of formation and include
such industries as films and television, footwear, gas and
electricity, shipping and civil aviation. They begin by
discussing training, safety and similar topics. Many are
moving steadily towards consideration of fringe benefits.
No pressure is brought to bear on those committees by the
Commission and they practically decide their own agendas.
These developments are slow and fluid, but the trend is
inexorable towards eventual European collective
bargaining, perhaps on minimum standards, not a hard
comprehensive framework, though it will take some time.

The problems to be solved are obvious. There are varied
bargaining patterns and procedures within as well as
between member states which involve plant and national
bargaining systems in different ratios. Secondly, wage
bargaining must be related to fringe benefit bargaining,
which is part of the overall cost of a collective agreement.
Here again, the patterns vary in member states. Broadly
speaking, the original six member countries of the
Community have given greater weight to the fringe
element in bargaining than the three new countries. The
same point could be made about Sweden, Norway, Austria
and Switzerland also.

Thirdly, many European countries are practising wage

restraint in one form or another and seem likely to do so for the foreseeable future, thus emphasising the problem created by wage differentials and making difficult the national discussion of harmonised bargaining at local level. In the long run, a type of European collective bargaining will develop but it seems likely to take the form of setting minimum standards at national and then at international level. The honest answer, therefore, is that the possibility of harmonised wage bargaining of any kind seems unlikely until the present economic difficulties of European countries ease substantially. The desirability of such moves should also be for the social partners to consider. European collective bargaining will only come if they want it. Harmonised wage bargaining, like good industrial relations, cannot be imposed from above. It must come from mutual trust between all the parties concerned.

Future industrial relations trends

I doubt if there has ever been a more difficult time to forecast future developments in the industrial relations field, but I accept the challenge. European industrial relations are in a state of dynamic change and there is considerable unrest. Some of the influences which have created this picture will continue to shape future developments. They are as follows:

The complexity of modern industry making it more vulnerable to stoppages of work. The interdependency of sectors means that strikes in a small sector can render thousands idle.

The pace of industrial change has brought elements of insecurity into the working lives of millions of people, in contrast to their expectations.

The challenge to authority patterns has begun to permeate all sections of our society and has wider sociological origins. It sometimes leads to outright rejection of the law and the rules of society.

Improved education and better communications have produced people who are less willing to be deferential and expect to get more out of life and work.

Bigness in industry has resulted from the fast pace of technological change in post-war years, which has been made necessary by persistent demands for greater influence. Size of organisations has in general been beneficial but it has produced two major human problems for shop-floor workers: exclusion from important work decisions and a tendency for work to become repetitive and monotonous. Alienation from key decisions in large firms and soul-destroying monotony at work have accordingly produced a happy hunting ground in which jostle genuine reformers, sincere idealists and unfortunately some whose motives are sinister and destructive.

The point about bigness can be made another way. The dominant institutions in the post-war Western economies have been the welfare state, the big trade unions and the big firm. They have provided the basis for political stability and material progress. The welfare state has given full employment until recently and social security by the means of liberal, parliamentary democracy. The big unions have ensured that most manual workers got their share of the cake and the big firm has generated technological momentum and induced the economy to produce more goods for the average citizen and made poverty an abnormal condition.

The very success of these institutions has created new problems which are difficult to solve. With their minds sharpened by better education, their bodies cushioned by the welfare state and their spirits bored by the even pace of material progress, people have become more demanding and more reckless in the actions they are prepared to take if their demands are not met. Having been hoist by our own petard in this way, we must not dismiss as hackneyed the phrases 'social justice', 'the quality of life' and 'worker participation'. They represent the deep feelings of people who are confused by the speed and complexity of social change.

There are six key influences or trends which are likely to shape future industrial relations techniques in Europe.

The first is unemployment, which persists at relatively high levels and will clearly dominate the agendas of most business meetings for the foreseeable future. Its intractability has focused attention on work-sharing, job creation schemes and earlier retirement. These topics will obviously become part of the collective bargaining spectrum because of their intrinsic importance. A reduction of working hours per week or an increase in annual leave may have a favourable influence on the employment situation if there is, in general, only partial wage compensation, though this is being contested by the unions, who point to the savings in unemployment benefit if people find work as a result of shorter hours being implemented.

Limits on overtime may be needed too. These could be achieved, in principle, by increasing the cost of overtime or by compensating for overtime in one period by reducing hours in another period. Flexible retirement schemes are being increasingly considered, especially for members doing difficult and hazardous work. It might be possible to offer early retirement to older people who have been unemployed for some time. The financing of such schemes, in particular, is very much in the domain of industrial bargainers. Earlier retirement for older, unemployed workers already oeprates under German law, whilst in Belgium male workers aged sixty or over and female workers aged fifty-five or more may be eligible for earlier retirement allowances if they are replaced by unemployed persons under thirty. High unemployment seems likely to stay with us for several years. It is therefore sensible to make work-sharing part of the bargaining agenda and a firm plank in social policy.

The second key influence on future industrial relations is the trickle (the cynics would say, a flood) of protective legislation emanating from national governments and in particular from the European Community. Some of these new European laws have been briefly mentioned in the section dealing with multinational companies, but there are others dealing with equal pay, migrant workers and safety, hygiene and health protection. A vocational training centre has also been established in Berlin and a foundation to study the working environment has been set up in Berlin.

These are just a few of the forty measures which formed the Social Action Programme carried out by the European Commission between 1973–6. The new Commission is deciding on its work programme, but a draft directive dealing with conflicts of law in intra-community employment relationships is already being studied by the Council and preliminary work is being done on new measures concerning protection of young workers, the rights of workers when their firm becomes insolvent and procedures for individual dismissals. This sample of legislative items already in train indicates the dimensions of the social shield, which is being constructed to counterbalance the social consequences of bigness in European industry. The industrial relations practitioner will do well to tune in these developments, both in his own country and in the European Commission.

The third influence is the persistence of incomes policies in one form or another in many European countries – implicit in Germany, more open in Sweden and Holland and quite explicit in Britain where new bargaining criteria are being sought to relate wage settlements more closely to the economic situation in the country and the industry concerned. This search for incomes policy is a response to general inflationary pressures. In the case of Britain, it is also an attempt to introduce more planning and economic realism into a bargaining system which has too often resembled a jungle – which is fine for the lions.

'Free' collective bargaining is a highly emotive phrase in the British trade union movement and for reasons which are concerned with resistance of Government interferences. But absolute freedom means anarchy and it is the much vaunted 'free' system which has produced the chaotic patchwork quilt of wage structures, the criteria for success not being skill, effort or responsibility, but the strength of the union concerned and whether the industry concerned was old and declining or new and expanding. In that sense, an 'ordered return to free collective bargaining' is a contradiction in terms. It spells economic suicide. Surely, suicide is bad whether you queue for it or drift into it slowly.

The fourth influence is worker participation, which is adequately covered elsewhere in this book. Suffice it to say that this is a psychological threshold we must cross gently and firmly, not a precipice to be rushed over wildly and blindly.

The fifth influence concerns fringe benefit bargaining which has long been established on the Continent and has substantially enhanced the quality of life of the workers so covered. It is less inflationary in its effects than wage bargaining and lowers the flashpoint in industrial relations.

The sixth influence is the increasing use of arbitrational systems of the institutional and *ad hoc* kinds, to provide the cushion between dead-locked negotiations and political confrontations. The persistence of inflation and unemployement alongside the use of incomes policy is creating great tensions in Europe's industrial relations systems. The role of arbitrational systems therefore assumes a crucial significance.

There are many other possible future influences on industrial relations, indeed, a veritable kaleidoscope, but the foregoing six are the highlights which should not be missed. Living abroad has confirmed an opinion I held strongly before emigrating – that political power is linked to economic strength and economic success depends on good industrial relations. It is no accident that the richer countries like Germany, Sweden, Denmark, Austria and Switzerland have progressive, harmonious industrial relations systems. This correlation rests on the predominance of industrial trade union structure and more professionalism and economic realism in management and trade unions. Profit is seen as a badge of honour and not as a term of opprobrium.

Good industrial relations are a careful mixture of idealism and realism. You can have the best blueprints in the plushiest board-room imaginable, but if the industrial relations scene is not right, they are worth nothing. Equally, all the trade union militancy on this planet cannot get from an industry more than it is capable of giving, without doing great damage to its workers. Such is the fascination of industrial relations – an art, a science and now an indispensable tool in the construction of a better society and a new Europe.

Table 13.1 List of organisations affiliated to the E.T.U.C.

Name		Country	Membership*
Fédération Générale du Travail de Belgique	F.G.T.B.	Belgium	900
Confédération des Syndicats Chrétiens	C.S.C.	Belgium	1,100
Landsorganisationen i Danmark	L.O.D.	Denmark	990
Fællesrådet for Danske Tjenestemands-og Funktionarorganisationer	F.D.T.F.	Denmark	210
Deutscher Gewerkschaftsbund	D.G.B.	Germany/Federal Republic	7,200
Union General de Trabajadores de España	U.G.T.	Spain	—
Solidaridad de Trabajadores Vascos	S.T.V.	Spain	—
Confédération Générale du Travail—Force ouvrière	C.G.T.–F.O.	France	1,000
Confédération Française Démocratique du Travail	C.F.D.T.	France	860
Trade Union Congress	T.U.C.	Great Britain	11,500
Irish Congress of Trade Unions	I.C.T.U.	Ireland	547
Althydusamband Islands	A.I	Iceland	42
Confederazione Italiana Sindacati Lavoratori	C.I.S.L.	Italy	2,100
Confederazione Generale Italiana del Lavoro	C.G.I.L.	Italy	4,300
Unione Italiana del Lavoro	U.I.L.	Italy	800
Confédération Générale du Travail de Luxembourg	C.G.T.L.	Luxembourg	30
Letzbuerger Chrëstleche Gewerkschaftsbond	L.C.G.B.	Luxembourg	15
General Workers Union	G.W.U.	Malta	26
Nederlands Verbond van Vakverenigingen	N.V.V.	Netherlands	700
Nederlands Katholiek Vakverbond	N.K.V.	Netherlands	340
Christelijk Nationaal Vakverbond	C.N.V.	Netherlands	210
Landsorganisesjonen I Norge	L.O.N.	Norway	200
Österreichischer Gewerkschaftsbund	O.G.B.	Austria	1,600
Schweizerischer Gewerkschaftsbund	S.G.B.	Switzerland	471
Christlichnationaler Gewerkschaftsbund der Schweiz	C.N.G.S.	Switzerland	106
Schweizerischer Verband Evangelischer Arbeitsnehmer	S.V.E.A.	Switzerland	14
Toimihenkilö ja Virkamicsjäjestöjen Keskusliitto	T.V.K.	Finland	240
Suomen Anmattilitojen Keskusjärjesto	S.A.K.	Finland	920
Landsorganisationen I Sverige	L.O.S.	Sweden	1,750
Tjänstemännens Centralorganisation	T.C.O.	Sweden	922
Confédération Générale du Travail de Grèce	C.G.T.	Greece	300

*In thousands members.